Multicultural America

Volume IV
The Asian Americans

Multicultural America

Volume IV
The Asian Americans

Rodney P. Carlisle
GENERAL EDITOR

Facts On File
An imprint of Infobase Publishing

Multicultural America: Volume IV: The Asian Americans
Copyright © 2011 by Infobase Publishing

Facts On File, Inc.
An Imprint of Infobase Publishing
132 West 31st Street
New York, NY 10001

Library of Congress Cataloging-in-Publication Data
Multicultural America / Rodney P. Carlisle, general editor.
    v. cm.
    Includes bibliographical references and index.
    Contents: v. 1. The Hispanic Americans — v. 2. The Arab Americans — v. 3. The African Americans — v. 4. The Asian Americans — v. 5. The Jewish Americans — v. 6. The European Americans — v. 7. The Native Americans.
    ISBN 978-0-8160-7811-0 (v. 1 : hardcover : alk. paper) — ISBN 978-0-8160-7812-7 (v. 2 : hardcover : alk. paper) — ISBN 978-0-8160-7813-4 (v. 3 : hardcover : alk. paper) — ISBN 978-0-8160-7814-1 (v. 4 : hardcover : alk. paper) — ISBN 978-0-8160-7815-8 (v. 5 : hardcover : alk. paper) — ISBN 978-0-8160-7816-5 (v. 6 : hardcover : alk. paper) — ISBN 978-0-8160-7817-2 (v. 7 : hardcover : alk. paper) 1. Minorities—United States—History—Juvenile literature. 2. Ethnology—United States—History—Juvenile literature. 3. Cultural pluralism—United States—History—Juvenile literature. 4. United States—Ethnic relations—Juvenile literature. I. Carlisle, Rodney P.
    E184.A1M814 2011
    305.800973—dc22   2010012694

Text design and composition by Golson Media
Cover printed by Art Print, Taylor, PA
Book printed and bound by Maple Press, York, PA
Date Printed: March 2011
Printed in the United States of America

11 10 9 8 7 6 5 4 3 2 1

CONTENTS

Volume IV

The Asian Americans

PREFACE

AMERICANS HAVE HAD a sense that they were a unique people, even before the American Revolution. In the 18th century, the settlers in the thirteen colonies that became the United States of America began to call themselves Americans, recognizing that they were not simply British colonists living in North America. In addition to the English, other cultures and peoples had already begun to contribute to the rich tapestry that would become the American people.

Swedes and Finns in the Delaware River valley, Dutch in New York, Scots-Irish, and Welsh had all brought their different ways of life, dress, diet, housing, and religions, adding them to the mix of Puritan and Anglican Englishmen. Lower Rhine German groups of dissenting Amish and Mennonites, attracted by the religious toleration of Pennsylvania, settled in Germantown, Pennsylvania, as early as 1685. Located on the western edge of Philadelphia, the settlers and later German immigrants moved to the counties just further west in what would become Pennsylvania Dutch country.

The policies of the other colonies tended to favor and encourage such group settlement to varying extents. In some cases, as in New Jersey, the fact that each community could decide what church would be supported by local taxes tended to attract coreligionists to specific communities. Thus in the colonial period, the counties of southern New Jersey (known in colonial times as West Jersey) tended to be dominated by Quakers. Townships in New Jersey closer to New York City were dominated by Lutheran, Dutch Reformed, and Anglican churches and settlers.

Ethnicity and religion divided the peoples of America, yet the official tolerance of religious diversity spawned a degree of mutual acceptance. While crossreligious marriages were frowned upon, they were not prohibited, with individual families deciding which parents' church should be attended, if any. Modern descendants tracing their ancestry are sometimes astounded at the various strands of culture and religion that they find woven together.

To the south, Florida already had a rich Hispanic heritage, some of it filtered through Cuba. Smaller groups of immigrants from France and other countries in Europe were supplemented during the American Revolution by enthusiastic supporters of the idea of a republican experiment in the New World.

All of the thirteen colonies had the institution of African slavery, and people of African ancestry, both slave and free, constituted as much as 40 percent of the population of colonies like Georgia and South Carolina. In a wave of acts of emancipation, slaves living in the New England colonies were freed right after the Revolution, soon joined by those in Pennsylvania, New York, and New Jersey. Although some African Americans in the south were free by birth or manumission, emancipation for 90 percent of those living south of Pennsylvania would have to wait until the Civil War, 1861–65. Forcibly captured and transported under terrible conditions overland and across the ocean, Africans came from dozens of different linguistic stocks. Despite the disruptions of the middle passage, African Americans retained elements of their separate cultures, including some language and language patterns, and aspects of diet, religion, family, and music.

Native Americans, like African Americans, found themselves excluded from most of the rights of citizenship in the new Republic. In the Ohio and Mississippi Valley, many Native Americans resisted the advance of the European-descended settlers. In Florida, Creeks and Seminoles provided haven to escaped slaves, and together, they fought the encroachment of settlers. Some of the African Americans living with the Seminoles and other tribes moved west with them on the Trail of Tears to Indian Territory in what later became the state of Oklahoma. Other groups, like the Lumbees of North Carolina, stayed put, gradually adjusting to the new society around them. Throughout scattered rural communities, clusters of biracial and triracial descendents could trace their roots to Native-American and African ancestors, as well as to the English and Scotch-Irish.

The Louisiana Purchase brought the vast Mississippi Valley into the United States, along with the cosmopolitan city of New Orleans, where French exiles from Canada had already established a strong Creole culture. With the annexation of Texas, and following the Mexican-American War (1846–48), the United States incorporated as citizens hundreds of thousands of people of Hispanic ancestry. Individuals and communities in Texas and New Mexico preserve not only their religion, but also their language, cuisine, customs, and architecture.

As the United States expanded to the west, with vast opportunities for settlement, waves of European immigrants contributed to the growth of the country, with liberal naturalization laws allowing immigrants to establish themselves as citizens. Following the revolutions of 1848 in Europe, and famines in Ireland, new floods of immigrants from Central Europe, Ireland, and Scandinavia all settled in pockets.

By the late 19th century, America had become a refuge for political and economic refugees, as well as enterprising families and individuals from many countries. More geographic-ethnic centers emerged, as new immigrants sought out and settled near friends and families who had already arrived. Neighborhoods and whole states took on some aspects of the ethnic cultures that the immigrants carried, with the Italians settling in New York City, San Francisco, and New Jersey; Azoreans and continental Portuguese in Rhode Island and southern Massachusetts; Scandinavians in Wisconsin and Minnesota; Germans in Missouri; and Chinese and Japanese in a number of West Coast cities and towns. San Francisco and Boston became known for their Irish settlers, and Italians joined Franco-Hispanic Catholics of New Orleans. In some other scattered communities, such as the fishing port of Monterey, California, later Portuguese and Italian arrivals were also absorbed into the local Hispanic community, partly through the natural affinity of the shared Catholic faith.

As waves of immigrants continued to flow into the United States from the 1880s to World War I, the issue of immigration became even more politicized. On the one hand, older well-established ethnic communities sometimes resented the growing influence and political power of the new immigrants. Political machines in the larger cities made it a practice to incorporate the new settlers, providing them with some access to the politics and employment of city hall, also expecting their votes and loyalty during election. The intricate interplay of ethnicity and politics through the late 19th century has been a rich field of historical research.

In the 1890s the United States suddenly acquired overseas territories, including Hawaii, Puerto Rico, and Guam. People from the new territories became American citizens, and although the great majority of them did not leave their islands, those who came to the continental United States became part of the increasingly diverse population. The tapestry of American culture and ancestry acquired new threads of Polynesian, Asian, Hispanic, and African-Hispanic people.

During the Progressive Era, American-born citizens of a liberal or progressive political inclination often had mixed feelings about immigrants. Those with a more elite set of values believed that crime, alcoholism, and a variety of vices running from drug abuse through prostitution, gambling, and underground sports such as cockfighting, all could be traced to the new immigrants. The solution, they believed, would be immigration reform: setting quotas that would restrict immigrants from all but Great Britain and northern Europe.

Other reformers took the position that the problems faced by new immigrants could be best dealt with through education, assistance, and social work. Still others approached the questions of poverty and adjustment of immigrants as part of the labor struggle, and believed that organizing through labor unions could bring pressure for better wages and working conditions. Meanwhile immigrants continued to work through their churches, community organizations, and the complexities of American politics for recognition and rights.

Ultimately two approaches emerged regarding how different ethnic groups would be viewed and how they would view themselves in America. For some, the idea of a melting pot had always held attraction. Under this way of thinking, all Americans would merge, with ethnic distinctions diminishing and the various cultures blending together to create a new American culture. Such a process of assimilation or integration appealed to many, both among American-born and immigrant groups. Others argued strongly that ethnic or racial identity should be preserved, with a sense of pride in heritage, so that America would continue to reflect its diversity, and so that particular groups would not forget their origins, traditions, and culture.

In 1882 the Chinese Exclusion Act prohibited further immigration of Chinese, and it was extended and made more restrictive in several amendments through 1902. Under the law, Chinese were prohibited from obtaining U.S. citizenship. In 1924 immigration legislation was enacted establishing quotas, based upon earlier census figures, so that the quotas favored those from northern Europe. Under that law, Chinese were excluded, although 1910–40 more than 50,000 Chinese entered under claims they were returning or joining families already in the United States. The racial nature of the Chinese Exclusion and Immigration Acts tended to prevent the assimilation of Chinese into American society, with many cities, particularly in the west, developing defined Chinatowns or Chinese districts.

Whether an individual ethnic group should become assimilated into the total culture, or whether it should strive to maintain its own separate cultural identity, was often hotly debated. For some, like the Chinese, Native Americans, and African Americans, armed power of the state, law, and social discrimination tended to create and enforce separate communities and locales. For others, self-segregation and discrimination by other ethnic groups, and the natural process of settling near relatives and coreligionists led to definable ethnic regions and neighborhoods. Among such diverse groups as African Americans, Asians, Hispanics, Italians, Arab Americans, and Native Americans, leaders and spokesmen have debated the degree to which cultural identity should be sacrificed in the name of assimilation. In the 21st century, the debates have continued, sometimes with great controversy, at other times, the dialogues went on almost unnoticed by the rest of the country.

Armed conflict, race-wars, reservation policy, segregation, exclusion, and detention camps in time of war have shown the harsh and ugly side of enforced separation. Even though the multiethnic and multicultural heritage of the United States has been fraught with crisis and controversy, it has also been a source of strength. With roots in so many cultures and with the many struggles to establish and maintain social justice, America has also represented some of the best aspirations of humanity to live in peace. The search for social equity has been difficult, but the fact that the effort has continued for more than two centuries is in itself an achievement.

In this series on Multicultural America, each volume is dedicated to the history of one ethnocultural group, tracing through time the struggles against discrimination and for fair play, as well as the effort to preserve and cherish an independent cultural heritage.

THE ASIAN AMERICANS

The early history of Asian immigration to the United States differed greatly from that of other ethnic groups. Although the migration was almost entirely voluntary, in contrast to that of African people brought as slaves, Asians faced a unique set of institutional and legal forms of discrimination. Following on early discriminatory laws, the Chinese Exclusion Act of 1882, renewed and in effect until 1943, was an attempt to prevent any immigration of Chinese. Even though ways around the law were found, the effect of the law was to single out Asians, and Chinese in particular, as undesirable.

The laws reflected the circular thinking common in many forms of prejudice. Since Chinese women were prohibited from immigrating in large numbers, prostitution among the few Chinese women became common in the late 19th century. Bachelor society was the norm for Asians in 19th century America. This fact led to further efforts to exclude Chinese women on the ground that they were prostitutes. Similarly since Chinese men were excluded from many occupations and forced to take the lowest paying sorts of work, white workingmen formed organizations and even a political party based on the premise that since Chinese worked for low wages, they should be excluded. Such circular thinking or self-fulfilling forms of discrimination are common in many situations of racial prejudice; such thinking repeatedly formed the basis for policy with regard to Chinese immigrants in the United States.

Although Chinese represented the largest number of Asian immigrants to the United States, other groups suffered similar forms of discrimination, usually leading to the formation of enclave settlements, mostly in the western part of the United States. Koreans, Japanese, Vietnamese, settlers from the Philippines, and smaller groups from other Asian countries and Pacific Islands tended to cluster in specific locations, much as other ethnic groups had done, including those from various European countries.

Because of the diversity of Asian immigrants, including those from 23 different cultures, and from a variety of religions, ranging from Korean Protestant groups, through Sikhs, Hindus, and Buddhists, no single Asian identity emerged. Just as European immigrants have found communal roots through religious affiliation, so have many Asian groups; although providing communal institutions for activities and cultural identification, the diversity of religions has worked against the emergence of a single Asian identity with the United States.

Other factors contributing to the cultural and social complexity of Asian-American status in America include the fact that many Asian women have come to the United States as "war brides," the wives of American servicemen who have been stationed in Asian countries. Another group of people of Asian ancestry include hundreds of thousands of Asian children who were adopted by white American families, and who tended to be cut off from close ties to any broader Asian community within the American social structure.

The diversity of groups, with different languages, cultures, religions, cuisines, and traditions have all contributed to preventing any unified cultural expression of people with Asian ancestry within the broader American culture. It was this very diversity, especially among activist Asian youth, that contributed in the late 20th century, to the emphasis on a multicultural view of American society and to an emphasis on diversity. Unlike the African American community, which tended to define cultural alternatives as integration or separatism, assimilation or black consciousness, Asian youth have tended to support a view of American society as consisting of a quilt-like variety of ethnicities and cultural identities.

In the Chinese, Korean, and Japanese communities, family traditionally held great importance as the fundamental social unit. When coupled with the pressures of the difficulty of integrating as an identified and racially identifiable minority, family became even more crucial. One consequence was greater familial pressure on children to excel in education. As a result, while the percentage of Asian Americans has generally remained under five percent within the United States, the percentage of Asians attending colleges and universities has been much higher. In California, for example, in the first decade of the 21st century, over 30 percent of college and university students are Asian.

Rodney Carlisle
General Editor

CHAPTER 1

Beginnings in America: Precolonial to 1859

THE HISTORY OF ethnic groups is important to an understanding of modern American history and culture because it was these groups that brought to America the ideas and cultural traditions that shaped the country. In the case of Asian Americans, the roots of their presence and influence date from the very first populations in North America. Although some scholars disagree, the prevailing view is that the human population of North America originated in Asia between 9,000 and 50,000 years ago, when colder temperatures led to larger ice caps and a corresponding lower sea level. The lower seas resulted in exposure of a land bridge connecting northeastern Asia with northwestern North America across what is now called the Bering Sea. Gradually spreading east across the continent, and south into Central and South America, these early arrivals were the ancestors of the various groups of people that Europeans labeled "Indians." In fact modern DNA testing has established a link between Native Americans and people living in Siberia and East Asia.

In 2006 the results of research on DNA found in a 10,000-year-old tooth in Alaska linked it with indigenous groups residing in the western coastal areas of Central and South America. Other finds in South America have been linked, at least by some anthropologists, with Melanesians, while research on the skull of Kennewick Man, found along the banks of the Columbia River

1

A portrait of a Native American from 1902. Recent DNA testing has confirmed links between Native Americans and East Asians.

in the state of Washington, concluded that the 9,200-year-old remains closely resembled bone structures found among South Asians or the Ainu people associated with Japan. These, and other discoveries, have led some scholars to believe that there may have been multiple routes of entry for people from Asia and the Pacific islands into the Western Hemisphere. It is certain that peoples from Asia were among the very first inhabitants of North America, but once the land bridge was submerged, contact was at best sporadic.

Dating to the 3rd century, the Chinese poem *Fu Sang* is said to refer to the Birthplace of the Sun. It also refers specifically to a land called Fu-Sang that was known in Chinese writing as early as the 2nd century B.C.E., a mysterious land some scholars have located along the Pacific coast of North America. Other scholars believe Fu-Sang was simply an alternative name for Japan, Kamchatka, or other areas along the north Asian coast. The poem reads as follows:

East of the Eastern Ocean lie
The shores of the Land of Fu-Sang.
If, after landing there, you travel
East for 10,000 li
You will come to another ocean, blue,
Vast, huge, boundless.

Emperor Shi Huang of the Han Dynasty is said to have sent an expedition to this far-off land in 219 B.C.E., but the most extensive description came from a Buddhist monk named Hui Shen who claimed to have returned to the court of Emperor Wu Ti in 499 C.E. from an extensive visit to Fu-Sang. The monk's descriptions appear in the 7th-century C.E. *Book of Liang*, a history of the Liang Dynasty, by Yao Sia-lian. In his description, Hui Shen reported beginning his voyage in 455 C.E. and traveling along the coasts of China, Korea, Japan, Kamchatka, and then on to Fu-Sang. Although some scholars believe that Fu-Sang was really Japan, the monk described going to "Wo" and that Fu-Sang lay beyond that land, clearly indicating that Wo and Fu-Sang were two different places. Although the name Fu-Sang was later associated with Japan, Wo was the ancient Chinese name for Japan; thus it would seem Fu-Sang and Japan were distinct lands. Further the monk claimed that Fu-Sang lay some 20,000 *li* from the "Great Han," and east of the "Middle Kingdom" (China). Great Han (or Dahan) was described as a land northeast of Wo (Japan). The *li*, as a measure of distance, varied over time, but if one uses the ancient Chinese definition of about 435 meters (476 yards), then 20,000 *li* would be approximately equal to 8,700 kilometers, or 5,406 miles. This would place Fu-Sang roughly where modern British Columbia is located.

Although still a topic of often emotional debate, many scholars have noted similarities between Hui Shen's descriptions and aspects of Pacific coastal areas. Hui Shen noted that Fu-Sang trees were plentiful in the land he visited, and were used for food and to make items such as clothing and a form of paper. Similar qualities are found in the maguey, or yucca, that grows in Mexico; cactus of the western desert; and ancient forms of corn that grew along the northern Pacific coast. Ancient Chinese coins have been unearthed along the Pacific coast, Chinese ship anchors have been located in waters off the coast of California, and other archeological discoveries have been interpreted by some scholars as being of Chinese origin. Archeologists have also identified Japanese pottery from the Jōmon era (ca. 14,000–400 B.C.E.) found along the coast of the Pacific Northwest, and art historians have detected possible Chinese influence on the art and rituals of the Olmec civilization in Mexico. The identity of Fu-Sang remains speculative, but there is sufficient evidence to indicate at least some Asian presence in North America prior to and contemporaneous with the arrival of the Spanish.

THE MANILA GALLEONS

There could have been Asian explorers sailing the Pacific Coast of North America at the same time that Spanish explorers were penetrating the continent from the opposite direction. An interesting document found in the Naval Museum in Madrid reported that in 1540 Coronado's expedition sighted "exotic ships with figureheads of golden pelicans" off the mouth of the Colorado River. Later in the same century, the Franciscan Friar Juan de Luco wrote of seeing eight strange ships off Tepic on the western coast of Mexico in 1573.

The 16th century brought the first European documentation of Asians in North America. The Spanish arrived in the Philippine Islands, which they named for King Philip II, in 1542, some 21 years after Magellan's initial visit. This attempt at settlement was unsuccessful, but they returned under Miguel Lopez de Legazpi in 1565, established the first permanent colony,

This painting by Samuel Scott depicts the capture of a Manila galleon by the British ship Centurion, commanded by Commodore George Anson on June 20, 1743, in the Philippines.

and founded Manila in 1571. Beginning in 1565, Spanish ships, the Manila Galleons, set sail to the port of Acapulco in Mexico, opening a trade route that would be one of the most profitable in the Spanish Empire. Many of the crew members on these vessels were Filipinos and Chinese, some of whom adopted Catholicism and Spanish names to increase their opportunities for employment by the colonial rulers. Some of these crew members stayed in North America, but there is ample evidence that Filipinos and Chinese also began to immigrate to New Spain as merchants, skilled craftsmen, and laborers. In fact there is a record that as early as 1635, Spanish barbers in Mexico City protested competition by Chinese barbers. In Mazatlan there was a popular Chinese inn operated by Luën-Sing, the Fonda de Canton.

In his description of Acapulco under Spanish rule in *The Manila Galleons,* William L. Schurz wrote that the port "consisted of Indians and Orientals, and of mestizos and mulattoes of every possible degree of mixture." In fact Acapulco was often known as the *ciudad de los Chinos,* or "city of the Chinese," and its Asian inhabitants were referred to as *Chinos Españoles,* or "Chinese Spanish."

The last of the Manila Galleons arrived in Acapulco in 1815, but these early Asian arrivals exerted an influence on the culture of the area that eventually spread north into areas that would become part of the United States. Stan Steiner asserts in his *Fu-Sang: The Chinese Who Built America* that Antonio Rodriguez, a founder of Los Angeles, was really one of the Chinos Españoles. He also argued that the old California breed of horse called the *caballo chino* (Chinese horse), famous for its endurance and curly hair, and believed to be the ancestor of the famous western mustang, derived from similar Mongolian horses. Art historians have detected Chinese influences in some forms of Mexican pottery and embroidery, and the Spanish also adapted Chinese Buddhist temple lanterns to their own use. Brought to North America in the Manila Galleons, these *faroles de China* (Chinese lanterns) found their way into Catholic celebrations when priests began using them during Christmas celebrations as *farolitos de Navidad* (Christmas lanterns). These became very popular in areas that would later become New Mexico and Southern California.

THE CHINA TRADE

One of the primary causes of the American Revolution was the Tea Act, which led disgruntled people in Boston to dump British tea into Boston Harbor. The tea was only British through purchase, obtained by the East India Company from China. Following the Revolution, the fledgling nation quickly began to establish its own ties with Asia as eager entrepreneurs. Freed from the restraints of the British mercantilist system, Americans sought their own lucrative trade with Asia. On February 22, Washington's birthday in 1784, the *Empress of China* set sail carrying Samuel Shaw to his post as the first American consul in China. The ship's cargo, and the merchandise it brought back to the United States, returned a 25 percent profit on the original investment. Between 1794 and 1812, American ships made some 400 trips to China, carrying U.S. products to Asia and returning with valuable cargoes of ivory, jade, porcelain, lacquer, bronze, copper, silver, gold, teak furniture, rugs, and other commodities greatly valued in the new republic. By the 1830s, U.S. trade with China reached over $75 million, a sum greater than the entire debt incurred during the American Revolution.

In 1796 Andreas Everard Van Braam Houckgeest returned from a trip to China with an extensive collection of painting and sculpture, which became the basis for the first major exhibition of Chinese art in America. He also brought with him a porcelain tea service for Martha Washington, and five Chinese servants. His collection, and his research in China, led to publication of two volumes in 1798–99, the first books on China printed in the United States. A second exhibition of Chinese "curiosities" opened in Philadelphia in 1839, featuring exhibits on the customs, manners, dress, and life of people in that Asian land. In 1845 a similar museum opened in Boston with a 152-page catalog. Impressed, the famous entrepreneur P.T. Barnum purchased the contents for his own museum in New York City, which opened in 1850. Among Barnum's other exhibits were Pwan Yekoo, advertised as "a Chinese lady and her attendants," an "eight-foot giant" named Chang-yu Sing, a life-size replica of the entrance to a Chinese temple, and the "Siamese Twins" Chang and Eng Bunker, who were actually Chinese born in Thailand.

Chinese export porcelain from the 18th century.

Along with the imported goods, the China trade brought Asian people to America. Although the Immigration Commission reported arrival of the first Chinese in America in 1820, there is considerable evidence for their presence on the Atlantic Coast before that date, with Chinese appearing in New York as early as 1808. In 1785 the sailing ship *Pallas* arrived in Baltimore from Canton, China, with a crew made up largely of Asians. Unhappy with the conditions of their employment, some 30 went ashore and refused to return to the vessel. They remained in Philadelphia for about a year before obtaining passage back to Asia. In the same year, three Chinese seamen named Ah Sing, Ah Chuan, and Ah Cun landed in Baltimore. In 1800 ship captain James Magee brought a Chinese student to Rhode Island to learn the language and customs of the country so he could return to China as an interpreter.

During the 1830s, a number of Asian performers appeared in circuses and theaters in New York City, including Afong Moy, who gained some celebrity in the theater in 1834–35, and was the subject of the lithograph *The Chinese Lady*, the first known likeness of a Chinese person in America. The juggler Ah Fong rose to popularity in New York in the mid 1840s, and in 1845 a Cantonese man living in Boston known as Atit became the first known Asian to be naturalized as an America citizen. Two years earlier Manjiro Nakahama, believed to be the first Japanese man in the United States, was rescued at sea by an American vessel and settled in Fairhaven, Massachusetts. He later served

Chang and Eng Bunker

The original Siamese Twins, Chang and Eng, were born May 11, 1811, in what is today Thailand. The twins' father was Chinese and their mother was half-Chinese and half-Malay. Conjoined at the sternum, they were otherwise separate and complete individuals. In 1829 the Scottish entrepreneur Robert Hunter convinced their parents to allow them to go on a tour in the United States, Great Britain, and Europe, where people were charged an admission fee to view the unusual brothers.

In 1832, concerned that they were not receiving their fair share of the revenue from the tour, they signed on with P.T. Barnum, who featured them until 1839. In that year, they settled down to farming in North Carolina, became naturalized U.S. citizens, and adopted the last name Bunker in 1844. The twins married local sisters and fathered 21 children. They died on the same day in January 1874.

Conjoined twins Chang and Eng Bunker moved to the United States in the 1830s.

as an interpreter when the first Japanese diplomatic delegation arrived in the United States in 1860.

The first permanent Chinese settlement in the United States appeared in New York in the early 19th century, with Chinese boardinghouses listed in city directories along Cherry Street in 1840. By 1855 the *New York Times* estimated the Chinese population of the city at 150, including a wide variety of occupations from laborers to merchants and professionals. This small initial settlement gradually grew into the city's famous Chinatown.

In 1847 Rev. Samuel R. Brown, who had worked as a missionary teacher with the Morrison Education Society in Macao and Hong Kong 1839–46, returned with three Chinese students who enrolled in the Monson Academy in Massachusetts. One of them, Wong Hsing, soon dropped out due to health reasons, but the other two enjoyed considerable success. Wong Foon completed his studies at Monson and enrolled in the University of Edinburgh in

The visit of the Chinese junk Ke Ying to New York harbor on July 12, 1847, is depicted in this Currier & Ives print from the same year.

Scotland. Yung Wing enrolled at Yale in 1850, was naturalized as a U.S. citizen in 1852, and became the first Asian to graduate from an American college in 1854. For the next five decades, he was engaged in promoting American technology in China, and overseeing the education of some 120 Chinese students in the United States.

In the same year that Brown arrived with the three students, the 700-ton Chinese junk *Ke Ying* arrived in New York from Hong Kong on July 12 carrying some 35 to 40 Chinese, and several English officers. Spectators were allowed to board the vessel for a fee of 25 cents, and a newspaper reported that some 4,000 people visited it in a single day. The ship remained in the United States for several months, sailing to Providence, Rhode Island, where it was billed as the "greatest curiosity every experienced in this city" and "a perfect model of Chinese ship building 2000 years since." From Providence it went to Boston, where it was estimated another 6,000 people visited the ship.

The China trade, which began as a business enterprise, led to the development of Asian museum exhibits that increased interest in Asian history and culture, and to the arrival of a wide variety of permanent residents who laid the groundwork for New York's Chinatown and other urban Atlantic Coast Asian communities.

MANILA ON THE BAYOU

In 1763 a group of Filipino seamen serving on Spanish galleons jumped ship in New Orleans and fled into the nearby swamps and bayous where they established a small fishing community on Bayou Saint Malo. More than a century later, Lafcadio Hearn, a reporter for *Harper's Weekly*, described the houses these "Manilamen" had constructed atop supports erected in the marshes. "All are built in true Manila style, with immense hat-shaped eaves and balconies, but in wood; for it had been found that palmetto and woven cane could not withstand the violence of the climate. Nevertheless, all of this wood had to be shipped to the bayou from a considerable distance, for large trees do not grow in the salty swamp."

Speaking Tagalog and Spanish, they lived a largely secluded life under their own local laws, their diet based on fish seasoned with oil and vinegar. Eventually they began interacting with nearby Spanish-speaking populations, especially in New Orleans, where they later established the first Filipino organization in America, La Union Philipina. Since the initial settlers were all men, they began to intermarry with Indians, Cajuns, and others from the local area. As the community grew, members began to settle in other locations, founding communities at Alombro Canal and Camp Dewey in Plaquemines Parish, and at Leon Rojas, Bayou Cholas, and Bassa Bassa in Jefferson Parish. The largest of these new settlements was Manila Village on Barataria Bay.

Though initially small in number, the Filipinos who settled in Louisiana founded the area's shrimp drying industry, the first of its kind in the United States. Descendants of the original settlers also fought with Jean Lafitte's men as members of Andrew Jackson's force that defeated the British at the Battle of New Orleans in 1815.

TAN HEUNG SHAN—FRAGRANT SANDALWOOD HILLS

They called them Tan Heung Shan, the "fragrant sandalwood hills." We call them the Hawaiian Islands. The first small group of Chinese recorded arriving in Hawaii appeared in 1789, and with them began a booming trade in sandalwood between the islands and China. From 1790 to 1840, some 36 million pounds of the popular wood was sent to China, forming the first major export crop between the two regions.

In 1802 Wong Tze-Chun, described as a "sugar master," arrived in Hawaii, bringing his boiling pans and other refining equipment. By the 1830s, several Chinese sugar-making facilities were in operation on the islands of Maui and Hawaii, using Chinese equipment, methodologies, and contract laborers to facilitate large-scale production. Their success brought others into the industry, with the resulting formation of the Royal Hawaiian Agricultural Society in 1850, largely to enable Caucasian planters to band together to import Chinese labor for their plantations. Two years later, the society's president explained: "We shall find Coolie labor to be far more certain, systematic, and economic than that of the native. They are prompt at the call of the bell, steady in their work, quick to learn, and will accomplish more." The reference was to native Hawaiian labor, which the planters sought to replace with cheaper Chinese labor that they believed to be more productive.

Chinese contract laborers began to arrive in Hawaii in larger numbers in 1852 with the disembarkation of 195 men. They had contracted to work for five years in return for $3 per month plus their room and board and the cost of their transportation. Yet not all of the arrivals were contract laborers. In the same year, 37 Chinese entrepreneurs were reported in Honolulu as proprietors of bakeries, dry goods stores, restaurants, and other businesses. Two years later, the Chinese in Hawaii founded their first community organization, a funeral society to provide appropriate services on the death of a member, including a traditional parade. Together these entrepreneurs and laborers formed the basis for today's rich, multicultural Hawaiian society.

PUSH AND PULL FACTORS

When historians examine migration patterns, they often discuss the push and pull factors that influence people's decisions on whether or not to leave an area and where to select as a destination. Push factors are the conditions that cause people to choose to leave, while pull factors are those that influence the choice of destination. When Asians looked to the United States, they found in Hawaii, and later California, opportunities to earn a better living as laborers and growing markets for merchants and skilled craftsmen. Economic opportunity, the same lure that attracted people from Europe and others regions of the world in the 19th century, attracted Asians as well. But motivations to leave the familiarity of their families and native culture differed.

For Filipinos, the motivation was a lack of employment opportunities and land that caused many to seek service as seamen in the Spanish Navy or on merchant vessels. For the Chinese, there were multiple factors that pushed them from their homeland. The first of these was a series of disastrous wars and rebellions that cost millions of lives and led to major societal upheavals. The Opium Wars in 1839–42 and 1856–60 brought conflict with Britain that resulted in the loss of Hong Kong, the occupation of Beijing, and the opening of a number of coastal ports, including Canton and Shanghai, to foreign traders. The disastrous Taiping Rebellion (1850–64) cost hundreds of thousands of lives and further disrupted the economy and society, creating upheavals in population and uncertainty that caused people to seek more stable regions.

Exacerbating the destructive warfare were natural disasters and increasing overpopulation. Between 1787 and 1850, the population of China increased 47 percent, while that of Guangdong Province grew by a massive 79.5 percent. Overpopulation led to significantly less land per capita in Guangdong than the average for China, while floods and crop failures caused widespread famine. Significantly the vast majority of Chinese who moved to the United States during this period came from Guangdong Province and the surrounding area.

MEI KUO—FLOWERY FLAG

To 19th-century Chinese people, the United States was *Mei Kuo*, the Flowery Flag. Though sparse in number, a few hundred Asians already lived in California before it became a state in 1850. A brisk trade had been established, especially between San Francisco and China. In 1849 Bayard Taylor, a correspondent with the *New York Tribune*, reported seeing in that city "Chinese with long tails, Malays armed with their everlasting creeses," the latter probably a reference to the *kris*, a typical Southeast Asian wavy-bladed knife. In the same year, William Ryan noted that silks and other items from China were in great demand in San Francisco and "large consignments from China are sold at very high prices." Some of these early Chinese residents were merchants who made a living from this trade, while others were restaurateurs and other businessmen. One of these, Yuan Sheng, known locally as Norman As-sing, proprietor of the Macao and Woosung Restaurant, was elected leader of the Chew Yick Kung Shaw, the first Chinese mutual aid society in America.

Among the estimated 300-member Chinese community in San Francisco in 1848, there was also a large number of laborers. Together with their countrymen who were of the merchant and professional classes, they generally enjoyed a positive reputation in the community, so much so that Thomas Larkin, an American official in California, wrote that "one of my favorite subjects

This 1851 view of San Francisco by the British artist Francis Samuel Marryat includes a group of Chinese residents in traditional clothing at right in the foreground.

or projects is to introduce Chinese emigrants into this country. . . . Any number of mechanics, agriculturalists and servants can be obtained."

Four years later, James A. Carson wrote in the *San Joaquin Republican* that "we have among us several thousand of the inhabitants of China; a great many of them are intelligent men, from which much reliable information can be obtained in regard to the introduction of the tea plant into California, and the value of our lands for the cultivation of rice. . . . These emigrants are, as a class, the best people we have among us—they are sober, quiet, industrious, and inoffensive. . . . Thousands of these men are ready to become citizens of the U.S., settle down, and turn our waste lands into beautiful fields, as soon as proper inducements and protection is offered them; and no better class of men could be chosen to develop the agricultural resources of the Tulare Valley than the Chinese who are among us." At the same time, the *Daily Alta California* noted that "scarcely a ship arrives that does not bring an increase to this worthy integer of our population . . . the China boys will yet vote at the same polls, study at the same schools and bow at the same altar as our own countrymen." Mark Twain, on a western visit, observed that "They are quiet, peaceable, tractable, free from drunkenness. A disorderly Chinaman is rare, and a lazy one does not exist."

Aside from the generally positive impression they made, the founders of this nascent Asian community in America were voluntary immigrants. Some paid their own passage to America, some were supported by loans from relatives and friends that would be repaid from anticipated profits, and laborers often used the "credit-ticket" system. Under the latter, an agent provided passage to a laborer on credit with the expectation of being repaid with interest from the money the laborer earned on arrival in America. Interest rates could be high, but the potential income of a common laborer in California could be 10 times what could be earned in Guangdong. The Chinese who moved to California were not involuntary coolies as is so often portrayed in stereotypes of the era, but free men who contracted voluntarily for their labor. Further evidence of this came from Sir John Rowring, the British consul in Hong Kong, who certified in 1852 that the vast majority of Chinese leaving for America had paid their own way.

GAM SAAN—GOLD MOUNTAIN

The most important event influencing 19th-century Asian migration to America occurred in 1848 with the discovery of gold near John Sutter's sawmill north of San Francisco. As word spread, people began to flock to California in hopes of becoming wealthy, among them a growing wave of Asians. To the Chinese, California was *Gam Saan*, or Gold Mountain. In 1849 records identified 325 Chinese who entered what would become a state in the following year, and 450 in 1850, but this number quickly increased to 2,716 in 1851 and 20,026 in 1852 as word reached Asia and the slow sailing ships began to

These Chinese gold miners are using rockers to sort sand and gravel from gold while placer mining beside a stream in mid-19th-century California.

carry more human cargoes. J.D. Borthwick, a California observer, reported that "crowds of China men were also to be seen, bound for the diggings, under gigantic basket-hats, each man with a bamboo laid across his shoulder, from each end of which was suspended a higgledy-piggiledy collection of mining tools, Chinese baskets and boxes, immense boots and a variety of Chinese 'fixins,' which no one but the Chinaman would tell the use of." By 1860 the census reported 34,933 Chinese living in the United States, with about 77 percent of all Chinese in the United States residing in California. Some 85 percent of these were working in the mines. Most of the new arrivals were from Guangdong, and they were almost exclusively male. By 1852 the gender ratio among Chinese in California was 1,685 males to each female. The majority were also *wah gung*, sojourners who came, usually with the aid of the credit-ticket system, with the intention of temporary residence until they had earned enough money to return to China as wealthy men.

As early as 1854, E.C. Capron wrote in his *History of California* that the "Chinese rank with the most successful foreigners in the mines." This is all the more amazing because they often purchased claims that had already been given up by other miners who believed them to have been "worked out." One of their methods was to use what was referred to as "the Chinese water wheel," a system of buckets attached to rope pulleys that was used to drain creek beds to retrieve gold from the bottom. One "Yankee" miner recalled that the Chinese "were hated by most of the white miners for their ability to grub out fortunes which they themselves had left—for greener pastures."

For the most part, they used a method called *placer mining*. Derived from the Spanish word for sandbank, placer mining refers to extraction of bits of gold from among the sand or gravel of riverbeds. It usually appeared in two forms. One was called "panning" and involved the use of a pan into which the prospector placed gravel and water, gently rotating the pan so the heavier gold would sink to the bottom while the lighter sand and gravel were washed over the side of the pan. The other involved the use of a rocker, a piece of equipment that resembled a baby's cradle that could be rocked back and forth so that sand and gravel could be filtered away from the gold. The Chinese referred to this method as "rocking the golden baby." Although some authors, pointing to experience with the use of hydraulics on Asian rice paddies, credit the Chinese for introducing this type of mining to the United States, this is erroneous. The method was well-known in Europe at least since the time of the Roman Empire, was used extensively in the gold fields of northern Spain, and was also common among Mexican miners. What the Chinese were most noted for was their expertise and perseverance, which allowed them to profit from the claims others had given up as unproductive.

By mid-1852 Chinese miners had penetrated into the Rouge River Basin in Oregon, and by 1855 they had reached the Carson River in Nevada. By 1859 they were prominent among the miners attracted to Virginia City by the Comstock Lode, and had moved north into British Columbia and Alaska, and east into Idaho, Utah, Colorado, Wyoming, and Montana. Though most were directly engaged in mining, some Chinese who accompanied them were merchants or professionals. An example of the latter was a physician named Ah Sang who treated both Asian and Caucasian patients in the Yankee Hill mining camp. His success led to the directorship of a 50-bed hospital, the largest medical facility in the mining camps, and one of the largest in California.

DIA FOU—BIG CITY

While more than three-quarters of the Chinese in California in 1860 resided in the mining areas, 7.8 percent resided in San Francisco, known to them as *Dia Fou*, the Big City. They made quite an impression on the visiting Englishman J.D. Borthwick: "There were Chinamen in all the splendor of sky-blue or purple figured silk jackets, and tight yellow continuations, black satin shoes with thick white soles, and white gaiters; a fan in the hand, and a beautifully plaited glossy skullcap, with a gold knob on the top of it." These "were the swell Chinamen; the lower orders of the Celestials were generally dressed in the immensely wide blue calico jackets and bags, for they really could not be called trousers, and on their heads they wore enormous wickerworks . . . which would have made very fine clothes-baskets."

The Asian community in San Francisco grew slowly until the gold rush, but quite early there were a number of entrepreneurs in the city catering to both Asian and Caucasian clients. To inform the community of activities and opportunities, newspapers began to appear during the 1850s. The first Chinese newspaper in California, the San Francisco *Golden Hills' News* (*Kim Shan Jit San Luk*), appeared in April 1854, followed in the next year by the San Francisco *Oriental* (*Tung Ngai San Luk*) and in 1856 by the Sacramento *Chinese Daily News*. By 1856 the city directory listed 33 Chinese merchandise stores, 15 apothecaries, five barbers, five butchers, five herbalists, five restaurants, three boarding homes, three tailors, three wood yards, two bakers, two silversmiths, a carver, an engraver, an interpreter, and one broker specializing in working with U.S. merchants. There were also a number of laundries and other service businesses. Many of the merchants imported goods from China for the U.S. market, including: manufactured goods, tools, utensils, clothing and textiles, and a variety of foodstuffs including grains, rice, tea, sugar, spices,

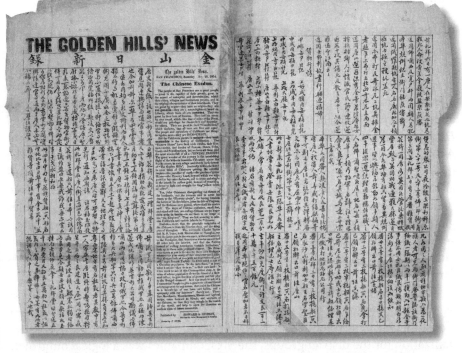

The May 27, 1854, issue of the Golden Hills' News included a note in English welcoming American "merchants, manufacturers, miners, and agriculturists" to "come forward as friends, not scorners of the Chinese, so that they may mingle in the march of the world, and help to open America an endless vista of future commerce."

and dried fruits. J.D. Borthwick commented on one "large bazaar in particular where . . . [there was] a stock of the costliest shawls, cabinets, workboxes, vases and other articles of Chinese manufacture, with clocks, bronzes and all sorts of drawing-room ornaments." Most goods were sold locally in the city, but some of the merchants also acted as suppliers for the mining camps. One of the white miners acknowledged their importance in 1850 when he wrote: "Were it not for the Chinese we might have starved the first year."

One of the more unique businesses that Chinese entrepreneurs operated was the importation and assembly of prefabricated homes. These structures, locally known as "Chinese houses," came in pieces that were assembled by Chinese carpenters. They were used in the city, but because they were movable, they were also used in the gold fields. William Redmond Ryan's *Personal Adventures in Upper and Lower California in 1848-9, with the Author's Experiences in the Mines*, published in London in 1850, explained that "the houses they brought with them from China, and which they set up where they were wanted, were infinitely superior and more substantial than those erected by the Yankees." In 1849, Ryan asserted, "Houses that cost $300, sell readily for $3,000; and the demand is constantly increasing. At least 75 houses have been imported from Canton, and are put up by Chinese carpenters."

CHINESE ASSOCIATIONS—*FONGS, HUIGUANS, AND TONGS*

With the expansion of the Chinese population and the growth of businesses, various types of organizations emerged. Primary among these was the *fong*, a group of people linked through family or by virtue of coming from the same village. Taking this general concept a step further, in 1851 the first two *huiguan* appeared with the formation of the Sam Yup Benevolent Association (*Sanyi Huiguan*), also known as the Canton Company, and the Sze Tup Benevolent Association (*Siyi Huiguan*). The huiguan was an association based on the district or region where a person originated in China, with members usually sharing a common dialect. The huiguan provided a number of services to members, beginning with locating lodging and jobs for new arrivals. The huiguans administered the credit-ticket system, ensured the payment of debts, settled disputes among members, raised funds for community projects, provided medicine to members, maintained cemeteries, covered burial expenses for the poor, and returned the bones of the deceased to China.

The number of huiguan increased to six during the 1850s, at which time they further organized themselves into the *Chung Wai Wui Koon*, the Chinese Consolidated Benevolent Association or Six Companies. As an umbrella organization for the district groups, the Six Companies was a logical outgrowth of normal Chinese social organization that they used to administer their own communities, and to interact on their behalf with the larger community. Led by prominent merchants with access to city government and non-Asian businessmen, the Six Companies represented the Chinese population to the general community, resolved disputes between the huiguan, and provided health and educational services to their community.

Another form of community organization was the *tong*. The first formed in the United States was the *Kwang-tek-tong* (Chamber of Far-reaching Virtue) founded in California in 1852. The tong originated in 18th-century China as a secret society with the purpose of overthrowing the government. In the United States, tongs were formed by immigrants for their mutual self-protection, but they eventually became associated with gang and criminal activity, including "tong wars" over the control of gambling, prostitution, and other illegal activities.

THE BACKLASH BEGINS

Early reactions to Chinese immigration among Californians ranged mostly from benign to positive. Often referred to as *celestials* by the English-speaking population because of Chinese references to the Celestial Kingdom in their religions, Chinese businesses were patronized by Caucasians, Chinese products circulated throughout the community, and the Chinese community was invited to participate in the ceremonies surrounding California's admittance as a state in 1850. In the same year, the San Francisco newspaper *Alta California* wrote: "These celestials make excellent citizens and we are pleased to notice their daily arrival in large numbers." As the Asian population increased in number and success, the good feelings did not last. The change is best illustrated in the editorial opinion of the same newspaper. When it changed editors in 1853, its previous positive attitude toward Asians underwent a dramatic change that found it characterizing the Chinese as ". . .morally a far worse class to have among us than the negro. They are idolatrous in their religion—in their disposition cunning and deceited [*sic*], and in their habits libidinous and offensive."

The backlash against Asian immigrants originated in the competitive search for gold. White miners resented the success the Chinese enjoyed profiting from claims they had given up as unproductive, as well as the general competition from all "foreigners" who arrived in search of the hidden wealth. In 1849 the first expulsion of Chinese from mining camps took place in Tuolumne County, but it is not clear if this was aimed specifically at the Chinese, or whether it was a consequence of a general anti-foreign movement. In the following year, California levied a tax of $3 per person on miners who did not intend to become citizens, which may have been aimed at the Chinese, since it was not clear at that time whether they qualified for citizenship. In the same year, a Foreign Miners' License Tax of $20 per month was imposed after calls for "protection" by white miners. Again this was probably intended more to address the large numbers of Mexicans and other Central and South Americans coming to the gold fields, but it also applied to the Chinese. The

Railroad Reports

Aside from work in the mines and urban business of the west coast, thousands of early Chinese immigrants were employed building the railroad network that connected western cities and mining areas with each other and the east. In the first report below, taken from a reprinted article in the *Bulletin of the Southern Pacific Railroad*, the employers comment of the industrious work ethic of the Chinese. The second, though reflecting the Central Pacific's bias in paying Chinese less than other workers, speaks to their value to the company and the method of payment employed among them.

Swarms of laborers, Chinese, Europeans and Americans were hurrying to their work. . . . By the side of the grade smoked the camp fires of the blue clad laborers who could be seen in groups waiting for the signal to start work. These were the Chinese, and the job of this particular contingent was to clear a level roadbed for the track. They were the vanguard of the construction forces. Miles back was the camp of the rear guard–the Chinese who followed the track gang, ballasting and finishing the road bed. Systematic workers these Chinese–competent and wonderfully effective because tireless and unremitting in their industry." —From a Southern Pacific Railroad report.

The greater portion of the laborers employed by us are Chinese, who constitute a large element of the population of California. Without them it would be impossible to complete the western portion of this great national enterprise, within the time required by the Acts of Congress.

As a class they are quiet, peaceable, patient, industrious and economical—ready and apt to learn all the different kinds of work required in railroad building. They soon become efficient as white laborers. More prudent and economical, they are contented with less wages. We find them organised into societies for mutual aid and assistance, These societies, that count their numbers by thousands, are conducted by shrewd, intelligent business men, who promptly advise their subordinates where employment can be found on the most favorable terms. No system similar to slavery, serfdom or peonage prevails among these laborers. Their wages, which are always paid in coin, at the end of each month, are divided among them by their agents, who attend to their business, in proportion to the labor done by each person. These agents are generally American or Chinese merchants, who furnish them their supplies of food, the value of which they deduct from their monthly pay. We have assurances from leading Chinese merchants, that under the just and liberal policy pursued by the Company, it will be able to procure during the next year, not less than 15,000 laborers." —From a report to the Secretary of the Interior by the Central Pacific Railroad.

enforcement of this was often accompanied by violence, and even demands that the tax be paid more than once by different tax collectors, since the collectors were paid from the money they collected. It is estimated that the tax on foreign miners raised between a quarter and one half of the revenue gathered in California during the 1850s.

"NO CHINESE SHOULD . . . "

In April 1852 the situation took a dramatic turn for the worse when Governor John Bigler expressed public opposition to "the present wholesale importation to this country, of immigrants from the Asiatic quarter of the globe . . . I allude particularly, to a class of Asiatics known as 'Coolies,' who are sent here, as I am assured, and as is generally believed, under contract to work in our mines for a term; and who, at the expiration of the term, return to their native country." Bigler objected to "the exportation by them of the precious metals which they dig up from our soil without charge and without assuming any of the obligations imposed on citizens." Although almost all of the miners who came to California from China either paid their own way or arrived through the credit-ticket system, the governor's endorsement of this early stereotype of Chinese immigrants as coolies went far toward supporting latent prejudices. His message led to a decade of increasing calls for restriction of Asians, increasing violence against them, and movements to exclude them not only from the mines, but also from the entire state.

The month after Bigler's message, the *Marysville Herald* reported that local miners had adopted a resolution calling for the elimination of Chinese who were "overrunning and occupying a large portion of the mining lands, . . . to the injury and disadvantage of the American citizens" and demanding that "no Chinese should thereafter be allowed to hold mining claims." Under increasing pressure from miners and businessmen who came to resent competition from the Asians, on April 28, 1855, the California legislature enacted An Act to Discourage the Immigration to this State of Persons Who Cannot Become Citizens Thereof. Directed specifically at Asians, the new law required the master of a ship to pay a $50 tax for each such person brought to California ports. Three years later, this was followed on April 26, 1858, by An Act to Prevent the Further Immigration of Chinese or Mongolians to This State. The statute subjected any new entrants to a fine between $400 and $600, and imprisonment for three months to one year.

THE *PEOPLE V. GEORGE W. HALL*

In 1853 in a mining camp along the Bear River in Nevada County, California, a Chinese miner named Ling Sing was shot dead by a Caucasian man and two accomplices. The three were arrested by local authorities and charged with murder. Rev. William Speer, who had spent time in China and knew the language, was engaged by the Chinese community to assist at the trial by translating the testimony of three Chinese witnesses. With this testimony, the accused, George W. Hall, was found guilty of murder.

Hall appealed his conviction to the Supreme Court of California on the basis that the testimony of the three Chinese witnesses should not have been admissible as evidence. The appeal rested on Section 394 of the Act Concerning Civil Cases, which provided that no Indian or negro could testify in a trial involving a white person, and Section 14 of an act regulating criminal proceedings adopted on April 16, 1850, which read: "No black or mulatto person, or Indian, shall be allowed to give evidence in favor of, or against a white man." Hall's attorney argued that the exclusion applied to the Chinese witnesses, and thus their testimony (presumably the basis for the conviction), should not have been admitted.

JUSTICE MURRAY'S DECISION

In rendering his decision, Chief Justice Hugh Murray noted that the key point was "the legal signification of the words, 'black, mulatto, Indian, and white person,' and whether the Legislature adopted them as generic terms, or intended to limit their application to specific types of the human species." Another key point was the federal naturalization law of 1790, which limited citizenship to "white" people. In an amazing exercise of flawed logic, Justice Murray found that the term "black" was meant in a generic sense to include everyone who was not "white." Were this not the case, he argued, if Asians were allowed to testify, then by extension the more restricted definition of "black" to mean only negroes would "admit [Asians] to all the equal rights of citizenship, and we might soon see them at the polls, in the jury box, upon the bench, and in our legislative halls."

Then, in a clearly racist continuation of his thinking, the justice explained that allowing Asians to testify would result in "The anomalous spectacle of a distinct people, living in our community, recognizing no laws of this State, except through necessity, bringing with them their prejudices and national feuds, in which they indulge in open violation of law; whose mendacity is proverbial; a race of people whom nature has marked as inferior, and who are incapable of progress or intellectual development beyond a certain point, as their history has shown; differing in language, opinions, color, and physical conformation; between whom and ourselves nature has placed an impassable difference, is now presented, and for them it claims, not only the right to swear away the life of a citizen, but the further privilege of participating with us in administering the affairs of our Government."

Based in this specious reasoning, Justice Murray, supported by Justice J. Heydenfeldt, then announced that "we are of opinion that the testimony was inadmissible. The judgment is reversed and the cause remanded." Hall was free, his conviction reversed on appeal, and the testimony against him thrown out because of the race of the witnesses. But the results of the decision went far beyond the effect on Hall. The decision effectively eliminated constitutional protections for Asians, thereby actually encouraging crimes against Asians, since it would henceforth be extremely difficult to convict white people without the testimony of the victims or other Asian witnesses. It was a serious setback for the protection of Asian civil rights.

CULTURAL INFLUENCES

The development of the Asian area of San Francisco introduced Americans to what would later become Chinatown, along with bits of culture that would be adopted by other Americans. These "celestial" immigrants brought with them Buddhism, Confucianism, and Taoism, and introduced Americans to the joyous celebrations of the Chinese New Year. The first Chinese theater was constructed in San Francisco in 1852 from one of the Chinese prefabricated kits, a building large enough to seat 1,000 people. In the same year, the first Chinese play was presented in the city by a cast of 123 actors of the Hong Fook Tong, a group of Chinese opera performers.

One of the most prominent pastimes among Chinese immigrants in California was gambling. Mark Twain observed wryly that "about every third Chinaman runs a lottery." These games of chance became quite popular

Chinese men, women, and children attend the performance of a historical play in a large theater in San Francisco in the mid-19th century.

among non-Asians as well, and some survive today as recognizable elements of Chinese culture adapted to the American environment. One of these was *fan tan*, a game that was exceptionally popular into the early 20th century, but has since lost much of its appeal. In fan tan, players bet on squares numbered one through four. The croupier then takes a double handful of beans or other small objects and places them on the table. Four objects are withdrawn at a time until there is only one group left, the number of pieces in that group determining the winner who received three times his bet, less a five percent commission for the croupier. More well-known today are two other games that are still played widely. One is *mah jongg*, a game in which players draw domino-like tiles bearing various designs until one player achieves four combinations each with three tiles and a matching pair. The most popular throughout America today is *pak kop piu*, in which people select numbers on a card from one to 80. Twenty numbers are then selected at random, and winners are determined by the number of matches on their card. Known by Americans as keno, it is played in casinos throughout the country.

CUISINE

The most influential of the cultural elements brought to America by these early Chinese was food. Street vendors abounded, selling all manner of food from wicker baskets suspended from each end of a bamboo pole, while restaurants catered to Asians and non-Asians alike. William Redmond Ryan told English readers that he "once went into an eating house kept by one of these people, and was astonished at the neat arrangement and cleanliness of the place, the excellence of the table, and moderate charges . . . As I had always been given to understand that these people were of dirty habits, I feel it only right to state that I was delighted with the cleanliness of this place, and I am gratified to bear testimony to the injustice of such a sweeping statement." Bayard Taylor explained to readers of the *New York Tribune* that Chinese restaurants were "denoted by their long three-cornered flags of yellow silk. [They] are much frequented by Americans, on account of their regard to quantity. Kong-Sung's house is near the water, Whang-Tong's is in Sacramento Street, and Tong-Ling's in Jackson Street. There the grave celestials serve up their chow-chow and curry, besides many genuine English dishes; their tea and coffee cannot be surpassed." Further acclaim came from William Shaw, who maintained in *Golden Dreams and Waking Realities* that "the best eating houses in San Francisco are kept by the Celestials and conducted in Chinese fashion. The dishes are mostly curries, hashes and fricasee served up in small dishes and they are exceedingly palatable."

Since most of the early immigrants were from Guangdong and Fujian Provinces, the cuisine they served reflected traditional dishes from those areas: rice, duck, chicken, pork, fish, and foods imported directly from China such as dried vegetables, noodles, beans, tea, vinegar, soy sauce, oil, bean paste, dried mushrooms, bamboo shoots, cured eggs, salted fish, and dried shrimp. Enjoying early popularity was something Americans called *chop suey*, a stir-fry mixture of vegetables with sliced meat. With the rice replaced by noodles, it became the American favorite chow mein. Probably nothing epitomizes the early influence of Asian culture on the United States more than Chinese food.

CONCLUSION

The influx of Chinese into California during the gold rush established the basis for permanent Asian settlement in the United States. These years also saw the beginnings of the intense discrimination various groups of Asians would face in America in the years to follow. By 1860 the wheel had begun to turn quite quickly against Asians. In 1857 the Oregon Constitutional Convention determined that Chinese would not be able to own land or mining claims, and two years later when Oregon became a state, it levied a $5 poll tax on Chinese. Between 1858 and 1859, Chinese miners were expelled from the Buckeye, Columbia, Coyote Flat, Douglas Flat, Rock Creek, Sacramento Bar, Sand Flat, Shasta, Tuolumne, and Vallecito mining regions. Excluded from the mines, Chinese began to move into urban areas, where competition with locals grew to feed the increasing calls for exclusion. In 1859 Chinese children were excluded from the San Francisco public schools, setting the stage for increasing social and civil segregation to accompany the economic discrimination. Eventually this would lead to the onerous Chinese Exclusion Act of 1882, the first of a series of racist federal legislation designed to eliminate or restrict what were increasingly believed to be "undesirable" groups.

JAMES S. PULA
PURDUE UNIVERSITY NORTH CENTRAL

Further Reading

Chang, Iris. *The Chinese in America: A Narrative History.* New York: Viking, 2003.

Chen, Yong. *Chinese San Francisco, 1850–1943: A Trans-Pacific Community.* Stanford, CA: Stanford University Press, 2000.

Chiu, Ping. *Chinese Labor in California, 1850–1880.* Madison: State Historical Society of Wisconsin, 1963.

Chow, Lily. *Chasing Their Dreams. Chinese Settlement in the Northwest Region of British Columbia.* Prince George, BC: Caitlin Press, 2000.

Christman, Margaret C.S. *Adventurous Pursuits: Americans and the China Trade.* Washington, DC: Smithsonian Institute Press, 1984.

Dirlik, Arif, ed. *Chinese on the American Frontier.* New York: Rowman & Littlefield, 2001.

Espina, Marina. *Filipinos in Louisiana.* New Orleans, LA: A.F. Laborde & Sons, 1988.

Fessler, Loren W., ed. *Chinese in America: Stereotyped Past, Changing Present.* New York: Vantage Press, 1983.

Leland, C.C. *Fu-Sang or The Discovery of America by Chinese Buddhist Priests in the Fifth Century.* New York: Barnes & Noble, 1973.

Miller, Stuart Creighton, *The Unwelcome Immigrant: The American Image of the Chinese, 1785–1882.* Berkeley: University of California Press, 1969.

Steiner, Stan, *Fu-Sang. The Chinese Who Built America.* New York: Harper & Row, Publishers, 1979.

Takaki, Ronald. *Strangers From a Different Shore.* Boston, MA: Little, Brown and Company, 1989.

Tchen, John Kuo Wei. *New York Before Chinatown: Orientalism and the Shaping of American Culture, 1776–1882.* Baltimore, MD: Johns Hopkins University Press, 1999.

Zhu, Liping. *A Chinaman's Chance: The Chinese on the Rocky Mountain Mining Frontier.* Boulder: University Press of Colorado, 1997.

CHAPTER 2

The Civil War to the Gilded Age: 1859 to 1900

IN THE SECOND half of the 19th century, the Chinese were the largest Asian immigrant group to enter the United States. About 90 percent of all Chinese immigrants in the 19th century lived in the western states, over two-thirds of them in California alone. Immigrants from other Asian nations numbered much fewer than those from China. For example, in the late 19th century, Japanese leaders began to imitate the Western powers in order to turn Japan into a modern nation. The modernization was financed with taxes that left hundreds of thousands of Japanese destitute, but the Japanese were not allowed to emigrate until 1885. Similar to Japan, Korea was closed to Western powers until the mid-19th century. In 1882 the United States ratified a treaty with Korea, and soon treaties with other Western powers followed. Yet Korean immigration to Hawaii and the United States did not take place until after 1900. Large-scale immigration from the Philippines also did not occur until after the turn of the 20th century. The Philippines was a Spanish colony until 1898, when it was won by the United States in the Spanish-American War. The Filipinos then demanded independence from the United States and fought a bitter guerrilla war for several years.

Various laws and taxes that targeted Chinese immigrant workers were introduced in the 1850s and 1860s; for example in 1862, the Act to Protect Free White Labor against Competition with Chinese Coolie Labor, and to

Discourage the Immigration of the Chinese into the State of California, also known as the Chinese Police Tax, fixed a tax of $2.50 on all Chinese who worked in the mines. They did not have to pay this tax if they produced or manufactured sugar, rice, coffee, or tea. While laws like this were not successful in curbing Chinese immigration to the West Coast, they encouraged many Chinese to move into occupations where they posed no threat to whites. Some found work in agriculture where they cleared forests, reclaimed swamplands, or planted and harvested vegetables and fruit; others worked in textile or cigarette factories, or in the fishing industry where they caught fish, shrimp, and abalone, cured fish, and canned salmon. Many Chinese also opened laundry businesses and worked in domestic service. Their willingness to work in what were regarded as women's occupations, however, led to the stereotype of Chinese men as feminine.

The press on the West Coast increasingly portrayed Chinese immigration as an invasion, and claimed that unless the Chinese were excluded, they would soon dominate entire regions. Racism had been institutionalized in the United States by the Naturalization Act of 1790, which stipulated that only whites were eligible for naturalized citizenship. Since there was no universal definition of who actually belonged to the white race, some Chinese argued that they were in fact white, and therefore were entitled to U.S. citizenship. While in some eastern states Chinese immigrants were naturalized, most states refused to grant U.S. citizenship to Chinese immigrants, claiming that they were not part of the white race. In 1854 *People v. Hall* reinforced the

This 1880 newspaper cartoon titled "The Tables Turned" evoked fears that Chinese workers would take jobs away from European-Americans, while playing up that fact that these jobs were traditionally held by women.

These Chinese fishermen were photographed on a boat in San Francisco Bay, where they worked catching shrimp in the late 1880s.

racialization of Chinese immigrants as nonwhite by stipulating that Chinese were not allowed to give testimony against whites. Since they could not take legal action, Chinese immigrants became an easy target for racist mobs and discrimination.

CHINESE COMMUNITIES IN THE UNITED STATES

Chinese immigrants were mostly young and male. This facilitated their exploitation by U.S. employers, who made them work and live in miserable conditions for low wages, taking advantage of the fact that the Chinese workers did not have to support families in the United States. The fact that hardly any Chinese men brought their wives to the United States also meant that there would be no Chinese children who could apply for citizenship because they had been born on U.S. soil. Many states had laws that forbade intermarriage between Chinese and whites (although some Chinese men married Irish women), and so Chinese communities were mostly dominated by men.

The high percentage of men among the Chinese immigrants also led to another stereotype: that of the Chinese sojourner. Although it was quite common for immigrants in the United States to return to their country regardless of their nationality, the Chinese were stigmatized as sojourners by those who demanded their exclusion on the grounds that the Chinese were unable to assimilate into U.S. society. Proponents of Chinese exclusion also pointed out that the Chinese tended to settle down in ethnic communities, and refused to mingle with other ethnicities.

However this was by no means proof of the Chinese inability to assimilate. In fact it was common for immigrants (even from European countries) to settle in areas where their ethnicity was dominant. In this respect, the Chinese were no exception. However the Chinese did not always choose to live in Chinese communities; they were often forced to live there. They were discriminated against by landlords and harassed by their (white) neighbors until they found shelter from racial hatred in their own ethnic communities. Thus the Chinese communities (some of which later became Chinatowns) were by no means proof of a Chinese inability to assimilate—they were presented as such because it allowed proponents of Chinese exclusion to uphold the image of the United States as a nation of immigrants.

One effect of forced segregation was that Chinese communities (even when their populations were mostly male) developed considerable cohesion. Immigrants in Chinese communities began to form their own institutions for mutual support, such as clubs (known as *tongs*). They were also able to retain or develop their own distinctive culture in areas such as cuisine and architecture.

The concentration of Chinese in specific areas also made them an easy

Chinese workers often lived in segregated, mostly male, communities even outside of urban Chinatowns. This cluster of houses at Point San Pedro was home for some of the Chinese fishermen of San Francisco Bay around 1889.

target for anti-Chinese agitation. Soon Chinatowns were associated with values that were deemed immoral or uncivilized, like gambling, filth, disease, and crime. For example, the press often depicted Chinese immigrants as opium and gambling addicts who lacked morals and were incapable of progress of any kind.

This in turn raised fears of a degeneration of U.S. society if it continued to be swamped with Chinese immigrants, and pseudoscientific arguments about the need to protect Anglo-Saxon purity were used to argue against Chinese immigration. The notion of the Chinese body as a threat to U.S. society was also constructed by associating

This 1891 funeral for a Chinese man conducted by a small group of his compatriots in Deadwood, South Dakota, drew a crowd of spectators.

it with disease, and often Chinese immigrants were blamed for spreading epidemics and sexually transmitted diseases in communities.

WOMEN AND CHILDREN

The few Chinese women and children who arrived in the United States were also targets of racial hatred. In 1857 Chinese children in San Francisco were no longer allowed to go to schools for white children (African-American and Native-American children had already been forced to go to segregated schools). In 1866 a California law officially forbade all African-American, Native American, and Asian-American children from attending white schools. Various laws also limited the immigration of Chinese women. Since Chinese men could not get married and raise families in the United States, many turned to prostitutes. The majority of Chinese women in the United States were prostitutes, many of whom had been kidnapped or purchased in China from poor families or lured to the United States under false pretenses. This had the effect of even fewer Chinese women being admitted to the United States because it was claimed that they were all prostitutes. For example, in 1870, the Act to Prevent the Kidnapping and Importation of Mongolian, Chinese, and Japanese Females, for Criminal or Demoralizing Purposes stipulated that Asian women could only enter California if they could prove to the immigration officer that they were of good character and had come to the United States voluntarily. In 1875 the Page Law prohibited the entry of Chinese, Japanese, and Mongolian contract laborers (coolies), felons, Chinese prostitutes, and women who were suspected of being prostitutes. This meant that immigration officers could refuse entry to Chinese women by claiming that they suspected them of being prostitutes. As a consequence, practically no Chinese women were allowed to immigrate to the United States after 1875 except for merchants' wives, and it became impossible for Chinese immigrants to send for their wives and children.

Throughout the 19th century, only five to seven percent of the Chinese immigrants to the United States were women, and Chinese society was a "bachelor society" where prostitution thrived. However Chinese brothels were frequented not only by Chinese, but also by white men, which further increased fears of the degeneration of U.S. society. The exclusion of Chinese women, therefore, served to ensure that hardly any Chinese-American children were born in the United States who could claim American citizenship. Also because the white race, and especially American society, were seen as superior to the Chinese, the exclusion of Chinese women was also part of an effort to keep the white race "pure" and avoid degeneration by mixing races. Laws like the Page Law stigmatized Chinese women as prostitutes (and presented them as the opposite of idealized American women) and were used by proponents of Chinese exclusion to argue that since all Chinese women were prostitutes, they were all immoral, diseased, and depraved and had to be excluded.

This photograph taken in San Francisco's Chinatown around 1896 is titled "slave girl in holiday attire."

In Hawaii, however, where Chinese had immigrated to work on plantations, the situation was different. After they fulfilled their contracts on the plantations, many remained in Hawaii and became farmers. Since they were allowed to marry native Hawaiian women, many Chinese workers decided to settle down and start a family, something that was impossible

Yellow Peril

Since the 18th century, scientists had been categorizing human beings according to races that they put in a hierarchical order. On top were usually whites, on the bottom blacks. Asians, such as the Chinese, Japanese, and Koreans, were usually grouped together as the yellow race, and were placed in between whites and blacks in the racial hierarchy. In the United States, racial theories had traditionally been used by colonists to portray Native Americans and African Americans as naturally inferior, to justify slavery and later segregation. After the arrival of Chinese immigrants in the United States, racial theories were used by supporters of Chinese (and later Asian) exclusion. The Yellow Peril was not so much a national as a racial image and essentially described the yellow race as a threat to the white race. Various versions of the idea existed in the United States in the second half of the 19th century. The most popular one focused on the numbers of Chinese immigrants to the United States and described them as hordes invading the country. The dehumanization of Chinese immigrants not only presented them as a threat to American society, it also legitimized violence against the Chinese.

In the following excerpt, Huie Kin, who immigrated to the United States in 1868 when he was 14, recalls the anti-Chinese movement in Oakland, California, in the 1870s:

The sudden change of public sentiment towards our people in those days was an interesting illustration of mob psychology [. . .]. The useful and steady Chinese worker became overnight the mysterious Chinaman, an object of unknown dread. When I landed [in 1868], the trouble was already brewing, but the climax did not come until 1876–1877. I understand that several causes contributed to the anti-Chinese riots. It was a period of general economic depression in the Western States, brought about by drought, crop failures, and reduced output of the gold mines, and on the top of it came a presidential campaign. [. . .] There were long processions at night, with big torchlights and lanterns, carrying the slogan "The Chinese Must Go," and mass meetings where fiery-tongues flayed the Chinese bogey. Those were the days of Denis Kearney and his fellow agitators, known as sandlot orators, on account of their vehement denouncements in open-air meetings. To Kearney was attributed the statement which showed to what extremes political demagogues could go: "There is no means left to clear the Chinamen but to swing them into eternity by their own queues, for there is no rope long enough in all America wherewith to strangle four hundred millions of Chinamen." The Chinese were in a pitiable condition in those days. We were simply terrified; we kept indoors after dark for fear of being shot in the back. Children spit upon us as we passed by and called us rats. However, there was one consolation: the people who employed us never turned against us, and we went on quietly with our work until the public frenzy subsided.

for the majority of Chinese immigrants to the United States in the 19th century. Thus the Chinese immigrant community in Hawaii with its family structure was very different from that of the U.S. Chinatowns dominated by men.

THE LABOR MOVEMENT AND ANTI-CHINESE SENTIMENT

Since Chinese workers were willing to work for low wages, unions and (white) workers blamed Chinese immigrants whenever wages decreased in the west; for example, the arrival of Chinese workers in the gold mines resulted in anti-Chinese sentiment there. The employment of thousands of Chinese during the period of railroad construction spread the anti-Chinese movement farther across the west. For example, about 12,000 Chinese were employed for the construction of the Central Pacific Railroad 1865–69 because they were much cheaper than white workers. Even though they were supervised by whites and carried out the most dangerous tasks (over 1,000 Chinese died because of the harsh living and dangerous working conditions), hostility among white workers and unions against Chinese laborers increased. However because of the contributions of Chinese workers, the railroad was finished much faster. After the railroad was completed, the Chinese laborers immigrated to other regions in their quest to find work, but there, too, they were soon met by anti-Chinese sentiment and talks of an invasion of Chinese workers.

Chinese laborers also helped maintain railroads after construction. Here they are shown shoveling out a snowbound Union Pacific train in Ogden, Utah, in 1872.

The American labor movement tended to describe Chinese workers as coolies and claimed that because their presence in the United States had resulted in degrading wages and working conditions, the Chinese had to be excluded. In the 1860s, anti-coolie clubs were founded in San Francisco, and in 1870 the Act to Prevent the Importation of Chinese Criminals and to Prevent the Establishment of Coolie Slavery stipulated that Chinese were allowed to enter California only if they could prove they were not coolies, but had come to the United States voluntarily. Especially after Chinese laborers were used in the south to replace slaves on sugar, cotton, and rice plantations, op-

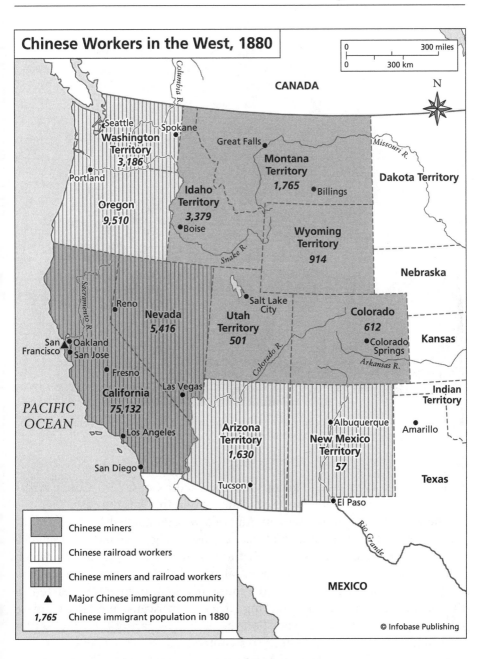

Chinese Workers in the West, 1880

ponents of Chinese immigration claimed that because the Chinese worked as coolies, a kind of slave labor was reintroduced to the United States, even though slavery had been outlawed in the Civil War. While Chinese coolies were indeed used in some parts of the world to replace slaves as a cheap workforce after slavery was abolished, they did not work as coolies in the

A factory owner or manager teaching Chinese strikebreakers in North Adams, Massachusetts, to use a pegging machine for shoe manufacturing in 1870.

United States, even though groups like the Pacific Coast Anti-Coolie Association, which was founded in 1867, claimed that this was the case.

The anti-Chinese movement in America was dominated by Irish immigrants who in the 1840s and 1850s had themselves been victims of prejudice in the United States because of their Catholic faith and Celtic origin (which were believed to be contrary to the racial and religious basis of American society, which was Anglo-Saxon and Protestant). Irish immigrants reacted to this hostile environment by attacking African Americans, and later Chinese immigrants, in an effort to reposition themselves as part of the white settler community in the United States. This contributed to many Chinese stereotypes similar to those of African Americans; for example, anti-Chinese stereotypes about the biological and cultural incapability of the Chinese to assimilate into American society and customs were similar to stereotypes about African Americans. Moreover, in popular culture, the stereotypical African-American characters Jim Crow or Zip Coon had a Chinese equivalent, namely, the character John Chinaman, which stood for the cultural and racial differences of Chinese Americans and was very popular in songs, poems, stories, and musical performances. While white performers in minstrel shows blackened their faces to portray African Americans, they used a similar technique called yellowface to portray Chinese.

The fact that Chinese workers were sometimes used as strikebreakers increased the anti-Chinese sentiment in the U.S. labor movement. In 1870, 75 Chinese laborers arrived in North Adams, Massachusetts, where they were used as strikebreakers in a shoe factory that workers had picketed for more pay. Soon Chinese workers were imported to other factories in the north, either as strikebreakers or cheap labor. Until then, the anti-Chinese movement had been mostly concentrated in the west. Now, however, unions in the northeast also began to demand the exclusion of Chinese immigrants, resulting in nationwide spread of anti-Chinese sentiment that was based on the image of the Chinese as a threat to white workers.

When the west was hit by an economic depression in the 1870s, the Chinese were blamed for lower wages and the loss of jobs. As a result, the anti-Chinese movement gained momentum, and anti-Chinese laws were implemented in rapid succession. Some ordinances specifically targeted the Chinese. For example, in 1870, the Cubic Air Ordinance of San Francisco stipulated that every room in a house that was occupied by people had to have at least 500 cubic feet of air per person. This law was only enforced against Chinese lodging houses, even though there were other lodging houses that violated its provisions. Another law prohibited people on the pavement from carrying baskets suspended from a pole over the shoulder. Since this was a typical Chinese way of carrying goods, it was also clearly aimed at the Chinese.

Often anti-Chinese sentiment erupted in violence. White mobs looted and burned Chinese settlements, driving away or lynching their inhabitants. In October 1871 a mob murdered and lynched about 20 Chinese in Los Angeles, and looted and burned their houses. In 1873 an influx of Chinese immigration led to the founding of the People's Protection Alliance, an

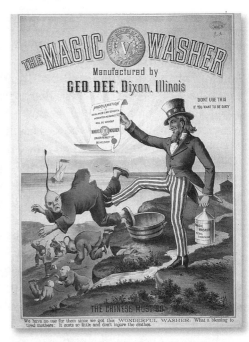

This 1886 ad from Illinois for "Magic Washer" detergent employs racist imagery of the era and shows Uncle Sam kicking Chinese out of the country.

Men on horseback assaulting a Chinese man in a small town in the west around 1880. Such anti-Chinese attacks and riots occurred in a number of towns and cities in the late 19th century.

anti-Chinese umbrella organization that had as its goal the exclusion of Chinese immigrants. More anti-Chinese measures were taken. For example, the Laundry Ordinance stipulated that laundries in San Francisco had to pay $2 every three months if they had a delivery horse, $4 if they had two horses, and $15 if they had no horse.

Since Chinese laundries did not use horses, but had their employees carry baskets, the law targeted them. Hundreds of Chinese were arrested for violating the law. After most of them chose to go to prison instead of paying a fine, the San Francisco Board of Supervisors came up with another anti-Chinese order that was called the Queue-Cutting Order. The sheriff had to cut the hair of prisoners to one-inch length.

Since for the Chinese the queue was crucial to their social standing and mandatory for any Chinese, having it cut off was an extreme humiliation. Eventually both ordinances were vetoed by the mayor of San Francisco because they violated the Burlingame Treaty (ratified between China and the United States in 1868), which guaranteed the protection of Chinese immigrants in the United States.

The labor movement, however, increasingly pressured the U.S. government to act against Chinese immigration and coolie labor. In December 1874 President Ulysses S. Grant confirmed such views by stating that most

Chinese immigrants did not come to the United States voluntarily, and that such practice had to be stopped. Now even the U.S. government agreed with the labor movement. Meanwhile the economic situation worsened, but Chinese immigration continued (16,500 arrived in the United States in 1875, and 22,800 in 1876), and further increased demands for Chinese exclusion. The popularity of anti-Chinese organizations and clubs grew rapidly, resulting in 1876 in an anti-Chinese demonstration with 250,000 participants in California. Chinese immigrants also became the focus of two legislative committees, one in the California State Senate, and one in Congress. Both concluded that Chinese immigrants were naturally inferior to whites, psychologically unfit for democracy, and had to be excluded because they would turn the United States into an Asian colony if they were not stopped.

THE CHINESE EXCLUSION ACT
Pressure on the U.S. government increased further when the Workingman's Party of California was founded in 1877 in San Francisco under the leadership

The Race for Possession

The following is an excerpt from the Senate Report of the Joint Special Committee to investigate Chinese Immigration (1877):

[T]he Pacific coast must in time become either American or Mongolian. There is a vast hive from which Chinese immigrants may swarm, and circumstances may send them in enormous numbers to this country. These two forces, Mongolian and American, are already in active opposition. They do not amalgamate, and all conditions are opposed to any assimilation. The American race is progressive and in favor of a responsible representative government. The Mongolian race seems to have no desire for progress, and to have no conception of representative and free institutions. While conditions should be favorable to the growth and occupancy of our Pacific possessions by our own people, the Chinese have advantages which will put them far in advance in this race for possession. They can subsist where the American would starve. They can work for wages which will not furnish the barest necessities of life to an American. They make their way in California as they have in the islands of the sea, not by superior force or virtue, or even industry, although they are, as a rule, industrious, but by revolting characteristics, and by dispensing with what have become necessities in modern civilization. To compete with them and excel them the American must come down to their level, or below them; must work so cheaply that the Chinese cannot compete with him, for in the contest for subsistence he that can subsist upon the least will last the longest.

of Denis Kearney. The party adopted as its slogan "The Chinese must go!" In 1880 a new treaty between China and the United States allowed the United States to restrict immigration from China (until then the Burlingame Treaty protected Chinese immigration to the United States), resulting in 25 petitions in Congress against Chinese immigration in 1881. Although President Chester A. Arthur was opposed to such measures, and even vetoed a Chinese exclusion bill in 1881, he eventually gave in. On May 6, 1882, he signed the Chinese Exclusion Act, which suspended the immigration of Chinese workers to the United States for 10 years, and allowed only Chinese teachers, students, merchants, and tourists to enter the United States.

The main argument of supporters of Chinese exclusion, namely, that hordes of Chinese were invading the United States, was completely unrealistic. Even in 1880, the Chinese constituted only 0.2 percent of the total U.S. population. They were neither swamping the United States, nor did they pose a realistic threat to white workers, especially since they tended to work in occupations that were rejected by white workers. Thus the exclusion of the Chinese was not based on rational facts, but was clearly racist. In fact, while Chinese immigrants were excluded from the United States, European immigration was encouraged; out of the five million immigrants who came to the United States in the 1880s, over two-thirds came from western Europe.

After 1882 various acts further limited Chinese immigration. In 1888 the Scott Act made it impossible for Chinese workers to return to the United States once they left. In 1892 the McGeary Act not only prolonged Chinese exclusion until 1902, but also made it mandatory for all Chinese to prove that they were legally residing in the United States. In 1902 Chinese exclusion was made permanent, and was not repealed until 1943. Although the Chinese Exclusion Act reduced the numbers of Chinese immigrants, it also convinced many Chinese to enter the United States illegally. Some of them came via Canada or Mexico, and hid on the train or posed as Native Americans, Mexicans, or even African Americans to cross the border. Some took legal action after they were denied entry to the United States; others claimed they were born in the United States. Many were also taken in as so-called paper sons by Chinese men who had a permit to reside in the United States. Although U.S. immigration officials tried to reduce the numbers of these paper sons by detailed and scrupulous interrogations, they were not always successful.

The Chinese Exclusion Act did not stop anti-Chinese violence; massacres of Chinese immigrants, which had occurred since their arrival, continued in the 1870s and 1880s. Especially in the 1880s, widespread unemployment and the use of Chinese workers as strikebreakers contributed to anti-Chinese agitation, which was rampant in the west, especially in those areas where Chinese made up a significant percentage of the population. In California, Montana, Oregon, Washington, and Colorado, racist mobs massacred Chinese, burned their homes, demolished their laundries, and drove entire Chinese communities from towns. The most infamous example is the Rock Springs Massacre in Wyoming in 1885. In Rock Springs, 331 Chinese and 150 white workers were employed by Union Pacific in a coal mine. Tensions between the ethnic groups rose, and eventually erupted in a massacre of the Chinese workers by white mobs. The Chinese were hunted down, robbed, beaten, and lynched, and their shacks burned. Those who survived fled the village, but they lost all their possessions. No whites were charged with the murders. In all, 28 Chinese were killed, and the entire Chinese population of Rock Springs was driven away. Similar incidents of mass expulsion occurred in other towns including Seattle, where unemployment caused by the economic depression increased

This newspaper engraving depicts the anti-Chinese riot in Denver, Colorado, on October 31, 1880.

hostility against Chinese immigrants, resulting in anti-Chinese riots that forced almost the entire Chinese population of Seattle to leave the city under the protection of the police and other officials.

THE ANTI-JAPANESE MOVEMENT
Although the Japanese were allowed to emigrate after 1885, most Japanese decided to go to Hawaii, not to the United States. There they worked as contract laborers on sugar plantations. By 1900 about 40 percent of the population in Hawaii were Japanese or of Japanese descent. Some Japanese came to the United States, especially the West Coast, from Hawaii. By 1890 there were about 2,300 Japanese in the United States (compared to about 106,700 Chinese), and Japanese communities formed in various areas along the Pacific coast.

The Japanese soon began to replace the Chinese in the labor force because Chinese workers were no longer allowed to enter the United States, and the Chinese in the country were aging. Soon, the press focused on the Japanese as the new threat for white workers. An anti-Japanese movement then began in America in the 1890s as a continuation of the anti-Chinese movement. For

A Chinese Immigrant's Response to Discrimination

The following excerpt is a letter to the San Francisco *Argonaut* in 1878 by the Chinese immigrant Kwang Chang Ling:

You demand every privilege for Americans in China but you would deny the same privileges to Chinamen in America, because in your opinion the presence of Chinese among you is a menace to your civilization. You shrink from contact with us, not because you regard us as mentally or bodily inferior, for neither fact nor argument will support you here—but rather because our religious code appears to be different from yours, and because we are deemed to be more abstemious in food, clothing, and shelter [. . . Let me] correct one great misapprehension in respect to the Chinese. You are continually objecting to his morality. Your travelers say he is depraved; your missioners call him ungodly; your commissioners call him uncleanly [. . .] . Yet your housewives permit him to wait upon them at table; they admit him to their bed-chambers; they confide to him their garments and jewels; and even trust their lives to him by awarding him supreme control over their kitchens and the preparation of their food. There is a glaring contradiction here [. . .] . The slender fare of rice and the other economical habits of the peasant class [of China], which are so objectionable to your lower orders and the demagogues who trumpet their clamors, are not the result of choice to Chinamen; they follow poverty. The hard-working, patient servants that you have about you today, love good fare as well as other men, but they are engaged in a work far higher than the gratification of self-indulgence; they are working to liberate their parents in China [. . .] and as long as their labor continues to strike off the fetter from their beloved ones will they continue to practice their nobel self-abnegation. When this emancipation is complete, you will find the chinaman as prone as any human creature to fill his belly and cover his back with good things.

example, whereas Denis Kearney demanded "The Chinese must go!" in the 1870s, now it was "The Japs must go!" While the anti-Japanese movement did not grow into a full-blown phobia in the 1890s because the number of Japanese immigrants still remained relatively small, by 1900 fears concerning the numbers of Asian immigrants had grown to such a degree that demands for Asian exclusion grew louder.

CONCLUSION

Between 1859 and 1900, the majority of Asian immigrants to the United States were Chinese. While the immigration of whites from Europe was actively supported, demands increased to exclude Chinese—and later Japanese—immigrants because they were seen as a threat to American society. Most Chinese came to the United States to make enough money so that they could support their families back in China.

Their willingness to work for low wages led to claims by the American labor movement that the Chinese took away the jobs of white workers and lowered wages so much that it was impossible for whites to survive. The employment of Chinese workers was also often denounced as a modern slavery that would eventually turn white workers into slaves.

Not only Chinese men, but also Chinese women were the target of racial discrimination: Asian women were portrayed as prostitutes who had to be excluded from the United States. As a result, especially on the West Coast, laws and ordinances targeted Chinese immigrants, and throughout the second half of the 19th century, white mobs massacred and lynched Chinese. Even after the Chinese Exclusion Act in 1882 outlawed the immigration of Chinese workers to the United States, anti-Chinese sentiment did not disappear. However, slowly the focus of racial hatred began to shift more and more toward the Japanese immigrants who had been arriving since the 1880s.

ARIANE KNUESEL
UNIVERSITY OF ZURICH

Further Reading

Aarim-Heriot, Najia. *Chinese Immigrants, African Americans, and Racial Anxiety in the United States, 1848–1882.* Champaign: University of Illinois Press, 2003.

Chan, Sucheng. *Asian Americans: An Interpretive History.* Boston, MA: Twayne, 1991.

Choy, Philip P., Lorraine Dong, and Marlon K. Hom. *The Coming Man: 19th Century American Perceptions of the Chinese.* Seattle: University of Washington Press, 1995.

Daniels, Roger. *Asian America: Chinese and Japanese in the United States since 1850.* Seattle: University of Washington Press, 1988.

Hoobler, Dorothy, and Thomas Hoobler. *The Chinese American Family Album.* New York: Oxford University Press, 1994.

Lee, Erika. *At America's Gates: Chinese Immigration during the Exclusion Era, 1882–1943.* Chapel Hill: University of North Carolina Press, 2003.

Lee, Robert G. *Orientals: Asian Americans in Popular Culture.* Philadelphia, PA: Temple University Press, 1999.

Library of Congress, "The Chinese in California 1850–1925." Available online, URL: http://memory.loc.gov/ammem/award99/cubhtml/cichome.html. Accessed August 2009.

McCunn, Ruthanne Lum. *Chinese American Portraits: Personal Histories 1828–1988*. San Francisco, CA: Chronicle Books, 1998.

Miller, Stuart Creighton. *The Unwelcome Immigrant: The American Image of the Chinese, 1785–1882*. Berkeley: University of California Press, 1969.

Moon, Krystyn R. *Yellowface: Creating the Chinese in American Popular Music and Performance, 1850s–1920s*. New Brunswick, NJ: Rutgers University Press, 2005.

Takaki, Ronald. *Strangers from a Different Shore: A History of Asian Americans*. New York: Penguin Books, 1989.

Wu, William F. *The Yellow Peril: Chinese Americans in American Fiction 1850–1940*. Hamden, CT: Archon Books, 1982.

Yung, Judy, Gordon H. Chang, and Him Mark Lai, eds. *Chinese American Voices: From the Gold Rush to the Present*. Berkeley: University of California Press, 2006.

CHAPTER 3

The Progressive Era and World War I: 1900 to 1920

IN 1898–1900, THE United States dramatically changed its involvement in Asia, and this was to have a major effect on the number and the distribution of Asian Americans in the United States. The first of the events that altered U.S. links with Asia was the war with Spain that broke out in April 1898. This saw U.S. soldiers fighting the Spanish in their colonies, including the Philippines, and in the Caribbean island of Cuba. By the Treaty of Paris on December 10, 1898, the Philippines were officially ceded to the United States. After a short struggle against independence fighters, the United States was soon in unchallenged charge of the islands until the Japanese invasion of December 1941. This saw U.S. administrators posted to the Philippines, and gradually, significant numbers of Filipinos moved to the United States for education or training, or in search of work. This was particularly true of Hawaii, with many Filipinos settling there. The Spanish-American War also led to the United States gaining the island of Guam in the Pacific, which had a significant Asian population as well.

In 1899 the Boxer Rebellion (an uprising by anti-colonialists) in China led to the siege of the foreign legations in Beijing and the dispatch of U.S. marines from the Philippines. This culminated in U.S. soldiers taking part in the storming of Beijing in August 1900, and the United States becoming a major foreign power involved in Chinese affairs. Although there had been many American missionaries in China before the Boxer Rebellion, the number increased after 1900. More and more wealthy Chinese saw business opportunities in the United States, or sent their children there for education.

From the period of the war with Spain, the United States had also become interested in expanding its power into the Pacific. In 1898 President William McKinley signed the Newlands Resolution, which on July 7, 1898, led to the official U.S. annexation of Hawaii. On February 22, 1900, Hawaii became a U.S. territory, and finally gained statehood in 1959. Because of Hawaii's position in the Pacific, there were many Chinese, Japanese, Filipino, and other Asian migrants already there when it became the Hawaii Territory of the United States, although it was not long before the U.S. restrictions on labor migration were imposed in Hawaii.

THE CHINESE

From 1900 until 1920, the vast majority of Asian Americans—as in previous decades—were Chinese, and a large number of factors continued to influence the establishment of many Chinese-American communities throughout the country. Some were from families that had settled in California and had been connected with the gold rush of 1849 and/or the subsequent building of the railroads. The descendants of these Chinese had settled throughout the West Coast, and in many other cities and towns in the United States, and small

This photograph shows Pell Street in New York City's Chinatown around 1900. By this time, a number of U.S. Chinatowns had been established, but the overall population of Chinese was in decline.

Chinatowns were established in San Francisco, Los Angeles, New York, Boston, and some other major cities.

However there were also many new immigrants from China who moved to California and elsewhere. Figures from the U.S. Census Bureau's *Historical Statistics of the United States* show that the number remained relatively constant throughout the 1900s and 1910s, with occasional rises. In 1900 some 1,247 Chinese immigrated to the United States, and this rose in the following year to 2,459. It remained between these two figures until 1915, with the exceptions of 4,309 in 1904 and only 961 in 1907. In 1914 the figure rose to 2,502, and then in 1915 to 2,660, but then fell back to its previous levels. This was a period during which many tens of thousands of migrants arrived

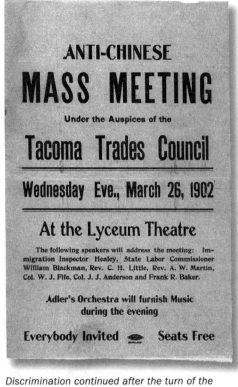

Discrimination continued after the turn of the century, as shown by this poster from Tacoma, Washington, calling for an anti-Chinese meeting.

each year from all over Europe and elsewhere, so the numbers were not comparatively high. Overall the number of Chinese in the United States fell during the 1900s and 1910s. Part of this came from natural attrition (death), and many Chinese having made (or not made) their fortunes and returned to China. Some left the United States to settle in the Philippines or other parts of southeast Asia or in Hong Kong. Some moved to Latin America and the Caribbean.

Most of the Chinese who came to the United States did so in search of greater economic advantages. The majority of these still came from southern China, and there was still the worry that the Chinese were capable of providing a labor force that could undercut many U.S. workers. In 1901 there were so many Chinese in San Francisco that the Chinese community established its own telephone exchange. In 1904 bilateral trade between the two countries was approaching $40 million a year. But then the United States started a process of trying to exclude Chinese laborers. Chinese delegates to the St. Louis World's Fair in 1903 were discriminated against when U.S. authorities wanted all Chinese delegates to be photographed

Spectators watching Chinatown burn on April 18, 1906, after the San Francisco earthquake. The reconstruction of Chinatown after the disaster was a turning point for many Chinese, and demonstrated the durability of the community.

and examined, and have a $500 bond posted against them absconding. It was not long before these measures led to anti-American protests in China, and many Chinese boycotted U.S. goods after 1904.

Although the number of Chinese in California and elsewhere was declining, there was still a large degree of racial tension. In the San Francisco earthquake of 1906, large numbers of homes and businesses in San Francisco's Chinatown were destroyed. Many of the Chinese fled to escape the fires, and others were forced to leave by local police and others. Although much of Chinatown was burned down, the rebuilding efforts that followed showed many local residents that the Chinese were settlers, rather than temporary immigrants.

The fires also created a window of opportunity for many people. The fires that followed the earthquake destroyed many of the city records. This, in turn, enabled many Chinese to falsely claim that they had been born in San Francisco—because birth records had been lost and the authorities were unable to disprove their claims. The Chinese were not the only group who took advantage of this—Britons, Germans, and others all filed for U.S. citizenship. Thus the fires enabled many Chinese to gain U.S. citizenship, which at that time applied to anybody born in the United States. Having acquired U.S. citizenship, the Chinese were able to return to China knowing that they would not face any problems reentering the United States. The Chinese community, which, at that time was largely focused on San Francisco and New York, started spreading, with Lonie Quan establishing a Chinatown in Los Angeles in 1909.

TENSIONS WITHIN CHINESE COMMUNITIES

With a larger Chinese community, and one that overwhelmingly kept to itself, it was not long before various secret societies started to operate. Some of these were self-help groups, and they took on the tasks of looking after members, their families, and paying for funerals, through benevolent associations. Some were also involved in looking after the savings of members. In 1904 there had been a clash in the Chinese community in San Francisco with the new generation led by Walter U. Lum, Joseph K. Lum, and Gunn Ng establishing the Native Sons of the Golden States to provide leadership for Chinese who wanted to take part actively in American society. They wanted to ensure that all Chinese who would play a part in the United States should have their civil rights, and should exercise them. They wanted the Chinese to be able to get U.S. citizenship, but they also wanted this to come with the responsibility of being active U.S. citizens, working with non-Chinese and promoting relations with people outside the Chinese community. It was not long before chapters of the Native Sons of the Golden States were established in Oakland, Fresno, Los Angeles, and San Diego—and the association soon changed its name to the Chinese American Citizens Alliance.

However there were a small number of Chinese who were connected with crime, making money from illegal gambling and prostitution. They often vied with others for control over areas in Chinatowns, and these conflicts could get violent, with people assaulted and some killed. It gained the Chinese community a reputation for being dangerous, even though the vast majority had as little to do with crime as did Italians of the same era with the Italian organized crime gangs.

San Francisco's Chinese Telephone Exchange

San Francisco's Chinese telephone exchange (an office with operators who connected calls) was a popular tourist venue. Its directory even included an invitation to both non-Chinese and Chinese to visit the exchange. By 1910 Chinese subscribers were being listed both in English and in Chinese characters in the telephone directory, but by the 1920s, the exchange was producing its own directories printed entirely in Chinese characters. The following description of the original telephone exchange as it appeared before the 1906 earthquake and fire ran in the *San Francisco Examiner* on November 17, 1901:

The new Chinese Telephone Exchange is open and ready for business, after months of preparation. The exchange differs from all others in this city or in the world in that it is gorgeous with Oriental beauty and a marvel of luxurious good taste and splendor. The telephone company has made it a point to make the new exchange one of the show places in Chinatown. It has spared no expense to obtain this result, and Chief Engineer Cantin, under whose direction the work was done, feels justly proud of the results of his labors. The new exchange is in the three-story building at 743 Washington Street.

The first floor is occupied by a store, which has been refitted and decorated by its owners to be in accord with the remainder of the building. The entrance to the exchange is up a long flight of narrow stairs, at the head of which is a gayly decorated sign in Chinese letters announcing the presence of the telephone, which, strangely enough, is one of the most popular of the American inventions among the Chinese. . .

The walls are hung with banners in red and yellow and gold. Along one side of the room is a row of teakwood chairs with cushions of silk, while near the switchboard are the small black stools which are to be seen all over the Chinese quarter. The switchboard itself is exactly like those in the other exchanges of the city, except that the operatives are men and Chinese. They used the same cry of "hello" in answer to a call—a pleasant tone, cheerful and good-humored.

The work of the exchange would drive an American operator insane. For, in addition to the 255 numbers on the exchange, there are at least 125 telephones which are either in Chinese lodging-houses or in clubs. The operatives have nearly 1,500 names to remember, together with their owner's place of residence. For example, Woo Kee rings his telephone and says he wants to talk to Chung Hi Kin. He gives no number, for Chung lives in some big tenement and has no telephone number. It is the duty of the operative to remember all these names, and it is claimed he does so without effort.

The Chinese telephone company has been in existence since 1887 and has slowly made its way from place to place as its increasing business made larger quarters necessary.

The tensions between the Chinese and other immigrants worried many U.S. legislators, and President Theodore Roosevelt, in a speech to southern textile manufacturers, noted: "We cannot expect China to do us justice, unless we do China justice. The chief cause in bringing about the boycott of our goods in China was undoubtedly our attitude toward the Chinese who came to this country . . . Our laws and treaties should be so framed as to guarantee to all Chinamen, save of the excepted coolie class, the same right of entry to this country, and the same treatment while here, as is guaranteed to any other nation. By executive action, I am as rapidly as possible putting a stop to the abuses which have grown up during many years in the administration of the law. I can do a great deal and will do a great deal even without the action of Congress, but I cannot do all that should be done, unless some action is taken . . ."

If Roosevelt's aim was to encourage wealthier and better-educated Chinese to come to the United States, this was partially achieved. Some Chinese boys were already attending schools in America, and in 1904, Soong E-ling (Song Ailing), the oldest of the three Soong sisters, arrived in the United States to attend Wesleyan College at Macon, Georgia. Her father, Charlie Soong, had spent some of his early life in Boston, and by the 1900s was emerging as a wealthy publisher and printer in Shanghai. Soong E-ling was later joined by her two sisters Soong Ching-ling and Soong Mei-ling, the three going on to dominate the Chinese political scene—themselves and through their husbands—from the 1920s to the 1950s.

Just a few years before Soong E-ling arrived in Georgia, Dr. Sun Yat-sen, the man for whom she would work (and who would marry her sister), returned to Hawaii as a revolutionary intent on the overthrow of the Chinese Manchu government, which finally occurred in 1911. In 1904 Sun managed to acquire U.S. citizenship—he claimed to have been born in Hawaii (although he was actually born in China)—and he mixed freely with the Chinese Americans in Hawaii and on the U.S. mainland where he raised

Sun Yat Sen in an undated portrait made during a visit to San Francisco.

funds for his activities. Sun helped raise the profile of the Chinese revolutionary movement throughout Chinese communities in the United States.

He was traveling from Denver to Kansas City when he heard about the 1911 uprising in Wuchang that would lead to the Chinese Revolution. After the revolution and the end of Manchu imperial rule in China in 1912, Sun's nationalist party, the Kuomintang, began to establish branches throughout the United States and elsewhere, and this helped bring a political aspect to the leadership of Chinese community groups in many U.S. cities.

Another Chinese-American political activist was Yung Wing, who had graduated from Yale and returned to China where he was a supporter of the reforms that were ended in 1898 by imperial rule. He fled China with a price on his head, and although Secretary of State John Sherman revoked his U.S. citizenship, he still managed to enter the United States illegally and saw his youngest son Bartlett graduate from Yale University. Yung Wung died in Hartford, Connecticut, in 1912, three months after the abdication of the last Manchu emperor.

THE KOREANS

Sun Yat-sen was not the only revolutionary Asian American in the United States during this period. Syngman Rhee also arrived in the United States in 1904. A descendant of the eldest brother of the first king of the Yi royal family of Korea, he had been agitating against Japanese control of Korea. He lived in the United States for six years, studying at George Washington University and then Princeton University, where he gained his doctoral degree. During his time in the United States, he raised the consciousness of many Americans about the plight of the Koreans, and was active among the small Korean-American population in California and Hawaii. He was largely responsible for maintaining the concept of Korean independence among the overseas Korean population. In 1948 Syngman Rhee became the U.S.-backed leader of South Korea.

At the same time that Syngman Rhee moved to the United States, a Korean social activist named Ahn Chang Ho settled in Los Angeles, and also

Korean leader Syngman Rhee, who lived and studied in the United States in the early 1900s.

became an outspoken opponent of Japanese rule over Korea. Using the pen name Dosan, he established the Young Korean Academy and helped found, with Syngman Rhee, the Provisional Government of the Republic of Korea, a government-in-exile, based in Shanghai. The father of the Hollywood actor Philip Ahn, and Susan Ahn Cuddy, the first Asian woman to serve in the U.S. Navy, Ahn Chang Ho is one of the two men who are credited with writing the lyrics of the South Korean national anthem.

Both Syngman Rhee and Ahn Chang Ho moved to the United States at a time when a number of Koreans were moving doing the same. This was because of the restrictions being imposed on Chinese and Japanese laborers—regulations on immigration that did not apply to Koreans. As a result, some 1,000 Koreans moved to Hawaii and then to San Francisco 1904–07, and ended up working along the U.S. West Coast as laborers in mines, as farm workers, or on the railroads—in some of the same occupations where the Chinese had found employment. However Korean immigration came to a halt in 1910 when Japan annexed the Korean Peninsula, and Koreans were regarded, for immigration purposes, as Japanese.

THE JAPANESE

It was not until the 1880s that the Japanese started to immigrate overseas. Until 30 years earlier, they had been forbidden to have any contact with foreign people on pain of death. With the passing of the Chinese Exclusion Act in 1882, an opportunity arose for Japanese to find work in the United States. Many Japanese laborers started to move to the United States; in 1900, there were only 23,326, but by 1910 there were 72,157, many of whom were women, with many Japanese Americans born.

Dislike of the Chinese had led to discrimination against them by many Californians, and they became more aggressive toward the Japanese, who were treated even worse. However the Japanese complained to their government in Tokyo, and it was not long before the U.S. representatives in Japan were being called in to hear these problems. At one point, Theodore Roosevelt felt that if the anger in Japan over the treatment of Japanese Americans became worse, there was a real possibility of war between the two countries. In 1906 the California state government ordered the segregation of Japanese children in schools, and soon afterward, Roosevelt asked his Secretary of the Navy for details on the Japanese fleet and a comparison of it with the U.S. Navy in case of possible war.

Eventually, in 1908, the Gentleman's Agreement was introduced by which the Japanese government promised not to issue as many emigration permits to laborers. This had briefly created a demand for Koreans, as mentioned earlier. However when Korea was annexed by Japan, this source dried up, and the United States sought another place for cheap labor—this led to an influx of migrants from India.

California Governor Asks for Curb on Japanese

California Governor William D. Stephens (in office 1917–23) joined in attempts to limit Japanese immigration to the state in the early 1920s, as evidenced by a letter he wrote to the U.S. Secretary of State in 1920. The *New York Times* excerpted his letter in the following story, which ran on June 22, 1920:

Sacramento, Cal, June 21—the influx of Japanese into California has brought about "alarming" conditions and it has become necessary to protect the sovereignty of the State against this "growing menace" through diplomatic negotiation or a strict exclusion act, Governor William D. Stephens said in a letter addressed to Secretary of State Colby today.

Governor Stephens expressed the hope in the letter that the initiative measure now being projected in the State to deny Asiatics the right to all land purchases or leaseholds would be adopted by the electorate by an overwhelming majority. While California harbors no animosity against the Japanese people, he said the State does not wish them to settle within her borders and to develop a Japanese population in her midst. He asks that immediate negotiations be entered into with the Empire of Japan to make impossible any further "evasions" of existing immigration agreements and to make such agreements as rigorous as possible.

"Twenty years ago our Japanese population was nominal," the letter said. "Ten years ago the census reports of the United States Government showed a Japanese population in California of 41,356. A computation and survey recently made by the Board of Control of the State of California indicates that this Japanese population has been more than doubled—amounting now to 87,279."

Governor Stephens said he feared that the initiative measure, if passed, might fall short of its purpose through the Japanese retaining possession of agricultural lands through personal employment contracts, and that therefore Government action was necessary.

Although respecting Japanese culture and advancement and the right of Japan to true development, Governor Stephens held that "the people of California are determined to repress a developing Japanese community in our midst. They are determined to exhaust every power in their keeping to maintain this State for its own people."

. . . . The spirit of existing anti-alien land laws and immigration agreements has been evaded through the employment of legal and other subterfuges to such an extent that the purposes of the measures have been frustrated, Governor Stephens charged. He referred to the suspension of anti-Asiatic legislation in the State during the Peace Conference at the request of Secretary of State Lansing, but held that decisive action was necessary now.

By 1910 there were 72,157 Japanese in the United States. Although Japanese students were segregated in California schools, this photo shows a solitary Japanese student, at right, in a New York City classroom in 1913.

THE INDIANS

Indian immigrants appear in U.S. newspaper reports and books of the period as "Hindoos," although it is not certain all of them were actually Hindu—some were Buddhist, and a few were also Muslim. Between 1898 and 1902, there had been about 30 Indian families a year immigrating to the United States, and in 1906, there were 271, some of whom came via Canada. Within a few years, hundreds were arriving in the United States each year, and Samuel Gompers, president of the American Federation of Labor (AFL), remarked in 1908 that "sixty years contact with the Chinese, 25 years' experience with the Japanese and two or three years' acquaintance with Hindus should be sufficient to convince any ordinarily intelligent person that they have no standards . . . by which a Caucasian may judge them."

There were a few racial attacks, and soon some American politicians became involved with the Asiatic Exclusion League, working to end Indian immigration as well. One of the worst incidents of this period was when timber cutters from Saint John, Oregon, physically drove the Indians from the town.

The *San Francisco Chronicle* also led attacks on the Indian presence in San Francisco, in particular against the steady arrival of Indian women. In 1909 Canada introduced laws to prevent Indians immigrating there, and more sought admission to the United States. U.S. authorities were instructed to use existing measures to keep out Indian migrants, and any who immigration officials felt would be a burden to the U.S. taxpayer were rejected. As a result, between 1911 and 1920, although 1,460 Indians did immigrate to the United States, 1,782 were rejected, and a larger number were put off from applying because of the rigorous physical examination that was introduced to reduce the number entering America.

Another deterrent to Indians, and to other Asians immigrating to the United States at this time, was the Alien Land Law of 1913 that (although amended in 1920–21) prevented non-U.S. citizens from owning land in the United States. Wealthier Asian Americans then started working through American business partners or agents, but poorer ones were prevented from putting down roots in the United States.

INDIAN ACTIVISTS

As with the Chinese and Korean communities, there were a number of Indian political activists arriving in the country. In 1901 the first Indian student came to the United States, and there were soon a number of Indian students at the University of California, Berkeley; the San Luis Obispo Polytechnic College; and a number of agricultural colleges elsewhere in California. In 1905 Lala Lajpat Raj, an Indian nationalist who was campaigning against the British presence in India, spoke at a meeting of the Boston Anti-Imperialist League, where he urged for support for the Indians working against the British.

Lala Har Dayal studied in England and then, after some time in Paris, moved to Boston, then to California, and finally settled in Hawaii, where he was involved in studying the works of Karl Marx and other philosophers. Gradually he expanded his interested into communist activism and soon became secretary of the San Francisco branch of the Industrial Workers of the World; he then founded the Bakunin Institute of California, and became heavily influenced by anarchism. His support, published in a pamphlet, for the attempted assassination in India of the British Viceroy, Lord Hardinge, gained him increased attention from the U.S. government, which arrested him in April 1914. After his release, he went to Berlin, and then to Sweden, returning to the United States where he died in 1939.

By contrast, although Taraknath Das also advocated Indian independence, he never became as radical as Lala Har Dayal. His *Free Hindustan* newspaper urged that "To protest against all tyranny is a service to humanity and the duty of civilization." He went on to become a professor at Columbia University. Other Indian anti-British activists who worked in the

United States included Barkatullah, Ram Chandra, and Bhai Parmanand. To bring their supporters together, the Hindu Association of the Pacific Coast formed the Ghadar Party in Oregon, and issued *Ghadar*, a weekly newspaper that was circulated among Indian nationalist circles around the United States, Canada, and elsewhere.

The focus of the Ghadar party rapidly became San Francisco, and the British started to urge U.S. authorities to crack down on them. With the outbreak of World War I, Indians in the United States made common cause with the Germans—sharing the same enemy—and in 1915, a large amount of weapons were shipped from the United States to Indian nationalists when they were intercepted by U.S. authorities. In 1917 with the entry of the United States into the war, the British and U.S. governments operated together against the Ghadar party, and many were prosecuted for subversion for their support for Germany.

Members of San Francisco's Indian community built the Vedanta Society building, shown above, in San Francisco in 1905. It was billed as the first Hindu temple in the Western world.

Asian sugar plantation workers filling and weighing sacks of raw sugar at a Hawaiian sugar plantation mill 1910–20.

THE FILIPINOS

The restrictions on Chinese, Japanese, and later, Korean migrants resulted in a small influx of Filipinos from 1909. Many were able to take the place of other Asians as laborers in plantations in Hawaii. However this led to tensions, with many Japanese in Hawaii unhappy as their role was supplanted by the Filipinos. This was exacerbated when, in 1909, the U.S. authorities in Hawaii took a series of heavy-handed measures against the editor of the *Jiji* newspaper and the Higher Wage Association, both in Honolulu. Although many of the early Filipinos in Hawaii and California in the 1900s were semi-literate, as U.S. schooling had an effect in the islands in the 1900s, and English replaced Spanish as the second language (after Tagalog), by the late 1910s, numbers of English-speaking Filipinos were moving to the United States to take up a range of employment.

HO CHI MINH

The end of World War I led to the emergence of a range of other Asian political activists who had been living in the United States. One of these was a Vietnamese called Nguyen Ai Quoc (later called Ho Chi Minh). It is uncertain exactly when he was in the United States, but he later wrote about his time in New York City, in awe of the great skyscrapers, and earning $40 per month as a laborer, far more than he had received elsewhere. He also became a domestic servant to a wealthy family, and found time to visit the Universal Negro

Improvement Association (UNIA). It was during his time with UNIA in New York that he heard the Jamaican-born black nationalist speaker Marcus Garvey give a talk about the rights of African Americans, and was sympathetic to the ideas Garvey expressed.

Ho Chi Minh also claimed that he went to Boston and worked as a pastry chef at the Parker House Hotel—and there is independent confirmation of this in a postcard to a colleague in France. There is also a postcard to a French colonial official in Annam (central Vietnam) dated December 15, 1912, signed by Paul Tat Thanh, the alias he was using at the time. Ho Chi Minh later related a visit to the southern states, where he saw the lynching of African Americans. As he found work on ships, and these called into various ports, his visits to these places are probable, but his actually being an eyewitness to lynchings has been questioned by some scholars.

CONCLUSION

Although Sun Yat-sen, Syngman Rhee, Ho Chi Minh, and many of the Indian intellectuals used the United States as a base for their political activities, most of the Asian Americans in the United States in the 1900s and 1910s were politically inactive—at least as far as involvement in U.S. politics. For the most part, they held menial jobs, but many established their own small businesses as soon as they had saved enough money—corner stores, laundry businesses, or cafés. By the 1920s, all cities and most towns boasted a number of Chinese or Japanese businesses, with U.S. interest in Asia increasing through missionary activity and the pages of the *National Geographic* magazine and other similar publications. Although at home most immigrant families continued to speak Chinese, Japanese, Korean, or other native languages, the U.S. education system resulted in most second-generation Asian Americans, even from this period, becoming fluent in English. It was from this that Asian Americans in the 1920s came to play a more and more important role in U.S. society.

JUSTIN CORFIELD
GEELONG GRAMMAR SCHOOL, AUSTRALIA

Further Reading

Bautista, Veltisezar. *The Filipino Americans from 1763 to the Present: Their History, Culture, Traditions.* Farmington Hills, MI: Bookhaus, 1998.
Beck, Warren A., and David A. Williams. *California: A History of the Golden State.* New York: Doubleday, 1972.
Buchholdt, Thelma. *Filipinos in Alaska 1788–1958.* Anchorage, AK: Aboriginal Press, 1996.

Dicker, Laverne Mau. *The Chinese in San Francisco: A Pictorial History*. New York: Dover, 1980.

Duiker, William J. *Ho Chi Minh*. New York: Hyperion, 2000.

Jones, Claire. *The Chinese in America*. Minneapolis, MN: Lerner, 1972.

Kwong, Peter, and Dusanka Mscevic. *Chinese America: The Untold Story of America's Oldest New Community*. New York: New Press, 2005.

Lal, Brij V. *The Encyclopedia of the Indian Diaspora*. Singapore: Editions Didier Millet in conjunction with the National University of Singapore, 2006.

Lee, Rose Hsun. *The Chinese in the United States of America*. Hong Kong: Hong Kong University Press, 1960.

Leonard, Karen Isaksen. *The South Asian Americans*. Westport, CT: Greenwood Press, 1997.

Siu, Paul, and John Kuo Wei Tchen. *The Chinese Laundryman: A Study of Social Isolation*. New York: New York University Press, 1988.

Sung, B.L. *Mountain of Gold: The Story of the Chinese in America*. New York: Macmillan, 1967.

Yin Xiaohuang. *Chinese American Literature since the 1850s*. Champaign: University of Illinois Press, 2000.

CHAPTER 4

The Roaring Twenties and the Great Depression: 1920 to 1939

BY 1920, THERE were Asian-American communities throughout the United States, with significant numbers in Hawaii (still a territory), California, Oregon, and Washington, as well as in New York, Chicago, and some other large cities. Most American towns had Chinese-, Japanese-, Korean-, or Indian-owned businesses. One of the major changes was that the disparity of males to females in the Asian-American population was being redressed. In 1860 there were 18.5 Chinese males to every Chinese female; by 1890, this had risen to 27 males to every female. But by 1920, there were only seven males to every female, and by 1930, there were slightly less than four males to every Chinese female. The male-female ratio disparity in the Japanese-American community also decreased, as did that in the Korean-American community.

Overall by 1930 ethnic Japanese vastly outnumbered ethnic Chinese on the U.S. mainland. There were well over 140,000 ethnic Japanese in the United States—including 112,000 living on the West Coast in the late 1930s—compared to only about 77,000 Chinese in the late 1930s. There were also groups of other Asians on the U.S. mainland throughout the 1930s, but their numbers remained comparatively small. Asians were concentrated in the Pacific Coast states, especially in California—42 percent of the total continental Japanese population lived there in 1900, and 70 percent lived there only 30 years later.

This poster from Senator James D. Phelan's failed 1920 re-election campaign played to fears of a "silent invasion" of Japanese, represented by a hand grasping at a map of California.

Asian Americans seeking to become naturalized U.S. citizens still encountered major roadblocks in the 1920s and 1930s. The 1790 federal law that granted citizenship only to white people was still in effect in the 1930s. It was used as a pretext to prevent any first-generation Asian immigrant from acquiring citizenship. Children born in the United States, however, were automatically citizens. In many states, laws prohibiting marriage between people of different races also kept Asian immigrants and their offspring fairly isolated from mainstream American society.

The changes that affected U.S. society beginning in the 1920s had a major effect on Asian Americans. This started in January 1919 with the passing of the Volstead Act leading to Prohibition—the banning of the production, sale, or consumption of alcohol throughout the United States. And in November 1920, Republican candidate Warren Harding was elected U.S. president, promising a "return to normalcy" by which the United States would try to distance itself from international conflicts, especially in Europe, through a policy of isolation.

The 1920s were also a period of economic boom in the United States, with the automobile and other mass-produced items transforming the economy and creating the powerhouses of Detroit and Chicago. The decade of Republican Ascendancy saw less government regulation, and the promotion of small businesses in which many Asian Americans worked.

In spite of the economic boom, there was continued worry by some people over the possibility of large-scale Asian immigration. Significant numbers of Asian Americans had assimilated, and many Asian-American children attended school, becoming fluent in English, although they continued to speak Chinese, Korean, or Japanese at home. Much of the greater acceptance of Asian Americans came with increased knowledge about Asia in the United States. Some depictions of Asian Americans improved, for example, the *Boys' Own* adventure stories in which American or British teenagers and young men fought off attacks by varied collections of Oriental pirates, gangsters, bandits, and the like were being replaced with instances of more thoughtful literature that would culminate in Pearl S. Buck's *The Good Earth* in 1931.

Some U.S. reporters were now based in Asia, and the newspapers were full of stories about the developing political situation in China after the death of Sun Yat-sen in 1925, the assassination of the "Old Marshal" Chang Tso-lin in 1928, and the emergence of Chiang Kai-shek and his nationalist Kuomintang Party. Chiang Kai-shek's wife had been educated in the United States, and this fact helped change American perceptions of Chinese generally and specifically of Asian residents in the United States.

In the 1930s, the Great Depression had a devastating impact on most Americans, but Asian Americans as a whole were generally less affected than most Americans. Most Asian Americans lived in California, where the agricultural economy was not as hard hit as many other areas of the United States. Furthermore many Asian-American communities had become so self-sufficient that, while they had little wealth, they could weather the turmoil of the era.

The knowledge that they could not get easy access to white venture capital had instilled in many of these communities certain protective habits such as frugality, reliance on family connections, and avoidance of deep debt. Families and friends protected and helped each other. Asian-American businesses had also established their own informal credit systems, which often saved businesses or families in desperate need. Japanese truck farmers and Korean rice farmers in California continually found demand for their products, and Asian farm laborers often had little difficulty finding work.

THE IMMIGRATION ACT OF 1924

The boom in the U.S. economy in the early 1920s created a wide demand for labor in factories, but the political policies of isolationism and protectionism led some politicians to support the Immigration Act of 1924, commonly known as the Asian Exclusion Act. Stories of tong wars, killings, immigration fraud, smuggling people into the country, and the alleged prevalence of opium dens and illegal gambling houses spurred some politicians into action. In Philadelphia, Captain of Detectives Alfred I. Souder banned all gambling during the playing of mah-jongg, carrying out raids, and seizing many sets of the game in that city's Chinatown. Similar raids occurred elsewhere in the United States.

The Immigration Bill of 1924 had been drawn up and supported by Congressman Albert Johnson and Senator David Reed, and was often called the Johnson-Reed Act after it became law. The basic aim was to stop a large number of immigrants from any particular country, and although six senators opposed

Angel Island

A young Chinese immigrant undergoing questioning at Angel Island in 1931.

Despite efforts such as the 1924 Johnson-Reed Immigration Bill to further clamp down on Asian immigration, a constant flow of Chinese, Japanese, and other Asians endeavored to enter the United States. Many claimed that they were the legal children or spouses of Chinese already living in the United States, which if true would allow them entry. But before they could enter, they had to pass through the Angel Island Immigration Station in San Francisco Harbor where their papers were examined, and many had to endure intensive questioning before they were granted or denied entry. The many Chinese and Japanese who tried to enter were routinely incarcerated on the island for months or even years until a decision could be reached concerning their eligibility to enter the United States. Detainees had little, if any, contact with friends or relatives on the mainland. For this reason, the immigration station on Angel Island was known among Immigration Service officials as the Guardian of the Western Gate.

The restored barracks are now testament to the grim existence of the detainees. There was little room to store belongings, detainees had to sleep on hard cots stacked in three levels, and no one was allowed outside except for supervised outings in small fenced-off areas. The food was poor and there was little to do. Responding to the harsh conditions of their detentions and to the anxiety they suffered over the uncertainty of their futures, detainees began to write poetry. The writing depicts a picture of the isolation these young men faced as they tried to enter the United States. Hundreds of poems like the one excerpted below were carved into the walls of the detention barracks, and many of them survive to this day.

Detained in this wooden house for
several tens of days
...Waiting for news of my release,
I am ready to snap my whip and gallop.
All my kinsmen and housemates
will be happy for me.

it in the U.S. Senate, and a few led by Emanuel Celler opposed it in the House of Representatives, it became law.

The Immigration Act of 1924 established a system that regulated the number of immigrants from any particular country. They would be limited to two percent of the number of people from that country living in the United States in 1890, as tabulated by that year's census.

This cut heavily into the number of immigrants from southern and eastern Europe, but more importantly, the Immigration Act specifically prohibited any further immigration of Asians. For this purpose, the Asia-Pacific Triangle from where immigrants were specifically excluded was defined as China, Japan and Korea, the Philippines, Siam (Thailand), French Indochina, British Malaya and Singapore, India, Ceylon (Sri Lanka), the Netherlands East Indies (Indonesia), and Turkey.

This major reduction in the number of Chinese admitted to the United States coincided with widespread problems in China itself. There, in the absence of any strong central government, warlords exercised control over large pieces of territory, and while some of them were benevolent, many were not; as a consequence, many people were eager to leave, and the United States was one of their favored destinations.

In addition to these poor immigrants, the 1920s saw great prosperity for the ruling class in China, and wealthy Chinese started to go to the United States to complete their education. More and more Chinese attended schools in the United States, with most coming for a university education. Part of this came from the rise of the Soong sisters during this time, and the emergence of Chiang Kai-shek, whose wife—the youngest of the Soong sisters—had been educated at Wesleyan College at Macon, Georgia. Her flamboyance and power persuaded many other wealthy Chinese to send not only their sons, but also their daughters to the United States, resulting in rich Chinese becoming commonplace at the major universities such as California, Chicago, Columbia, Cornell, Harvard, and Yale.

ANXIETY OVER CHINESE IMMIGRATION IN THE 1920s

Part of the reason Americans opposed Asian immigration was the perception from the late 1910s that the Asian, and especially the Chinese, communities were forming themselves into separate enclaves. This was especially true of San Francisco's Chinatown, where large numbers of Chinese people could operate for their entire life speaking only Chinese, mainly Cantonese because most of the Chinese there came from Guangdong Province. However the limitations on Chinese immigration resulted in the number of Chinese in San Francisco declining dramatically through the 1920s.

Like San Francisco's Chinatown, the Chinatown in New York was also almost a self-contained enclave. There were three Chinese-language newspapers, the main one the *Mun Hey Weekly* (*Public Sentiment Weekly*), which operated from its office at 16 Pell Street; the other two Chinese-language newspapers, *Chinese Republic News* and *The Republic News,* both contained extensive coverage of foreign news, as well as much about San Francisco's Chinatown. Although there were only 2,000–3,000 Chinese living in New York's Chinatown, many Chinese from outlying areas such as Brooklyn, the Bronx, and Newark made the journey there on Sundays and holidays, raising the population of Chinese quickly to nearly 10,000.

Certainly in New York's Chinatown, and also in San Francisco's, there was concern about the tongs ("friendly associations," some of which were clearly fronts for gangs). In New York, the most famous of the tongs was the On Leong Tong that operated around Mott and Pell Streets. As a mutual protection society, it looked after its members who paid "subscriptions." Most of its tasks were legal—providing for widows and orphans when their breadwinner died, helping with hospital care for sick or elderly members, and the like. It collected money from members for funerals, paying for wreaths and for gravestones. However, it also protected members from attacks, and it was not long before this group and others engaged in reprisals against other similar tongs. This led to a series of gang wars that overshadowed attempts by community leaders to integrate into mainstream U.S. society. This worry about the tongs coincided with Hollywood's producing films using racial stereotypes

A Washington, D.C., branch of the On Leong Chinese Merchants Association.

and a generation of non-Chinese Americans growing up with fictional figures such as the sinister villain Fu Manchu. Although living in London's Chinatown, Fu Manchu, who put poison in teacups and hid a dagger in the sleeve of his silk brocade gown, was seen as the epitome of evil, financing his dastardly deeds by the smuggling of white slaves, and selling illegal drugs in Chinese restaurants.

For many of the Chinese living outside the main Chinatowns, there was far greater assimilation and interaction. They did not worry about the tongs—and often operated in complete ignorance of how they actu-

Chinatown's Last Queue

In an attempt to answer some of the queries of members of the public about New York's Chinatown, the following article was printed in the *New York Times* on March 28, 1920:

New York's Chinatown, as it was known to its frequenters and to out-of-town visitors a few years ago, is no longer in existence. This compact and congested little parcel of Manhattan Island, to be sure, still has its picturesque shops with their attractive window displays of Oriental wares, its green groceries and flamboyant restaurants. In these respects it is the Chinatown of old as fervid sightseers knew it, yet it has undergone a transformation as complete that the change cannot escape the eye of its most casual visitor.

This change, then, is not in Chinatown itself, but in its inhabitants. They have become modernized and Americanized. Once-familiar Chinese in blouses, roomy pantaloons and sandals are almost as scarce in the quarter as doves among a flock of crows. They have discarded their native dress for garments of American style and texture. It is not uncommon to see young Orientals clothed in the latest and most stylish creations of the tailor's art. They are often the envy of their companions, wearing their clothes with ease and nonchalance of youths who have been born to them. The most startling change noted is the absence of the queue. A visitor may spend hours in the quarter without counting a single queue, but this is not strange since there is today but one Chinese living there with a queue. He is an old fellow who obstinately clings to it, refusing to part with it.

It is not only in dress that the Chinese are different. They have also changed somewhat in manner and deportment. Chinese are habitually closemouthed. They doubtless will always remain so since they have inherited this trait from countless backward generations, but they have become slightly more loquacious and outwardly, at least, a great deal more cheerful. Chinese of solemn face and mien once so common have given place to those who actually wear a smile, joke and laugh. It was not long ago that it was rare to find a Celestial with but the most elementary knowledge of English. Now any number possess a good knowledge of the language, and those who do not are studying and learning. In shops where Chinese literature is sold, there is a growing demand for English-Chinese dictionaries and textbooks. This desire to know our language is by no means confined to the young; it is being taken up by the old folk as well.

What has brought about this change in the Chinese? The principal reason an educated Chinese gave was the birth some years ago of the Chinese Republic. The queues were worn as a sort of mark of servile submission and respect to the sovereign power. When the Republic was born and equality among men was proclaimed, Chinese by their hundreds cut off their pigtails and donned the habitments of civilization.

ally worked. However, for the people in San Francisco and New York, the stories that tended to catch the attention of the press saw each attack, robbery, and death in Chinatown as a part of some major tong or gangster war. Traditional U.S. policing methods failed to deal with the problem, and Chinese tong leaders were known to hire "skilled counsel" when brought before the courts. It was argued that perhaps whenever a tong member was named, his family back in China should be arrested by the authorities there in retribution. Gardner L. Harding of the *New York Times* on December 14, 1924, even suggested that the Manchu government did this before 1911, "but in a republic such high-handed methods are not possible and the present Chinese Republic could not make an arrest in Canton if it wished."

However much of the problem was that some police avoided the Chinatown areas which, in New York, gained a reputation as the Jungle of Death. This was often the attitude taken by sightseers whose buses would drive through Chinatown, and in 1920, the third deputy police commissioner for New York stated that "the Police Department wants to put a stop to indiscriminate shouting in the streets by the bus barkers and the practice of referring to Chinatown and the Ghetto as 'the slums' will probably be prohibited." Negative press coverage continued with regular reports of police raids on gambling dens and the seizing of opium and the proceeds of crime. On June 24, 1922, a major raid by police in Boston's Chinatown led to the discovery of "opium, pipes and various paraphernalia valued at about $100,000," as well as information showing that some Chinese there were organizing a systematic method of misusing passports to allow new migrants to come into the country undetected. In early August 1922, Ko Low, the leader of the Hip Sing Tong, was shot dead, probably by men associated with the rival On Leong Tong.

THE CHINESE IN THE 1930s

The Chinese population decline was reversed in the 1930s as the number of Chinese having their own families increased somewhat. Nevertheless throughout the 1930s, 80 percent of the population was still male. The fact that the percentage of women had jumped from below 10 percent before 1920 to 20 percent just before World War II meant that there was increasing stability in the Chinese community, but not nearly the stability found in Japanese communities.

The Great Depression did not affect the Chinatowns of the 1930s as much as it did other American communities. Aside from their great sense of frugality and hard work habits, families and friends tended to work together and always took each other in during times of need. Chinese businesses had established their own informal credit systems. Aspiring entrepreneurs could readily borrow money from their own friends and relatives, or partner with other Chinese immigrants to form a *hui,* a self-generated pool of capital into which

Tourism in Chinatown

During the Great Depression, the Chinese in San Francisco worried about a downturn in business, deciding that they needed to find a new source of revenue. They soon had the idea of promoting tourism.

The result was a creation of a live fantasy version of the "wicked Orient," where Chinese deliberately exploited the worst stereotypes of the Chinese. Tour guides would tell tales of a hidden world in Chinatown, filled with opium dens, gambling halls, and brothels where slave girls, both Chinese and Caucasian, were held against their will. Other Chinatowns across the United States soon followed suit.

In New York, tour companies paid young Chinese residents to stage elaborate street dramas, including fake knife fights between opium-crazed men over possession of a prostitute. As phony as these acts were, they brought in needed money, but they also reinforced negative stereotypes about the Chinese. The *New York Times* described such tours in an article from September 25, 1927, which is excerpted below:

Chinatown has a civic record and its folklore and its history. Most of the truth in the annals of Chinatown can best be gleaned from the police records. The rest is of such little importance that no one has ever taken the time or trouble to write it. But there is another history of Chinatown. It is a shorter history and to learn it costs only a dollar. The classroom is a bus and the professor a man who seems to have eyes that are ever roaming and an uncanny insight into things Oriental. His patter never ceases as the bus wends its way downtown from Times Square to the storied streets of Chinatown.

Not even "New York's Finest" and Uncle Sam's Secret Service have developed the faculty of spotting a stranger in a crowd as rapidly and as surely as these guides spot him. They have, like the gold brick salesman of another day, so adequately pursued their study of types that they are almost able to tell from what city the stranger comes.

A daytime trip through Chinatown would be useless, for during the day the section seems not to differ from any other portion of a busy city. Nightly the "showman" takes his stand and so alluring are his running advance descriptions of the trip through Chinatown that he has little difficulty in drawing the attention of the stranger away from the bright lights of the Roaring Forties and in filling his car with expectant sightseers.

As the car is guided through the crowded streets en route, the course in history begins. Accounts of tong wars, tales of cruelty and anecdotes of mystery—all serve to build up the eagerness of the passengers. It may seem strange that the Chinese never have attempted to assure visitors that they are not so bad as the "historians" make them. The reason is that they find the sightseers much keener to take home a load of souvenirs after blood-curdling tales have been told.

The percentage of Chinese women in the United States continued to increase in the 1920s and 1930s, reaching 20 percent of the Chinese-American population just before World War II.

they could make regular deposits, and out of which loans could be made at mutually agreed rates of interest.

Working and living in their small shops, many lonely male Chinese felt caged. "Nobody can imagine such a life as ours in the 'Golden Mountain,'" one laundryman lamented. "I have been confined to this room for more than two years. Sometimes I feel so lonesome in this small jail, I just want to go back to China." But by the 1930s, famine, civil war and, after 1931, a major Japanese invasion of China made the prospects of returning home even more unappealing. Most of these Chinese men just resigned themselves to lives of misery in the United States, working to earn just enough money to survive. Any extra money they had might be spent in one of the many Chinese social clubs on a Saturday night, eating or gambling. One Chinese commenting on his sad situation noted with a sense of resignation, "I can't expect a life better than this and it is no use to try."

When the Chinese moved from rural areas and smaller towns to larger cities such as San Francisco or New York, they were employed mainly in such service occupations as restaurant, store, and laundry work. In 1920 of 45,614 gainfully employed Chinese, 12,559, or 28 percent (nearly one out of three), were laundry workers, and this ratio remained quite stable through the 1930s. In the city of Chicago, there were 209 Chinese laundries in 1903, and 704 by 1930.

Many Chinese found solace through the Six Companies, Chinese benevolent associations that helped Chinese survive in an alien environment. Most of the business transactions of the Chinese were done through the Six Companies. The Six Companies often contracted for large groups of laborers. Six Companies simply acted as clearinghouses for all sorts of transactions among the Chinese, who had found that they could handle more satisfactorily through such associations than they could individually.

Assistance programs made available by the Roosevelt administration, notably the Federal Emergency Relief Act, brought relief to 18 percent of the Chinese in San Francisco, but that number was considerably lower than the general U.S. population. The reason for this was that many Chinese refused to participate in these programs, scorning them as charity. One American-born Chinese woman who grew up in San Francisco in the 1930s remembers, "During the Depression I'd see these people taking canned goods [home] from school. And my dad refused. He told me simply, 'You're not going to bring back any canned goods here, period.' I think the pride of the Chinese is very strong. We're not going to accept food from anybody even to feed ourselves, even when we're eating less."

THE JAPANESE IN THE 1920s

The Japanese had started immigrating to the United States in large numbers in the 1900s, especially with the ban on Chinese immigration. Most Japanese in the United States lived in Hawaii or California, with a number in Washington, Oregon, and other parts of the country. Although those in Hawaii were largely accepted, many of the Japanese experienced discrimination, and some suspected that it would be only a matter of time before the U.S. government enacted legislation to ban immigration from Japan—which is what happened in 1924. As early as mid-1920, Japanese in neighboring Mexico were buying up land along the California border in anticipation of changes in U.S. immigration laws. This involvement in Mexico was not without its problems; the Chinese in Baja California had money extorted from them to finance the ill-fated Cantu Rebellion in August 1920, and there were worries that the same might happen to the Japanese.

Most of the Japanese in California were involved in working on farms, and some had prospered greatly. By the mid-1920s, almost half of employed ethnic Japanese were in one way or another employed in agriculture, and agriculture played an even greater role in the 1930s. What enabled the Japanese to become successful farmers was their timely entry into the field. Beginning in the late 19th century, industrialization and urbanization led to increased demands for fresh produce in the cities. The development of irrigation in California early in the 20th century opened the way for intensive agriculture, and a shift away from grain crops to fruit and vegetable production. By 1920 the value of crops representing intensive agriculture skyrocketed from only four percent in 1879, to over 50 percent and greater by 1930. This phenomenon occurred in tandem with the completion of national railway lines, and the development of the refrigerator car that made possible the rapid and safe transport of these goods to distant markets.

One very successful Japanese-American farmer was George Shima, the president of the Japanese Association of America, who had made his fortune from potatoes, earning himself the title of Potato King of California. In July 1920 he gave evidence before the House of Representatives Committee on Immigration and Nationalization, which was eager to discover the position of the Japanese in California. Shima, who said that he had lived in California for 30 years and had returned to Japan only once (to receive a decoration from the Japanese emperor), stated that he supported the assimilation of the Japanese population, but "to be sure, a good many Japanese do not make enough money to support Yankee girls. They are too expensive."

Shima, originally Ushijima Kinji, had immigrated to San Francisco in 1889, and by the 1890s, was renting land in the area around Sacramento. By 1913

Japanese fruit farmers working in California in the early 20th century. Nearly half of all employed Japanese Americans worked in agriculture by the mid-1920s.

he owned some 28,000 acres, and by 1920 he controlled 85 percent of the potato market in California—providing great hope for many later Japanese migrants. And there was Hideyo Noguchi, born in 1876, the son of peasant farmers, who managed to get through the Tokyo Medical School. He came to the United States, where he became a prominent bacteriologist, parasitologist, and immunologist working on tropical and other diseases in the United States during the 1910s and the 1920s. He died in 1928 while working on yellow fever in West Africa.

Japanese-American artist Yasuo Kuniyoshi. Despite his achievements, he was never able to become a U.S. citizen.

Another prominent Japanese American of this period was Yasuo Kuniyoshi. He had been born in 1893 at Okayama, Japan, and his father had sent him to the United States as a boy in the hope that he would learn English and find a job as an interpreter when he returned. After arriving in Seattle, Washington, in 1906, he started to work for the Spokane Railroad, but was so distressed at seeing so many poor Japanese working there that he found a position as a porter in an office building in Seattle. He later moved to Los Angeles, where he paid his way through night school. A teacher noted his skill in drawing, and he decided to take up painting. His first one-man exhibition was at the Charles Daniel Gallery in New York in January 1922, and he exhibited there each year until 1928, and again in 1930. Born in the Year of the Cow, many of his designs incorporated cows, and he also painted children, rapidly becoming influenced by the work of the French expressionist painter Marc Chagall. Except for tours in Europe in 1925 and 1928 and a visit to Japan to see his parents in 1931, he spent most of his life in the United States, but never acquired U.S. citizenship because of the 1924 Immigration Act.

Although the Japanese community in the United States was involved in regular gatherings around Shinto events and the New Year, they came together in 1928 with the coronation of the new emperor, Hirohito. To this end, the Japanese from Hilo, Hawaii, commissioned David Paris of Kona to build an outrigger canoe from Hawaiian mahogany to present to Hirohito as a show of their joint Japanese and Hawaiian heritage. Films about Hawaiian

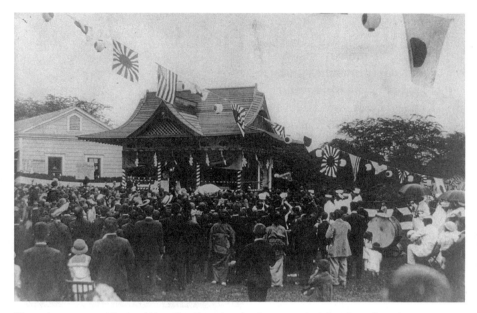

These Japanese residents of Hawaii gathered under Japanese and American flags for a ceremony honoring the Japanese emperor early in the 20th century.

volcanoes were also sent to Tokyo, and other gifts were given by the Japanese community in California.

JAPANESE AMERICANS IN THE 1930s

The 1930s were a time of general stability for many ethnic Japanese in the United States, despite the fact that the country was experiencing the Great Depression. Writers of Japanese-American history call the 1930s a time of great stabilization as many Japanese settlers—who had initially come to the United States as single men and had sent back home for "picture brides," or who brought their families with them—were by this time established with secure land, better houses, and young children.

Many Japanese had opened stores, restaurants, barbershops, tailor and dye shops, laundries, shoe shops, and the like before 1930, which also provided service jobs for thousands of their countrymen. Many of these businesses survived the 1930s because most of their customers were Japanese, and Japanese farmers were faring the Depression fairly well, since there remained great demand for the produce of their truck farms and orchards.

By the 1930s, Japanese farmers were producing over 70 percent of California's strawberries, and high percentages of other crops such as tomatoes, beans, onions, celery, and peas. Based on intensive cultivation, Japanese agriculture grew and flourished. In California, the Japanese owned or leased 486,056 acres of farmland in 1930, up from only 4,698 acres in 1900.

Farm labor was long and hard, but husbands and wives worked closely together. Initially many Japanese homes were no more than crude huts with oil lamps for light, boards nailed together with legs for furniture, and straw-filled canvases for beds. One farm wife remembered the hardship of farming in the 1920s and 1930s: "I got up at 4:30 AM and after preparing breakfast I went to the fields. I went with my husband to do jobs such as picking potatoes, and sacking onions. Since I worked apace with ruffians I was tired out and limp as a rag, and when I went to the toilet I couldn't stoop down. Coming back from the fields, the first thing I had to do was to start the fire [to cook dinner]."

THE INDIANS IN THE 1920s AND 1930s

During the late 1800s and early 1900s, tens of thousands of Indians emigrated to the British colonies and the United States in search of work as laborers. This resulted in large concentrations of Indians in such diverse places as South Africa, Fiji, Singapore, Hong Kong, and Trinidad. Indian immigrants in the United States were principally young men who worked as laborers. Like the Koreans, they did not develop a colony or a distinct ethnic community with geographical boundaries. A small and rather disparate group of men, there were not enough of them settled in any one place long enough to form a distinct Indiatown.

Like the Chinese and the Japanese, Indian Americans—often still called Hindoos—were also discriminated against by the Immigration Act of 1924,

Japanese men collecting sisal for the production of rope and mats on a plantation in Hawaii in the early 20th century. Many Japanese Americans continued to work in agriculture into the 1930s.

and by earlier legislation. In several court cases, arguments were made to define Indians as white demographically. For example Bhicaji Franji Balsara, a Parsi from Bombay, went to court, where it was argued that "Congress intended by the words 'free White persons' to confer the privilege of naturalization upon members of the White or Caucasian race only," and Balsara felt the definition "free White persons" should cover Parsis. Balsara eventually won his case. There was a similar court decision when Ahkoy Kumar Mozumdar managed to make a case that a "high-caste Hindu of pure blood" could also be regarded as white. These moves were overturned in November 1922 when the U.S. Supreme Court in the *Takao Ozawa* case argued that "white" was the same as "Caucasian"—it was later stated that this was a description of a person of European origin; Indians were thus Asians.

The result of these cases was that the Indian community in the United States declined during the 1920s, as no new immigrants arrived, and many already in the United States returned to India. In 1914 there were 10,000 Indians in California, but by the 1940 census, there were only 1,476 Indians in the state. The Sikh community in California also faced discrimination in their day-to-day lives. Some had tried to assimilate, and one, Vaisho Das Bagai, who had arrived in the United States in 1915, committed suicide in 1928, leaving a note saying that he had desperately tried to become as American as possible, but had been rejected.

Although there were restrictions on poor Indian immigrants, there were numbers of wealthier Indians who studied in the United States. One of these was anti-British activist, poet, and writer Rabindranath Tagore, who in 1913 was awarded the Nobel Prize for Literature. Tagore later went on lecture tours in the United States, proving himself highly influential in the Indian-American community.

By 1930 over 6,400 Indians had immigrated to the United States, a majority of whom were Sikhs. In the 1930s, Indians still tended to work as itinerant laborers, moving constantly from one job site to another; since few

The Nobel Prize–winning Indian activist and writer Rabindranath Tagore around 1916.

of them married, they rarely settled in one place. Plagued by discrimination despite the fact that most of them were Caucasians, by the 1930s many of them had either returned home to India, or had moved on to parts of the British Empire where they felt more welcome.

The Indians often lived, worked, and traveled from job to job together as work gangs. Their living conditions remained poor in the 1930s. They often slept out in the open or in tents. They were also housed in bunkhouses, barns, and sheds; at times, 12 men could be found crowded into a single room, sleeping under ragged blankets. In California, the gangs often became substitutes for families because, without wives and children, they came to depend on each other for companionship and security. By the 1930s, however, a few Indians had saved enough money to buy their own farmland or to become tenant farmers.

During the 1930s, many Indians worked in the Imperial Valley of California, gathering cantaloupes and picking cotton. A grower told an interviewer in 1930: "We are using Hindus for cleaning our ditches. The Japs won't do it and the Chinese have gotten too old. You can't get the younger generation of these peoples into any of this common work. But the Hindus are very efficient at this work."

KOREAN AMERICANS IN THE 1920s AND 1930s

Most Korean immigrants came to the U.S. mainland by way of Hawaii. They found hardships and little satisfaction in the plantation world of Hawaii and decided to move on to the West Coast of the United States with the hope of improving their lot. Once on the mainland, they had to struggle both to make a living, and to retain their ethnic community.

Unlike the Japanese and the Chinese in the United States, the Koreans did not have their own separate economy and communities. There were simply not enough of them. There were only 1,200 Koreans on the mainland (800 of them in California) in 1910, 1,677 in 1920, and only 1,700 in the late 1930s. There were simply too few Koreans to form their own Koreatown with its own stores, wholesalers, restaurants, churches, schools, and the like. They no longer had their own country to return to because Japan had seized Korea by 1910, and had turned it into a harshly treated colony. What held the Koreans in America together through the 1930s was their outrage against Japan, and their sense of obligation to do something to help free their shattered land.

Mainland Korean America before World War II was largely a community of bachelors. Of the 1,015 Koreans who arrived on the mainland from Hawaii, only 45 were female and 29 were children. Although a number of Korean picture brides soon arrived, the imbalance remained so disproportionate that in the 1930s, there were still two Korean men for every ethnic Korean female. Most of these women were married, and by the 1930s, there were several hundred Korean families on the American mainland, many families with one or more children.

A small minority of Koreans worked in urban areas during the 1930s. They were restaurant workers, gardeners, janitors, and domestic workers. A few enterprising Koreans went into the hotel business. Many of these hotel owners were also labor contractors, providing room and board to Korean workers and arranging work for them. Other Koreans became barbers or opened their own laundries.

The overwhelming number of Koreans were itinerant farm laborers. During the 1920s and 1930s, many small teams of Korean workers, usually about 10 workers supervised by a team head, moved from farm to farm wherever they were told they could find work. One day they could be picking tomatoes, another day grapes, and another peaches. They had no stable home life and no permanent abode.

While many Koreans remained migrant workers in the 1930s, at least a few of them were able to become farmers. Often several Koreans working together would combine their resources to lease and farm land. Like some Japanese and a few Chinese in the United States, they would all contribute money to their fund, and then allow individuals on a rotating basis to borrow funds to acquire land. The result was that Korean rice farmers in the Sacramento Valley of California were producing substantial amounts of rice, and Korean farmers in the San Joaquin Valley were shipping large amounts of fruit to Korean wholesale markets in Los Angeles.

Korean Americans in the were very active in their opposition to Japanese rule over their homeland. Many belonged to the American-based Korea

In many cases Koreans brought the Protestant faith with them from their home country. This Presbyterian church surrounded by worshippers stood in a village in Korea sometime before 1923.

National Association, which published harsh denunciations of Japanese rule, publicized the plight of Koreans back home, and organized rallies and other activities to voice their disapproval of what the Japanese were doing. Koreans, even those making low wages as farm workers, donated what they could to the Korea National Association and attended its rallies, distributed its publications, and worked to promote its cause.

Since many of the Koreans were Christians even before arriving on the mainland, Koreans established their own mainly Protestant churches wherever there were larger numbers of Koreans. These churches soon became the main community centers for Koreans. Worshippers would often convene on Sundays to worship, socialize, and renew their commitment to the liberation of their homeland. These churches often became forums for nationalistic education, sponsoring debates on such topics as "Jesus Christ and the Future of Korea" and "The Duty of Koreans Abroad."

By the 1930s, Korean families were placing a great emphasis on educating their children. Very often they opened their own Korean-language schools to teach the children the rudiments of their native language and culture. This emphasis on education worked very well: by 1930, Koreans had the highest literacy rate of all Asian immigrant groups—92 percent compared to 89 percent for the Japanese and 80 percent for the Chinese. Korean families were very determined to keep their families Korean—Korean was always spoken at home, and boys could date only Korean girls. There was very little effort to assimilate themselves into American society.

By the 1930s, however, second-generation Koreans were reaching adulthood. They had never been to Korea, and had no plans to go there as long as their country was occupied by the Japanese. Many saw America as their home, and cherished the fact that they had been born U.S. citizens. While their aging parents kept their nationalist movement alive, by the late 1930s, their grown children were showing decreasing interest in Korean nationalism.

FILIPINOS IN THE 1920s AND 1930s

The influx of Filipinos into mainland America was sudden and dramatic. Although the United States had seized the Philippines from Spain in 1899 as a result of its victory in the Spanish-American War, there were virtually no Filipinos in the United States at the time. As late as 1910, the number of Filipinos in the United States was only 406, but shortly thereafter, thousands of Filipinos immigrated to the United States. Because the Philippines was a U.S. possession, there were no entry restrictions in place until 1934. Any Filipino who could afford a boat ticket was free to come to the United States. Part of the incentive for this sudden rush of Filipinos after 1910 was the fact that exclusion laws and agreements severely truncated immigration from Japan and China at the very time that expanding agriculture in California and elsewhere needed migrant farm labor. The word spread to Filipinos in their country and in Hawaii that good money could be made in California. As usual, these dreams of rapid wealth were illusory, but they brought the workers nonetheless. By 1930 there were 45,208 Filipinos living in virtually every region of the United States, including 30,470 in California.

Filipinos worked in a wide variety of occupations. According to the 1930 census, 4,200 or nine percent worked in the Alaska salmon fisheries; 11,400 or 25 percent were service workers, including janitors, valets, kitchen staff, hotel workers, waiters, and so on, and many service workers were employed as domestic servants. Most of the Filipinos, 27,000 or about 60 percent, worked in agriculture, filling gaps created by the virtual termination of Japanese and Chinese immigration. The farm workers were often organized into gangs or crews under the leadership of a Filipino labor contractor who located their jobs and negotiated the terms with the employers. While Filipinos harvested a wide variety of crops ranging from cotton to oranges and lettuce, they were used extensively (and almost exclusively) to pick asparagus. They migrated great distances, working for a time in Fresno, California, and then moving to the state of Washington to pick cherries or apples, for example.

Dorothea Lange documented these Filipino farm workers cutting cabbages in Salinas, California, in June 1935. In 1930 as many as 60 percent of Filipino-Americans worked in farming.

As late as 1930, the Filipino population consisted mainly of single men. They had no permanent homes, sleeping in dilapidated bunkhouses near the farm where they were working that day. The bunkhouses were often made of old pieces of wood and had no sanitary facilities. A Filipino worker in 1930 remarked, "When I ate, swarms of flies fought over my plate . . . I slept on a dirty cot—the blanket was never washed." A Japanese grower told an interviewer in 1930 that he greatly preferred to employ Filipinos because they were single men and could be housed inexpensively. "These Mexicans and Spaniards bring their families with them and I have to fix up houses, but (pointing to a large old barn that was clearly a firetrap) I can put over a hundred Filipinos in that barn."

By the 1930s, a few Filipino women had found their way to the United States and had started raising families, but a far smaller percentage of Filipino women came as picture brides than was the case for other Asian immigrant groups in the United States. On the other hand, though the overall numbers were fairly small, there was a higher incidence of intermarriage between Filipino men and Caucasian women than was the case with other Asian groups.

ASIAN AMERICANS IN HAWAII

The Asian experience in Hawaii was vastly different from the experience of Asians in mainland United States. The experiences were similar in that they came as laborers to a society where whites controlled the economy and hired Asians as low-paid field hands, but demographically, Asians in Hawaii constituted a huge majority. Over 300,000 Asians immigrated to Hawaii 1850–20. In 1853 Hawaiians and part-Hawaiians represented 97 percent of the 73,137 inhabitants, while Caucasians represented only about two percent, and Chinese less than one percent. By the mid-1920s, Hawaiians and part-Hawaiians made up about 17 percent of the population, Caucasians eight percent, Chinese nine percent, Japanese 43 percent, Portuguese 10 percent, Puerto Ricans and Koreans a bit over two percent each, and Filipinos eight percent. At this time, Hawaii was very different from the mainland because Asian Americans totaled 62 percent of the island population, compared to less than four percent of the California population and 0.17 percent of the total mainland population.

The key to the economy of Hawaii through the 1930s was sugar. The Hawaiian sugar industry required the constant importation of workers from all over Asia, Portugal, and, later, from Puerto Rico. There were massive sugar plantations across the islands owned by Caucasians and managed by white foremen who maintained a harsh work ethic among the workers. The workers lived in dormitories or, in the case of families, small houses in or near the plantations. Work started as early as 5:00 AM each day, when the foremen would form teams of workers to cultivate or cut the sugar, dig up weeds, and so on. There were gangs of women workers, too—women made up over 15

The First Chinese Church of Christ in Honolulu, Hawaii, was built around 1929. In the mid 1920s the Chinese made up about nine percent of Hawaii's population, which was 62 percent Asian overall.

percent of the Asian workforce in 1930. Women were concentrated in field operations, hoeing, stripping leaves, and harvesting, or washing clothes or cooking in camp.

Over the years there were significant changes in the demographics of Asians in Hawaii. While most of the early immigrants were men, over the years the number of Asian women began to increase, and as their numbers grew, so did the number of families and children born in Hawaii. For example, married Chinese women increased from 559 in 1890 to 1,555 in 1910 to 3,212 in 1930. There were greater increases in the percentages of Japanese and Korean women. By 1920, 46 percent of the Japanese and 30 percent of the Koreans were women. By 1930, 40 or more percent of the Chinese and 45 percent of the Japanese were under the age of 20.

The fact that many Asians in Hawaii had young children in the 1930s had profound effects on the Asian-American population on the islands. Plantation owners wanted the children of their Asian workers to follow their parents and grandparents into the fields; they lobbied hard to restrict the education of workers' children to the sixth or eighth grade, but they did not always prevail. The older Asian workers strongly desired their children to become educated in English, and they did everything they could to see to it that the children got far more than a rudimentary education.

During the 1930s, there was notable unrest among young Asian Americans in Hawaii. Seeing their parents suffer from the drudgery of mindless plantation work, low wages, and discriminatory barriers, second- and third-generation Asians in increasing numbers resolved not to be tracked into plantation employment. They had a visceral dislike for the economic plantation pyramid with the white owners and foremen on top, and for the inherent racial inequality of the plantation system that kept their parents permanently poor, subservient, and uneducated. They aspired to be something more than just field laborers.

The problem for many young Asian Hawaiians in the 1930s was that, although they were becoming better educated and sought to break free from the plantations, Hawaii was still very much a society dominated by the plantations. Some succumbed to these conditions and returned to the agricultural ways of their parents and grandparents, but others began to open their own small businesses, to get jobs with the government, to work at places like the naval base at Pearl Harbor and the like. Asian society in Hawaii in the 1930s was very much in flux.

The fact that Asian immigrants came to Hawaii in great numbers, that they lived in large groups in plantation camps, and that they worked together in teams allowed each ethnic group to maintain much of its native culture. Also because Caucasians were few in number and kept themselves segregated from the laboring Asians, there was less need or desire to try to assimilate into American society. Living together with other Asians made it possible for them to weave together an amalgam of cultural traditions by the 1930s that made Hawaii a remarkably different place than mainland United States.

RACISM IN THE 1920s AND 1930s

Ever since they arrived in the United States in the middle of the 19th century, Chinese immigrants suffered from intense racism. But as the Chinese population dwindled or disappeared into large Chinatowns in the 1930s, the racial venom to a large extent was transferred to the growing, more prosperous, and more visible Japanese. The Japanese had to endure racist curses: "Jap Go Home," "Goddamn Jap," "Yellow Jap," "Dirty Jap." In California, the Japanese who entered white-owned barbershops reported being told, "We don't cut animal's hair." In theaters, Japanese were often denied admittance to the better seats and were forced to sit in segregated sections with blacks and other minorities. Throughout the 1920s and 1930s, Japanese were often denied entry into white schools, and had to endure boycotts of their stores by whites—but fortunately, whites continued to buy their agricultural products in increasing amounts. This anti-Japanese hysteria culminated in the detention of virtually all West Coast Japanese soon after the attack on Pearl Harbor in 1941.

Koreans were also victims of intense racism. Although many Americans were happy to hire Korean workers as temporary laborers, Koreans were not permitted to live in their neighborhoods, eat at their restaurants, sit with them at movies, and so on. If a single Korean family lived in a small community dominated by whites, the Koreans generally found themselves shunned. Very often Koreans were mistaken as being Japanese, and had to endure many of the same insults as their nation's colonizers.

Filipino and Indian immigrants also faced racial hostility from most of white America. Although they were nominally American nationals, Filipino immigrants found that they could not become naturalized citizens. They also found by the early 1930s that there was growing resentment in the United States against their free entry into the country. A law passed by Congress in 1934 forbade further entry by Filipinos, but by then the appeal of America had dwindled so much in the Philippines that immigration to the United States had come to a virtual halt.

CONCLUSION

The 1920s and 1930s represented a major change in the Asian-American population. On a statistical level, the previous heavy preponderance of men over women had gradually moved toward parity. With strict restrictions on immigration into the United States from many countries—especially from Asian countries—the number of migrants was severely reduced, and those within the United States started to assimilate. With the United States undergoing an economic boom in the 1920s, many Asian Americans established themselves in new cities and in suburbs, but the Chinatowns in San Francisco and New York remained the center of Chinese-American consciousness. The Japanese remained mostly in California and other West Coast states and in Hawaii, where there was also a large Chinese population; Koreans and Indians also lived primarily on the West Coast. The 1920s and 1930s were also a period when many of the stereotypes of Asian Americans had begun to be less important—most major universities had Asian students, and there were an increasing number of Americans who had traveled to Asia. However with the emergence of Hollywood as the center of the U.S. film industry and the production of silent films, and then the "talkies," some stereotypes reappeared and were reinforced to a new generation of Americans.

JUSTIN CORFIELD
GEELONG GRAMMAR SCHOOL, AUSTRALIA
DANIEL A. MÉTRAUX
MARY BALDWIN COLLEGE

Further Reading

Bautista, Veltisezar. *The Filipino Americans from 1763 to the Present: Their History, Culture, Traditions.* Farmington Hills, MI: Bookhaus, 1998.

Beck, Warren A., and David A. Williams. *California: A History of the Golden State—From Earliest Spanish Explorations in the Sixteenth Century to the Present.* New York: Doubleday, 1972.

Chang, Iris. *The Chinese in America.* New York: Penguin Books, 2003.

Chinn, Thomas W. *Bridging the Pacific: San Francisco Chinatown and its People.* San Francisco, CA: Chinese Historical Society of America, 1989.

Daniels, Roger. *The Politics of Prejudice: The Anti-Japanese Movement in California and the Struggle for Japanese Exclusion.* Berkeley: University of California Press, 1977.

Dicker, Laverne Mau. *The Chinese in San Francisco: A Pictorial History.* New York: Dover, 1980.

Jones, Claire. *The Chinese in America.* Minneapolis, MN: Lerner, 1972.

Kwong, Peter, and Dusanka Mscevic. *Chinese America: The Untold Story of America's Oldest New Community.* New York: New Press, 2005.

Lai, Him Mark, et al., eds. *Island: Poetry and History of Chinese Immigrants on Angel Island, 1910–1940.* Seattle: University of Washington Press, 1990.

Lal, Brij V. *The Encyclopedia of the Indian Diaspora.* Singapore: Editions Didier Millet in conjunction with the National University of Singapore, 2006.

Lee, Rose Hsun. *The Chinese in the United States of America.* Hong Kong: Hong Kong University Press, 1960.

Leonard, Karen Isaksen. *The South Asian Americans.* Westport, CT: Greenwood Press, 1997.

Lydon, Sandy. *The Japanese in the Monterey Bay Region: A Brief History.* Monterey, CA: Monterey County Historical Society, 1997.

Siu, Paul, and John Kuo Wei Tchen. *The Chinese Laundryman: A Study of Social Isolation.* New York: New York University Press, 1988.

Sung, B. L. *Mountain of Gold: The Story of the Chinese in America.* New York: Macmillan, 1967.

Takaki, Ronald. *Strangers from a Distant Shore: A History of Asian Americans.* Boston, MA: Little, Brown, 1998.

Wiley, Hugh, *Manchu Blood.* New York: Alfred A. Knopf, 1927.

Yin, Xiaohuang. *Chinese American Literature since the 1850s.* Champaign: University of Illinois Press, 2000.

CHAPTER 5

World War II and the Forties: 1939 to 1949

THE UNITED STATES underwent a number of significant changes between 1939 and 1949 that had both domestic and global consequences. The period began with war clouds gathering in Europe. Within two years, the United States had entered the struggle to fight tyranny and prevent worldwide aggression. By the time the 1940s gave way to the 1950s, the United States had become the dominant world power; life for Americans would never be the same. Inside the United States, the social scene was changing rapidly as the Great Depression ended in response to the war in Europe and racial, ethnic, and gender barriers began to break down. In June 1941 President Franklin Roosevelt signed Executive Order 8802, banning racial discrimination in federal employment. Two months later, Roosevelt secretly met with British Prime Minister Winston Churchill to identify the role of democratic nations in the new world order. Roosevelt's Four Freedoms, which became the cornerstone of the Atlantic Charter, detailed basic rights for all people, including the right to choose one's own government.

The Bureau of the Census recorded 254,918 Asian and Pacific Island Americans in residence in the United States in 1940. For them, the period was defined and shaped by World War II, and nowhere were those impacts felt more deeply than in the Japanese-American community. Entire families were forced to rebuild their lives after involuntary incarceration and loss of civil liberties forced them to reexamine what it meant to be Americans of foreign descent.

Before the 1940s, Asian immigration into the United States had been carefully controlled. Asian immigrants were not routed through New York's Ellis Island, but through Angel Island, located in the middle of San Francisco Bay. The chief purpose of the facility was to prevent "undesirable" Chinese workers from entering the country because of the 1882 Chinese Exclusion Act. This ban did not apply to other Asian Americans. Japanese immigration, for instance, was unrestricted until 1907, when the government closed loopholes that had allowed Japanese Americans to enter the United States from Hawaii, Canada, or Mexico.

Upon arrival in the United States, Asian-American immigrants were herded into wooden barracks to be carefully screened by immigration officials. While some immigrants were released in a matter of days, others remained

Minding the shop in a Chinese grocery store in New York City in 1942. Many Chinese Americans opened such businesses because they required only small amounts of capital.

for months. Even after admission to the United States, Asian-American immigrants were not allowed to become citizens. This lack of investment in their adopted land led many Asian immigrants to maintain close ties to their homelands. The Chinese were particularly hated in some western states, and thousands of Chinese immigrants had been killed by angry whites in the late 19th century. Because most Asian Americans were banned from labor unions, they were often relegated to low-paying jobs. Finally in order to avoid the competition that encouraged intolerance, Chinese Americans had begun opening groceries, restaurants, and laundries. Such businesses also required limited startup capital.

Chinese males generally traveled to the United States without their families, so many of them were single. They solved the problem of finding Chinese wives by marrying "picture brides." Typically a male would rent or borrow good clothing, and have a flattering picture taken to be sent to a potential bride. If she approved, he could designate a proxy to stand in for him in a wedding ceremony in China. The bride never laid eyes on her groom until she arrived in the United States. She then became dependent on him for her very survival.

Some states prohibited Asian Americans from possessing, purchasing, or leasing land. It was not until 1947 that such laws were overturned by the U.S. Supreme Court on the grounds that they violated the Fourteenth Amendment's guarantee of equal protection. Many states also banned the intermarriage of Asian Americans with other races. It was not until the 1960s that those laws were overturned. Use of the term Asian American to describe Americans of Asian descent did not come into common use until the civil rights movement of the 1960s. Before that time, Asian groups were referred to by their country of origin, or as Asians and Pacific Islanders.

By 1940 there were 77,504 Chinese Americans living in the United States. Most clustered in large cities such as San Francisco, New York, Los Angeles, Oakland, Chicago, Salt Lake City, Portland (Oregon), Boston, and Philadelphia. There were 126,947 Japanese residing in the United States. While the majority lived in the Los Angeles area, Japanese Americans also clustered in Seattle, San Francisco, New York City, Tacoma, Oakland, and Portland (Oregon). Like the Chinese, the Japanese tended to live in ethnic enclaves. Some wealthy Japanese families sent their children to Japan to be educated. However most Japanese Americans had never even seen Japan. The majority of their ancestors had come to the United States to escape land reforms instituted during the Meiji Restoration period of the late 19th century. There were also 45,563 Filipinos, 1,711 Koreans, and 3,193 "other" Asian and Pacific Islanders in the United States in 1940.

AN INFAMOUS DAY

The lives of all Asian Americans changed drastically when Japanese forces attacked the U.S. naval base at Pearl Harbor, Hawaii, around 8:00 AM on

Pearl Harbor and Korean Americans

On Sunday morning, December 7, 1941, Japanese planes bore down on the U.S. naval base at Pearl Harbor, Hawaii. A Filipino witness noted that the planes "looked like toys but they were shooting and dropping bombs on us." Many people who saw the planes initially thought they were part of a military exercise. Within hours, Japanese forces also attacked the Philippines and Hong Kong.

When news of the attack on Pearl Harbor reached the mainland United States, most Americans were sent into a spiral of outrage, shock, and fear. Many Asian Americans felt the same. Barry Saiki, a Japanese-American student at the University of California, Berkeley noted that reactions among his cohorts "ranged from stunned silence to uncertainty and frustration." While acknowledging that native-born Japanese Americans were "imbued with American concepts and ideals," they recognized the pull of two loyalties, not to Japan, but to their alien parents. Many Asian Americans were also worried about families in their homelands, which were in the direct path of Japanese aggression.

In the Korean-American community, many people responded to news of Pearl Harbor by gleefully shouting, "*Taehan. Toknip. Manse!*" (Long live Korean independence). In Los Angeles, the Korean National Association drew up a set of resolutions that pledged Korean Americans to promote unity, work for American defense whenever possible by such activities as buying war bonds and volunteering in the war effort, and identifying themselves as Koreans so they would not be mistaken for Japanese. Korean Americans were well aware that even though they hated Japan, the Alien Registration Act of 1940 classified them as "subjects of Japan." Most Korean Americans viewed the war as an opportunity for Japan's aggressive tendencies to be stopped before they spread all over Asia.

Once the United States entered the war, Korean Americans were classified as "enemy aliens" like the Japanese. In Hawaii, they were required to wear badges with black borders that equated them with Japanese workers. After they protested, the original badges were exchanged for new ones that proclaimed, "I am Korean."

Because many Korean Americans also spoke Japanese, the U.S. government employed them as Japanese-language teachers and translators. They also engaged in transmitting propaganda broadcasts to the Pacific front, and worked underground in occupied areas of Asia. In one area of Los Angeles, a group of Korean-American males between the ages of 18 and 65 joined the National Guard's Tiger Brigade, Manghokun. Other Korean Americans volunteered for the Red Cross, or worked as emergency fire wardens. They also bought war bonds, purchasing $239,000 worth between 1942 and 1943.

Sunday, December 7, 1941. The changes concerned not only the way Asian Americans, particularly Japanese Americans, were viewed by U.S. society as a whole, but also how Asian Americans identified themselves, and how they related to the greater society. Japanese Americans, especially those on the West Coast, immediately became targets of suspicion and discrimination. Irrespective of citizenship, anyone who was at least one-16th Japanese was classified as an "enemy alien."

Before December 7 drew to a close, 737 Japanese Americans had been arrested under direct orders of Attorney General Francis Biddle. Detainees included Japanese Association officials, teachers at Japanese-language schools, Buddhists, priests, and community leaders. The following day, the United States declared war on Japan. Within three days, the number of Japanese Americans in custody had risen to 1,370. By February 1942 the number had grown to more than 2,000. Most were questioned and released. The war placed patriotic Japanese Americans in a quandary because restrictions were placed on their activities. Males were banned from the military, and both sexes were prevented from signing up for civil service work. So Japanese Americans bought war bonds to show their patriotism.

A Japanese-American man boarding up his shop in San Francisco in April 1942 before internment. Some Japanese Americans were given as little as an hour to leave their homes and businesses.

Before the end of December, the Agriculture Committee of the Los Angeles Chamber of Commerce had officially recommended that all Japanese nationals be placed under direct control of the U.S. government. Out of fear of espionage, all Japanese Americans living in California, Oregon, Washington, Montana, Idaho, Utah, and Nevada were ordered to turn in short-wave radios, cameras, binoculars, and weapons. Curfews were imposed, and all Japanese Americans were required to carry identification papers.

On January 29, 1942, Attorney General Biddle issued the first of a series of orders designating certain West Coast areas as "protected zones" and calling for the evacuation of all German, Japanese, and Italian aliens from such areas. However at no time were large groups of German or Italian Americans rounded up during World War II. The government called for voluntary relocation of Japanese Americans, but resistance forestalled the project from the outset. Prominent journalists, including Walter Lippman, Edward R. Murrow, and Henry McLemore, joined prominent political and business leaders in demanding that Japanese Americans be removed from areas where they could conceivably aid the enemy. Biddle and the Department of Justice resisted the notion of forcible internment, but they were overridden by the War Department and popular opinion.

President Roosevelt finally signed Executive Order 9066 in February 1942. As the roundup of Japanese Americans on the West Coast began, no concessions were made regarding citizenship status. Neither were formal hearings held to give Japanese Americans opportunities to answer specific charges and clear themselves. In March, the Federal Reserve Bank was assigned the responsibility of helping Japanese Americans to dispose of their possessions. The first group of internees was relocated from Bainbridge Island in Puget Sound. On Terminal Island in San Pedro, California, Japanese Americans were given only 48 hours to report for transfer to an internment camp. Others were given less than an hour to get ready to leave their homes for an indefinite period. The financial losses and the loss of dignity and privacy were catastrophic for most families. Worst of all were the losses of family members. One internee wrote that his father was picked up an hour after the attack, and was not seen again for three and a half years.

INTERNMENT CAMPS

In the months after the Japanese attack on Pearl Harbor, more than 120,000 Japanese Americans were interned in the United States. Two-thirds were native-born Americans (*Nisei*) born to immigrant parents (*Issei*) who had become permanent residents. Most internees were children and teenagers. On average, the confinement in the camps lasted from two to three years. To remove the internees as far as possible from other Americans and from sensitive defense areas, the camps were generally located in the deserts and swamplands of the west and southwest. Many Americans agreed with jour-

Executive Order 9066

In the aftermath of the Japanese attack on Pearl Harbor, anti-Japanese feeling was at its peak in the United States. The initial call for restraint soon gave way to calls for exclusion. Groups around the country began pressuring President Franklin Roosevelt to remove all Japanese Americans from the West Coast, allegedly to prevent their aiding the Japanese in attacking mainland America. Two of the leaders of the anti-Japanese sentiment were Los Angeles Congressman Leland Ford and right-wing columnist Westbrook Pegler. Ford sent a telegram to Secretary of State Cordell Hull on January 6, 1942, stating that he did not "believe that we could be any too strict to our consideration of the Japanese in the face of the treacherous way in which they do things." In Portland, Oregon, the American Legion post demanded that all "enemy aliens" be removed from critical areas of the West Coast, and a combined force of congressional delegates from California, Oregon, and Washington insisted that President Roosevelt remove all Japanese Americans from strategically significant areas of their states.

On February 19, 1942, President Roosevelt finally yielded to increasing pressure and signed Executive Order 9066, paving the way for the incarceration of Japanese Americans in internment camps. The order did not specifically name Japanese Americans, but assigned authority to the secretary of war and military commanders to ensure that citizens of enemy countries be prevented from posing threats of "espionage" or "sabotage to national-defense material, national-defense premises, and national-defense utilities" as defined by existing laws. The president's designated representatives were authorized to take any actions deemed "necessary or desirable to prescribe military areas in such places and of such extent" as was considered essential to national security. Once "enemy aliens" were interned, it became the responsibility of the federal government to provide them with "transportation, food, shelter, and other accommodations" in addition to medical aid, hospitalization, clothing, and "supplies, equipment, utilities, facilities, and services." The secretary of war and the military were also given authority to enforce compliance by using "Federal troops and other Federal Agencies" and "to accept assistance of state and local agencies." By February 20, Secretary of War Henry Stimson had charged Lieutenant General John DeWitt with carrying out the stipulations of Executive Order 9066.

nalist Henry McLemore who called for all Japanese Americans to be herded and packed up to the "bad lands" where they would be "pinched, hurt, hungry, and dead up against it." Between 1942 and 1946, Japanese Americans were detained at 10 internment camps: Gila River, Arizona (13,348); Granada, Colorado (7,318); Heart Mountain, Wyoming (101,767); Jerome, Arkansas

(8,497); Rohwer, Arkansas (8,475); Manzanar, California (10,046); Minidoka, Idaho (9,397); Poston, Arizona (17,814); Topaz, Utah (8,130); and Tule Lake, California (18,789).

Armed soldiers patrolled the grounds with unsheathed bayonets. Curfews of 9:00 PM to 6:00 AM were strictly enforced. While most internees cooperated with camp personnel, there were occasions when trouble erupted. In November 1942 workers at the Poston camp engaged in a work stoppage after an internee was killed in a truck accident. Martial law was declared, and 1,200 soldiers and eight tanks arrived at Poston. One of the most violent episodes occurred at Manzanar when Fred Tayama of the Japanese American Citizens League was beaten by masked attackers. After Harry Ueno of the Kitchen Workers Union was arrested, some 3,000 to 4,000 supporters staged a protest. Military police released tear gas into the crowd when it refused to disperse,

Japanese-American Internment

N

0		300 miles
0	300 km	

Puyallup
WA
Portland
OR
Fort Missoula
Kooskia
MT
ND
Fort Lincoln
MN
ID
Minidoka
Heart Mountain
SD
WI
Tule Lake
CA
WY
Marysville
Sacramento
Stockton   NV
Tanforan
Turlock
Merced
Salinas   Pinedale
UT
NE
IA
Topaz
CO
IL
Grenada
KS
MO
Fresno
Tulare
Santa Anita
Manzanar   Mayer
Pomona   Poston
AZ
Santa Fe
NM
OK
AR
Rohwer
PACIFIC
OCEAN
Gila River
Fort Stanton
TX
Jerome
MS
LA
Crystal City   Kenedy
Gulf of Mexico

Military district
Assembly points
▲ WRA* internment camps
□ Justice Department internment camps
* War Relocation Authority

© Infobase Publishing

A 1943 Ansel Adams photograph of a line of internees waiting to eat lunch at noon in a mess hall at Manzanar in 1943.

Life Inside the Camps

According to personal narratives, life behind barbed wire was generally harsh. The worst thing was losing all aspects of privacy. Families ate in mess halls with other internees, losing the dinner hour when most families come together to discuss the events of the day. A siren blast woke internees at 7 A.M., and lines started forming for baths and breakfast. Living quarters consisted of rows of hastily constructed wooden-framed tarpaper buildings. Each family lived in a room 18 feet x 20 feet that was furnished with a potbelly stove, army cots with straw-filled mattresses, blankets, and pillows. The unfinished walls were so thin that conversations on either side could easily be overheard. Adult males were often separated from the rest of their families.

Most internees were able to find comfort in family and friends, and in carrying out normal activities as much as possible. Children went to school and adults worked or attended classes on everything from embroidery to Japanese language. Some camps had libraries composed of donated books. For 10 cents, an internee could see a movie, and amateur talent shows were common. Religious services were held, and holidays were observed.

Each camp was under the control of an administrative staff composed of approximately 100 people. Because of the language barrier, selected internees were chosen as block managers to carry out the dispersal of goods, services, and information. Internees elected members to a community council, which had authority to make policy decisions subject to approval by camp directors. Three internees were killed by gunfire during internment, but for the most part, internees avoided physical mistreatment during the war by invoking the Geneva Convention's stipulations concerning the humane treatment of prisoners of war. Nevertheless internees were sometimes beaten, handcuffed, or sentenced to solitary confinement.

and an officer fired into the crowd, killing a 17-year-old male. Another male died later from wounds suffered in the riot.

In 1943 the government began administering loyalty oaths to Japanese Americans, attempting to weed out those who might pose a threat to national security. The oath read: "I, the undersigned, do solemnly swear (or affirm) that I will support and defend the Constitution of the United States of America against all enemies, foreign and domestic; that I will bear true faith and allegiance to the same; that I do hereby foreswear and repudiate any other allegiance which I knowingly or unknowingly may have held heretofore; and that I take these obligations freely without any mental reservation whatsoever or purpose of evasion. So help me God."

In all, five of every six respondents pledged loyalty to the United States. Japanese-American males in the relevant age group were asked whether or not they were willing to serve in the military. Because they were angry at the mistreatment of all Japanese Americans, 22 percent of eligible males stated that they would not be willing to serve. Over 1,000 volunteered for the military. Throughout the course of World War II, 33,000 Japanese Americans served in the U.S. military.

Most served with distinction. Lieutenant General Richard Sakakida, for instance, translated Japanese plans for a surprise attack at Burma. Armed with the knowledge he provided, Allied forces were able to stage an ambush as the Japanese landed. Other Japanese Americans crawled close enough to enemy lines to hear commands and relay them back to Allied commanders. They also tapped lines, listened in on radio transmissions, and translated documents and messages.

ASIAN AMERICANS IN THE MILITARY

Even before the outbreak of World War II, Filipinos tended to hate and fear Japan. Within hours of attacking the U.S. naval base at Pearl Harbor, Hawaii, Japanese planes headed toward the Philippines. There, on the Bataan Peninsula, they met significant resistance from combined U.S. and Filipino forces. It was a losing battle for the island's defenders, and on April 9, they surrendered after enduring what was described as four months of "the tortures of hell." The bravery of the Filipino soldiers impressed the entire free world. First Lady Eleanor Roosevelt declared, "Fighting in Bataan has been an excellent example of what happens when two different races [Americans and Filipinos] respect each other" and fight side by side praising one another's "heroism and courage." Poet Carlos Bulosan described the surrender in *The Voice of Bataan* in 1943:

> *Bataan has fallen.*
> *With heads bloody but unbowed, we yielded to the enemy . . .*
> *We have stood up uncomplaining*

Besieged on land and blockaded by sea,
We have done all that human endurance could bear
Our defeat is our victory.

On February 19, 1942, Secretary of War Henry Stimson announced that the First Filipino Infantry Regiment was being formed "in recognition of intense loyalty and patriotism" of Filipino Americans. In response 16,000 Filipinos enlisted in California, 40 percent of the state's Filipino population. In all, some 7,000 Filipinos served in the First and Second Filipino Infantry Regiment. Their motto became "On to Bataan."

Throughout the war, Filipino servicemen and women demonstrated their courage. On the battlefield, they often engaged in enemy sabotage. Nevertheless Filipinos on the mainland continued to be openly discriminated against. Some California restaurants refused to serve Filipino servicemen; and Filipinos were banned from hotels, movie theaters, and other public places. Ultimately, military officials stepped in to prevent overt discrimination. On February 20, 1943, 1,200 Filipino soldiers became U.S. citizens at a ceremony at California's Camp Beale.

By the beginning of 1942, the Selective Service status of all Japanese-American citizens had been changed to Class 1V-C, identifying them as "enemy aliens." Japanese Americans who were already in the service were either dismissed or relegated to mundane tasks such as kitchen duty. Despite initial attempts to keep Asian Americans out of the military during World War II, political and military decisionmakers came to realize that Asian Americans had unique talents that could be used to defeat the enemy. In June 1942 Asian Americans from the 298th and 299th Regiments of the Hawaii National Guard were organized into the 100th Battalion. They called themselves One-Puka-Puka. During training, members of the 100th were closely watched by both the Federal Bureau of Investigation and military officers. In September 1943 the 100th was attached to the 34th Infantry Division in North Africa. After reaching Europe, it suffered heavy casualties, but

Ansel Adams photographed Japanese-American corporal Jimmy Shohara at the Manzanar camp during a visit to his interned parents in 1943.

managed to win more than 900 Purple Hearts, earning the nickname the Purple Heart Battalion.

The group that became known as the 442nd Regimental Combat Team was initially formed from the 100th Battalion and Japanese-American volunteers from the 10 mainland internment camps. The 442nd was comprised of the 442nd Infantry Regiment, the 522nd Field Artillery Battalion, the 232nd Combat Engineering Company, and the 206th Army Grand Forces Band in addition to an antitank company, a cannon company, a medical detachment, and a service company. The 442nd was involved in eight major European campaigns, including the liberation of Bruyeres in France, the rescue of the Lost Battalion in Italy, and the liberation of the Dachau concentration camp in Germany. In most cases, the 442nd had to assure groups being rescued that they were Americans, and not Japanese.

By the end of World War II, the 442nd had suffered 9,486 casualties (dead and wounded). The regiment had also won 18,143 decorations for valor, seven Presidential Citations, and 9,486 Purple Hearts. In a special ceremony at the White House on July 15, 1946, President Harry Truman told surviving members of the 442nd, "You fought not only the enemy, but you fought prejudice—and you won." After a medal upgrade, surviving veterans of the 442nd were on hand on July 20, 2000, to receive Medals of Honor. A memorial located on

Japanese-American soldiers from the 442nd Regimental Combat Team marching along a road in France in 1944. The regiment won thousands of medals, including 9,486 Purple Hearts.

the Avenue of the 442nd Infantry Regiment in Bruyeres, France, reads in both English and French: "To the men of the 442nd Regimental Combat Team, United States Army, who reaffirmed an historic truth here—that loyalty to one's country is not modified by racial origin."

CHINESE AMERICANS IN THE 1930s AND 1940s

Many Chinese Americans continued to maintain close ties to their homeland in the 1930s and 1940s. The government of Chiang Kai-shek had been facing aggression from both Japan and Russia. Within the United States, the Great Depression had not been kind to Asian Americans because many of them were ineligible for New Deal benefits. Although some Americans still held onto old prejudices, overall reactions to the Chinese had been somewhat tempered since the publication of Pearl Buck's *The Good Earth* in 1931. Buck had been born in the United States to Presbyterian missionaries, but had spent the first 40 years of her life in China. She retained a lifelong interest in the country. Buck won the Pulitzer Prize in 1937, and the Nobel Prize for Literature in 1938. After Japan invaded Manchuria in 1937, the Chinese government turned to the United States for help. However President Roosevelt was limited in his ability to help because of the isolationism that had become entrenched in the United States since the end of World War I. Chinese Americans remained committed to the Chiang regime, raising $56 million in relief funds 1937–45. Both Chinese and Korean Americans organized boycotts of ships carrying iron from the United States to Japan. In July 1941 Roosevelt cut oil exports to Japan by 90 percent, well aware that Japan had no source of domestic oil.

The day after the attack on Pearl Harbor, China officially declared war on Japan. In Portland, Oregon, the Chinese-American community donated three fighting planes to the Chinese government, *For the People, By the People,* and *Of the People.* In order to avoid being taken for "enemy aliens," many Chinese Americans wore buttons proclaiming, "I am not a Jap" or "I am Chinese." Yielding to pressure from Asian-American groups and such notable figures as Richard T. Walsh, the husband of Pearl Buck and publisher of *Asia and the Americas* magazine, Congress repealed the Chinese Exclusion Act in 1943, allowing Chinese Americans to become naturalized citizens. In New York City, crowds cheered as 40 percent of the city's Chinese-American population was drafted into the U.S. military. In all, 13,499 Chinese-American males were drafted. Many Chinese-American females joined women's service organizations. As employees left for the military or took war-related positions, many establishments in Chinatowns were forced to close.

Because of China's status as an Ally, Congress instituted a quota of 105 Chinese immigrants per year. Between 1944 and 1949, 383 Chinese immigrants were admitted to the United States. After the passage of the War Brides Act of

Chinese-American women joined in the war effort, including the American-born Chinese actress Barbara Jane Wong, shown here in June 1942, performing a radio program with actor Walter Pidgeon for the U.S. War Production Board.

1945, Chinese women began immigrating to the United States. Approximately 6,000 Chinese wives of American G.I.s were admitted to the United States on a nonquota basis. Between 1944 and 1952, 1,428 Chinese Americans were naturalized. The amiability toward the Chinese did not survive the war, however, and restrictions were placed on remittances that Chinese immigrants were allowed to send to their homeland.

When the communist Chinese solidified their control of China in 1947 under Mao Zedong, the alliance between the United States and China was relegated to history. The following year, Congress passed the Displaced Persons Act, which allowed 3,500 Chinese visitors, seamen, and students who had been in the United States when diplomatic relations were broken off to become permanent U.S. residents.

FILIPINO AMERICANS IN THE 1930s AND 1940s

In 1940 there were 45,563 Filipinos living on the mainland, and another 52,659 living in Hawaii. Most came to the United States looking for riches, only to find that living expenses consumed most of their wages. Because many families had mortgaged their homes to send sons to America, Filipino males often arrived in the United States under obligation to help repay huge debts.

Even though they were considered American nationals in the early 1940s because the Philippines were a U.S. territory, Filipino Americans were sometimes treated as "enemy aliens," and some were deported to the Philippines. On July 4, 1946, two days after Congress passed legislation clearing the way for Filipinos living in the United States to become naturalized citizens, the Philippines won their long-coveted independence. From 1946 to 1965, 100 Filipinos were allowed into the United States each year. Despite the contributions of Filipinos during World War II, the U.S. government reneged on promises to provide veterans' benefits to Filipinos who had served in the military. In 1997 the Filipino Veterans Equity Bill finally granted military benefits to 70,000 surviving Filipino veterans.

KOREAN AMERICANS IN THE 1930s AND 1940s
There were 1,711 Korean Americans in the United States in 1940. Like the Chinese, Korean Americans had been ill-treated by the Japanese. After invading Korea in the 1930s, the Japanese had banned the Korean language in all public schools, and had forced Koreans to adopt Japanese names. Large numbers of Koreans had been transported to Japan to work in industry. As a result of that history, Korean Americans were united against the Japanese.

World War II proved to be a turning point for most Korean immigrants and their families as job opportunities opened in shipyards, aircraft plants, and other defense industries. Other Korean Americans opened laundries, groceries, trucking companies, restaurants, drug stores, and hat shops. By 1945 there were 6,500 Korean Americans residing in Hawaii, and another 3,000 living on the mainland, where they clustered on the edges of Little Tokyos and Chinatowns.

INDIAN AMERICANS IN THE 1930s AND 1940s
Asian Indians lived through many difficult years before they won the right to become U.S. citizens. Through the efforts of Mubarak Alikhan, a bill was introduced in Congress in 1939 to grant citizenship to all Indians who had lived in the United States since 1924. The bill was defeated, because opponents of the bill insisted that passage would mean the same right had to be extended to all other Asian Americans. The following year, Khairata Ram Samras challenged *United States v. Bhagat Singh Thind* (216 U.S. 204, 1923), which had denied all Indians the right to become citizens.

In the face of the president's declaration of the Four Freedoms and the strategic significance of India during World War II, the U.S. government was forced to reexamine its position on the role of Indians in the United States. In 1946 they were allowed to become citizens, and an immigration quota was established. Between 1947 and 1965, 12,000 Indians immigrated to the United States.

On March 20, 1946, the camp at Tule Lake, California, became the last internment camp to cease operations. Many Japanese Americans returned home to find that their lands and homes had been confiscated by others in their absence. In some cases, Japanese Americans had continued to pay taxes while in internment, but their homes were generally in disrepair, and many

Gordon Hirabayashi

An Asian-American Quaker, Gordon Hirabayashi was a student at the University of Washington when the Japanese bombed Pearl Harbor in 1941. Hirabayashi decided to challenge his orders to report for transfer to an internment camp. Along with his lawyer, he reported to the FBI office in Seattle, Washington, on May 16, 1942. Hirabayashi explained that as a Quaker he was experiencing "anguish" over being herded up like cattle. Furthermore he contended that the "order for the mass evacuation of all persons of Japanese descent denies them the right to live" and "forces thousands of energetic law-abiding individuals to exist in a horrible physical atmosphere." Hirabayashi insisted that Japanese Americans were being denied their right to due process of law and to civil liberties guaranteed by the U.S. Constitution. While Hirabayashi was in the King County jail awaiting transfer to a federal facility, his diary was confiscated. Because he had admitted to ignoring the curfew placed on Japanese Americans living on the West Coast, additional charges were filed. The American judicial system refused Hirabayashi's challenge. A judge ordered Hirabayashi's jury to find him guilty, and on October 20, 1942, he was sentenced to 90 days in a federal prison in addition to time already served.

On May 10, 1943, the U.S. Supreme Court heard arguments in *Kiyoshi Hirabayashi v. U.S.* (320 U.S. 81, 1943). The Court had decided to use Hirabayashi's case to examine whether the government's war powers outweighed a citizen's right to due process. While admitting that "distinctions between citizens solely because of their ancestry are by their very nature odious to a free people whose institutions are founded upon the doctrine of equality" and generally a denial of equal protection, Justice Harlan Stone contended that the government gained unique powers whenever the nation was at war. Although he concurred with the Court's decision, Justice Frank Murphy, the only Catholic on the Court, disagreed with the Court's reasoning, insisting that "distinctions based on color and ancestry are utterly inconsistent with our traditions and ideals. They are at variance with the principles for which we are now waging war."

By the 1980s the movement to redress Japanese-American grievances had succeeded in winning an acknowledgement that the internment had not been justified, and plans to award $20,000 to each internee were under way. Hirabayashi's convictions were finally overturned in 1987.

houses and barns had intentionally been set on fire. Bank accounts were still frozen, and many storekeepers refused to sell to Japanese Americans. Japan finally surrendered on August 14, 1945, after the United States dropped atomic bombs on the cities of Hiroshima and Nagasaki. Afterward, scores of Issei began demanding the right to be become citizens.

In 1946 sugar laborers in Hawaii went on strike, paving the way for a complete transformation of Hawaii's economic system. With the establishment of the International Longshoremen's and Warehousemen's Union (ILWU) Local 142, the various ethnic groups were united to fight not only for workers' rights, but also to battle racial discrimination. On the West Coast, however, Asian Americans had a much more difficult time getting along with prejudiced Americans. A sign posted in one California neighborhood read, "JAPS KEEP MOVING. This is a White Man's Neighborhood."

In 1948 Congress passed the Evacuation Claims Act to aid Japanese Americans in recouping some of their financial losses. However only 232 claims filed 1949–50 were ever adjudicated. Ultimately the government paid only 10 cents on the dollar for claims that were settled. In 1980 President Jimmy Carter established a panel to examine Japanese-American internment, and recommend measures to redress the grievances of former internees. The Commission of Wartime Relocation and Internment determined that the internment was a result of "race prejudice, war hysteria, and a failure of political leadership." They noted that not a single Japanese American was convicted of espionage or sabotage during World War II. The commission recommended a payment of $20,000 to each surviving internee. Congress confirmed the commission's findings, and offered a formal apology in the Civil Liberties Act of 1988. The first redress check was handed out on October 9, 1990, to the Reverend Mamoru Eto, who was then 107 years old. An additional $1.25 billion was earmarked for an educational fund for Japanese Americans.

One of the terms of the 1945 Japanese surrender was the division of Korea along the 38th parallel. South Koreans surrendered to U.S. forces, while North Koreans surrendered to Soviet forces. The following year, the United Nations called for general elections to be held under supervision. Only South Korea complied. The Immigration and Naturalization Service began considering Korean immigrants as a separate class in 1948. Only 39 immigrants from Korea were allowed into the United States each year until 1952. From 1950 to 1953, the United States aided South Koreans in their attempt to prevent North Korean communist forces from taking over their land.

CONCLUSION

Between 1939 and 1949, the lives of all Asian Americans were reshaped by events that took place around the world that echoed with devastating results in the United States and abroad. Throughout that period, the vast majority continued to exhibit loyalty to the American way of life, and many of them gave their service and lives to uphold inherent rights of all Americans. Those who remained at home worked hard to support their families with dignity, while contributing to American society in a myriad of ways.

Elizabeth R. Purdy
Independent Scholar

Further Reading

Bangarth, Stephanie. *Voices Raised in Protest: Defending North American Citizens of Japanese Ancestry, 1942–1949*. Vancouver and Toronto: UBC Press, 2008.

Commission on Wartime Relocation and Internment of Civilians. *Personal Justice Denied: Report on Wartime Relocation and Internment of Civilians*. Washington: Government Printing Office, 1992.

Daniels, Roger. *Asian America: Chinese and Japanese in the United States since 1850*. Seattle: University of Washington Press, 1988.

Daniels, Roger, et al., eds. *Japanese Americans: From Relocation to Redress*. Seattle: University of Washington Press, 1991.

Densho. Available online, URL: http://www.densho.org/. Accessed September 2008.

Fugita, Stephen S., and Marilyn Fernandez. *Altered Lives: Enduring Community: Japanese Americans Remember Their World War II Incarceration*. Seattle, WA: University of Washington Press, 2004.

Handley, Norris, Jr. *The Asian Experience: The Historical Experience*. Santa Barbara, CA: CLIO Books, 1976.

Hayashi, Brian Masaru. *Democratizing the Enemy: The Japanese American Internment*. Princeton, NJ: Princeton University Press, 2004.

Irons, Peter. *The Courage of Their Convictions: Sixteen Americans Who Fought Their Way to the Supreme Court*. New York: Penguin, 1988.

Kim, Hyung Chan. *Dictionary of Asian American History*. New York: Greenwood Press, 1986.

Knoll, Tricia. *Becoming Americans: Asian Sojourners, Immigrants in the Western United States*. Portland, OR: Coast to Coast Books, 1982.

Lyman, S. M. *The Asian in the West*. Reno: University of Nevada, 1971.

Mark, Diane Mei Lin, and Ginger Chih. *A Place Called Chinese America*. Dubuque, IA: Kendall/Hunt, 1982.

Ng, Wendy. *Japanese America: Internment during World War II: A History and Reference Guide*. Westport, CT: Greenwood, 2002.

"Transcript of Executive Order 9066." Available online, URL: http://www.ourdocuments.gov/doc.php?flash=true&doc=74&page=transcript. Accessed September 2008.

CHAPTER 6

Postwar Immigration: 1950 to 1959

THE 1950s WERE a time of prosperity in the United States, a time of increasing incomes that enabled average blue-collar families to participate in the growing consumerism. Work-saving household appliances proliferated, movies played to record audiences, and the new medium of television began to bring entertainment and news into individual homes across the nation. But the economic prosperity masked growing fears of international communism. By 1950 the cold war cast a threatening shadow over American society. The fall of China to Mao Zedong's communist forces in 1949, followed quickly by the beginning of the Korean War in June 1950, increased tensions not only internationally, but also domestically, leading to the rise of McCarthyism—Senator Joseph McCarthy's investigations of communist infiltration into government and society. This Red Scare led to passage of the Internal Security Act, and other legislation designed to control organizations and individuals suspected of being subversive. This atmosphere of distrust had a direct impact on many Asians, both in the United States, and for those seeking entry.

In 1950 the U.S. Census reported the largest Asian group to be Japanese (326,379), followed by Chinese (150,005), and Filipino (122,707). Totaling 599,091 people, the three groups accounted for only 0.4 percent of the total U.S. population. Other smaller groups raised the total to only about one-half of one percent of the population. During the decade, immigration and natural growth raised these counts to 464,468 people of Japanese ancestry, 237,292 Chinese, and 176,310 Filipino. These represented increases of 42.3, 58.2, and 43.7 percent, respectively. Prior to World War II, there had been no real Korean community in the United States, except perhaps in Hawaii. During the 1950s, approximately 8,000 Korean refugees, orphans, and war brides entered the country. By the end of the decade, the Asian population comprised 52 percent Japanese, 27 percent Chinese, 20 percent Filipino, and one percent Korean, with a negligible amount of others from southeast Asia. The majority of each population was female and resided in areas bordering the Pacific Ocean, with the largest Asian communities found in Honolulu, San Francisco, New York, Los Angeles, Oakland, Chicago, Sacramento, Boston, Washington, D.C., and Stockton (California).

IMMIGRATION LAWS

During the 1950s, Asian immigration to the United States was still governed by restrictive legislation, including: the Chinese Exclusion Act (1882), the First Quota Act (1921), and the National Origins Act (1924). Because of these regulations and quotas, only 185 Japanese could enter the United States as immigrants each year, and only 100 Chinese, defined by the federal government as people from Taiwan, plus 105 openings for other "Chinese" who might enter from any other nation around the world. Despite these restrictions, Asians were able to circumvent the strict quotas. The War Brides Act, amended by Congress in 1947 to include Chinese, allowed the wives of U.S. citizens to enter outside the quotas; while the Displaced Persons Act (1948) and the Refugee Relief Act (1953) provided other avenues of entry. For example, after the fall of China to communist forces, some 5,000 Chinese professionals and students in the United States were granted refugee status. The Refugee Relief Act provided up to 205,000 special immigrant visas for people from non-communist nations, or those fleeing communist countries. The same law made available up to 4,000 immigrant visas for orphaned or abandoned children, and allowed up to 5,000 people on non-immigrant visas who had arrived before July 1, 1953, to convert to immigrant status.

It is estimated that about 25,000 Japanese entered the United States during the 1950s under provisions of the War Brides Act, and the arrival of students, government officials, and tourists also increased steadily during the decade. Japanese immigration in general, aside from the war brides and children, remained relatively small as the Japanese economy provided increasing opportunities and correspondingly less incentive to leave. Aside from those granted refugee status, a large number of Chinese immigrants during this period were also spouses of U.S. citizens, as were Filipinos. There were no significant Korean communities in United States in 1950, but, largely because of the Korean War, some 6,000 Koreans entered the country during the decade, a trend that continued to increase thereafter. Most of these early arrivals were also war brides. In

Traditional Behavior

While some Chinese who came to America found a new freedom away from the constraints of traditional Chinese society, for others little changed. The following description, taken from Ruth Hum Lee's *The Growth and Decline of Chinese Communities in the Rocky Mountain Region*, recounts the reminiscence of the wife of a Chinese merchant in frontier Butte, Montana, who found herself subject to strict traditional behavior patterns.

When I came to America as a bride, I never knew I would be coming to a prison. I was allowed out of the house but once a year. That was during the New Year's when families exchanged New Year calls and feasts. We would dress in our long-plaited, brocaded, hand-embroidered skirts. These were a part of our wedding dowry brought from China. . . . The father of my children hired a closed carriage to take me and the children calling. Of course, he did not go with us, as this was against the custom practiced in China. The carriage would take us even if we went around the corner, for no family women walked. . . . Before we went out of the house, we sent the children to see if the streets were clear of men. It was considered impolite to meet them.

1956, when Harry Holt brought eight Korean orphans with him to the United States, he and his wife established the Holt Adoption Agency, which eventually led to the adoption of thousands of Korean children by American families.

An important change in U.S. immigration laws occurred in 1952 with passage of the McCarran-Walter Act. Although the so-called immigration reform legislation did not eliminate the strict nationality quotas, it did provide some benefits for Asians. A new quota of 100 was allotted for the Asian-Pacific Triangle in southern and eastern Asia, and, more importantly, it eliminated the restriction of naturalization to "free white persons" in force since the original Naturalization Act of 1790. This allowed Issei (Japanese immigrants) and other Asian immigrants to apply for naturalization as U.S. citizens for the first time. Later, the Immigration and Nationality Act of 1957 more clearly defined policies regarding stepchildren, illegitimate children, and adopted children, and provided that persons fleeing a communist-controlled nation where they would be subject to persecution could be admitted to the United States under refugee provisions.

Because of these changes in immigration law and the various pieces of legislation providing alternative channels of entry, Asian immigration increased dramatically during the 1950s. All of the Asian groups were predominantly female, and because the new laws reserved half of the available immigration slots to professionals and skilled workers who would benefit the U.S. economy, the male immigrants were heavily skewed toward such workers. The effect of this can best be seen in Chinese immigration. Prior to 1950, only about 1.5 percent of Chinese immigrants possessed a college education. Most earned a living as cooks, domestics, laundrymen, or waiters, but beginning in 1952, the majority who were not war brides were educated professionals.

THE CONFESSION PROGRAM

As fear of communism increased during the 1950s, the State Department and the Immigration and Naturalization Service (INS) came under increasing pressure to scrutinize anyone entering the country from communist-controlled areas—especially those from China—as well as aliens already in the United States. In one case, Eugene Moy, editor of the *China Daily News*, was accused of being pro-communist and imprisoned, while subscribers were investigated and warned by federal authorities to cancel their subscriptions. The sole basis for the accusation and imprisonment was that the newspaper had accepted an advertisement from the Nanyang Bank of Hong Kong. The ad merely promoted the availability of its financial services for those wishing to send money to relatives in China.

In December 1955 Everett F. Drumright, U.S. consul general in Hong Kong, submitted a report alleging that massive passport and visa fraud was taking place as the communist Chinese attempted to infiltrate agents into the United States. Drumright asserted that the communists were using phony birth certificates to claim nonexistent relations that would qualify Chinese to enter the United States under family reunification laws. This same fear was voiced in testimony before a committee of the U.S. Senate: J. Edgar Hoover, director of the Federal Bureau of Investigation, charged that "The large number of Chinese entering this country as immigrants provides Red China with a channel to dispatch to the United States undercover agents on intelligence assignments."

At the heart of the issue was the "paper son" ploy by which many Chinese had entered the United States earlier, claiming falsely to be the offspring of Chinese residents. Usually this occurred when a legal U.S. resident claimed one or more offspring still residing in China. In payment for a fee, forged documents could then be used by another person to enter the United States, claiming to be the child of the legal resident. Under increasing pressure from Hoover, McCarthy, and other leaders of the anticommunist investigations, the INS launched a series of raids on Chinese organizations in San Francisco, New York, and elsewhere seeking not only incriminating evidence of subversive activity, but to gather information on the paper son network in preparation for deportation hearings threatened by the Eisenhower administration.

Faced with the possibility of widespread deportations, the National Chinese Welfare Council and other Chinese organizations brokered a compromise agreement with U.S. immigration officials. Known as the Confession Program, beginning in 1956, Chinese with fraudulent immigration documentation could gain amnesty and be allowed to stay in the country if they confessed, provided information on any others they knew of who were involved in the paper son scheme, and swore they were anticommunist in sentiment. Thus one confession could implicate any number of other people. By requiring people to implicate family members and friends, the program spread fear within the Chinese community, and caused great stress as people were forced to choose between possible deportation, and betrayal of their kin.

Research by Mae M. Ngai estimates that about 25 percent of the Chinese in the United States in 1950 were there illegally. But the INS was more interested in the communist threat than it was in those who had entered under the paper son scam. During the course of the Confession Program, 13,895 people confessed, implicating 22,083 others, and 11,294 potential immigration slots were uncovered and eliminated. About 99 percent of those who confessed were allowed to remain in the United States—only those involved in communist activities were deported. As Ngai concluded, despite the unfairness of selective prosecution, the Confession Program "enabled Chinese immigrants to take a step out of the shadow of exclusion [and] served as a means of renegotiating the terms of Chinese Americans' membership in the nation." Another researcher, Xiaojian Zhao, largely agreed, noting that by the end of the program the Chinese community "began to play traditional American ethnic group politics, lobbying in Washington, and forming alliances with other ethnic groups."

ASIANS FIGHT FOR CIVIL RIGHTS

Beginning with the landmark *Brown v. the Board of Education* decision by the U.S. Supreme Court in 1954, the civil rights movement became a dominating theme in U.S. domestic affairs. Lesser known are several cases involving Asian Americans that likewise contributed to the advancement of civil rights in America. In 1913 the Webb Act made it illegal for any alien "ineligible to naturalization" to purchase land. This stipulation, which prevented Asians from purchasing land, had been obliquely attacked in the 1948 case of *Oyama v. California* in which the Supreme Court declared a section of California's Alien Land Law unconstitutional because it had been used to deprive Fred Oyama, a Nisei (native-born Japanese American), of land he had legally purchased. Yet the original law remained. In 1952 the issue resurfaced in the Supreme Court in *Fujii Sei v. State of California*. In a divided opinion, the Court found the Webb Act to be in violation of Fourteenth Amendment protections. In the same year, in the case of *Masaoka v. State of California*, an elderly Issei widow named Haruye Masaoka—who had sent five sons to fight in the famed 442nd Regimental Combat Team where one lost his life—had been given a home by her sons, the ownership of which was contested under the state's Alien Land Law. Using the *Fujii* case as precedent, the Court once again ruled the controversial law unconstitutional. These decisions led the California legislature to repeal the state's alien land laws in 1956, removing a discriminatory practice against land ownership by Asian residents.

Another case, in 1953, involved the right to due process. Kwong Hai Chew resided in the United States with permanent resident status. A seaman, he had served in the U.S. Merchant Marine during World War II, and after the war was employed on a merchant ship registered in the United States. Upon his return from an overseas trip where his ship had docked in several Asian ports, Chew was denied entry into the United States by the attorney general, who claimed that his residence in the country would be "prejudicial to the public interest." Further the attorney general refused any hearing on the grounds that the information used to exclude him was confidential. Chew sued. In deciding *Kwong Hai Chew v. Colding, et al.*, the Supreme Court found that because Chew was a permanent resident, his rights to due process under the Fifth Amendment had been violated. The ruling established the rights of all permanent residents to equal protection.

In another case, Kiyokura Okimura, a U.S. citizen by birth, had been sent to Japan for his education, as was frequently the case with children of Issei parents. When World War II broke out, he was still in Japan, and was conscripted into the Japanese Army, despite his protests that he was a U.S. citizen. When he attempted to return to the United States after the war, he was denied entry on the argument that he had relinquished his citizenship by serving in the Japanese Army and voting in a Japanese election. The courts found otherwise in *Okimura v. Acheson*, reasoning that he had not entered the Japanese military willingly, and restored his U.S. citizenship in 1952. In a similar case in 1958, *Nishikawa v. Dulles*, Mitsugi Nishikawa had been born a U.S. citizen in 1916. Like Okimura, Nishikawa had been conscripted into the Japanese Army during the war; however his case was somewhat different because at birth his father had entered him on the family register in Japan, thus giving him dual citizenship. The Supreme Court eventually agreed that the government could not unilaterally revoke a person's citizenship without specifically establishing that the person had willingly renounced his citizenship rights. Nishikawa argued that he could not refuse service in the Japanese Army because his dual citizenship required him to serve, and he would have suffered severe penalties for refusing his obligation.

In each of these cases, the civil rights upheld by the courts brought increasing equality for Asians, and affirmed these same rights for members of other ethnic groups and nationalities.

PACIFIC COAST

The Pacific Coast states of California, Washington, and Oregon were the traditional areas of the majority of Asian settlement in the United States. Settlement patterns for Japanese residents were disrupted by their forced relocation during World War II, but by 1950, about 85,000 of the approximately 168,000 Japanese who had been relocated during the war had returned to the West Coast, primarily to California. During the decade, the return migration con-

These Japanese-American farmers were cultivating crops at Tule Lake, California, on land near their interment camp. After the war, Japanese Americans on the Pacific Coast continued to work in agriculture, with as many as 19.5 percent in farming jobs by 1950.

tinued, and by 1960 some 157,000 people of Japanese heritage lived in California. The second-largest Asian group in 1950, the Chinese accounted for 67,584 people in the Pacific Coast states (58,324 in California); by 1960, this number had risen to 95,600 (an increase of 63.9 percent).

Among Japanese residents on the Pacific Coast, the largest traditional occupation had been farming and gardening, making significant contributions to the development of agriculture, especially in California and Hawaii. Their introduction of alternative irrigation methods opened previously unproductive lands to cultivation, and while they were interned during the war, many of the internees farmed lands adjacent to camps in Arizona and at Tule Lake, California, making those areas productive for the first time. By

1950 agriculture continued to be the largest single-employment source of for Japanese Americans along the Pacific Coast, with 19.4 percent employed as farm laborers or foremen, and the largest concentration in southern California and adjacent Arizona. The related field of gardening was also well represented, with about 5,000 Japanese occupied as gardeners in the Los Angeles area alone in 1958.

Given the large percentage of people involved in agriculture, the passage of Proposition 13 in a referendum by a two-thirds majority—legislation initiated by the Japanese American Citizens League to abolish the Alien Land Law of 1913—was particularly important. With the legal ambiguities of land ownership finally eliminated, the percentage of farm laborers and foremen declined to 9.2 percent during the 1950s, but farm ownership and farm management employment increased from 17.1 percent to 21.4 percent by 1960.

During the 1950s, Nisei veterans took advantage of the GI Bill in large numbers, and Japanese Americans, along with other Asian Americans, gradually began to look outside the confines of their ethnic communities for employment opportunities. In 1950 about four percent of Japanese-

This Chinese school in Locke, California, was renamed for the Chinese businessman and donor Joe Shoong in 1954. This classroom, featuring U.S. and Republic of China flags, is now part of a museum dedicated to the school, which served Chinese-American children until the mid-1980s.

American males held professional positions, but by the end of the decade, that had risen to about 15 percent, and it would double in the following decade. Among the most populous professions were medicine, engineering, and pharmaceuticals.

Chinese Americans residing on the Pacific Coast were subject to the ongoing anticommunist investigations. In addition to the Confession Program, much of Chinese-American organizational activity during the decade was also focused on the investigations in attempts to prevent massive deportations. The Six Companies in San Francisco led an anticommunist campaign in Chinatown, and in 1951, the Anti-Communist Committee for Free China was established as Chinese Americans attempted to reassure Americans of their loyalty.

The Filipino population of the United States almost doubled by the end of the 1950s, largely because of contacts during World War II. While the prewar immigrants were mostly poor, with few nonagricultural skills; the postwar immigrants tended to be younger, married with families, and to have a higher degree of education. Most moved to Los Angeles, Chicago, New York, and Honolulu. Among the contributions of Filipinos to U.S. society was the Filipino Farm Labor Union organized in 1956 by Larry Dulay Itliong. The first major successful organization of farm laborers in California, it provided the model for the later formation of César Chávez's United Farm Workers, of which Itliong became vice president.

HAWAII

The admission of Hawaii as the 50th state in 1959 increased the Asian-American population of the United States by some 275,000—the majority of Japanese heritage, and those of Chinese heritage as the second-largest group. Although the Filipino population was smaller (69,070), the admission of Hawaii meant that about half of all the Filipinos in the country lived in Hawaii by 1960.

With a tradition of a more racially tolerant society, Hawaii offered more opportunity for Asian Americans than the continental states. Koreans in Hawaii, for example, were mostly descendants of the earlier Korean immigration during the first decade of the 20th century. By 1950 they enjoyed middle-class economic status and higher rates of educational and professional attainment than the average for Hawaii. By 1959 the median income for male workers in Hawaii was $3,717, but for Japanese Americans in Hawaii it was $4,302, and for Chinese Americans $5,096. Each of the major Asian groups in Hawaii had higher median income levels than average for the new state.

By 1950 residents of Japanese heritage comprised 37 percent of Hawaii's population. Largely because of this numerical advantage, by the 1950s, the Japanese population began to assert its growing economic and political influence. Under its leadership, the International Longshoremen's and Warehousemen's Union (ILWU) organized the plantations, providing better salaries, benefits, and working conditions for the large number of Asians employed in agriculture. Taking advantage of opportunities offered by the GI Bill, Nisei veterans enrolled in colleges in large numbers, enabling them to take advantage of increasing managerial and professional positions available in Hawaii's expanding business and tourism economies. In 1954 Nisei veterans and largely Nisei investors founded the Central Pacific Bank, chaired by Koichi Iida. Over the succeeding decades, it grew to become the fourth-largest bank in the state by the 1980s. In 1950 Robert Taira, of Okinawan descent, established a business with about $500 and his recipe to produce and sell his sweetbread. By the 1980s, his company grossed some $20 million a year, and Taira was later elected to the state House of Representatives. These examples, and other economic and political successes, led to the nickname "model ethnic group" being applied to the Nisei, and later to Asian Americans in general.

During this time, Asian influence also became evident in Hawaii's political arena. The McCarran-Walter Act of 1952 granted Issei the right to be naturalized and to vote; two years later, Tetsuo Toyama established *The Citizen*, a bilingual Japanese-English newspaper that encouraged Japanese residents to apply for citizenship, and provided free citizenship classes in his office. That same year, 1954, a coalition of Nisei and young activists led by John Burns and Daniel Inouye engineered a stunning Democratic Party victory over the previously entrenched Republicans in the territorial legislature. When the new session of the legislature opened in February 1955, Democrats controlled both houses for the first time, with Asians holding prominent positions.

With statehood, Hiram L. Fong became Hawaii's first U.S. Senator and the first Chinese American to win a Senate seat. Fong was born in Kahili, Honolulu, in 1906. Both of his parents were from Guangdong Province, and both of their stories were rather typical of immigrants in the late 19th cen-

tury: his mother was a maid, and his father was an indentured worker on a sugar plantation. Hiram worked his way through college, graduated from Harvard Law School in 1935, served in the Army Air Corps during World War II, and eventually ran several financial services companies, along with other business enterprises.

Daniel Inouye was a decorated World War II veteran who won the Medal of Honor and lost an arm while fighting in Italy as part of the renowned 442nd Regimental Combat Team. Inouye was also a Japanese American born in Honolulu. He became Hawaii's first member of the House of Representatives.

Senator Hiram L. Fong, who served in the Senate 1959–77.

Daniel Ken Inouye

Born in Honolulu, Hawaii, on September 7, 1924, Inouye is a second-generation Japanese American who grew up in a primarily Chinese neighborhood in the Bingham Tract in the city. A student enrolled in premedical studies at the University of Hawaii, he left school to enlist in the U.S. Army in 1943, when the ban on Japanese-American enlistments was eliminated. He served in the Italian Campaign with the celebrated 442nd Regimental Combat Team, the most decorated unit of the entire war, where he earned a battlefield commission and was decorated with the Bronze Star, Purple Heart, and the Medal of Honor. Seriously wounded, he returned to the United States for a lengthy convalescence after amputation of his right forearm and other wounds.

Daniel Inouye during his military service in the early 1940s.

After the war, Inouye returned to college under the GI Bill, majoring in political science. After earning his bachelor's degree in 1950, he went on to complete a law degree at George Washington University. He was elected to the Territorial Legislature, and when Hawaii was admitted as the 50th state in 1959, he became Hawaii's first member of the House of Representatives—and the first Japanese American to serve in the House. He was re-elected to the House in 1960, and in 1962, he became the first Japanese American elected to the U.S. Senate. He served on the Watergate Committee and the Iran-Contra Committee, as well as chairing the Select Committee on Intelligence (1975–79) and the Committee on Indian Affairs (1987–95 and 2001–03). In 2009 Inouye was third in seniority in the Senate.

Three years later, in the first regular election following statehood, Inouye was elected senator, and Masayuki "Spark" Matsunaga and Patsy Takemoto Mink were elected to the U.S. House of Representatives.

SCIENCE AND ENGINEERING

Asian Americans have long been leaders in fields related to science and engineering. Both Minoru Yamasaki and I.M. Pei first rose to prominence during the 1950s, and became regarded among the most noted architects of the second half of the 20th century. A Nisei born in Seattle, Yamasaki attended the University of Washington and New York University before working for firms in New York and Detroit in the 1940s. In 1951 he opened his own firm designing public buildings, notably the U.S. Consulate in Kobe, Japan (1954). He went on to a distinguished career that included designing the Pacific Science Center in Seattle, Century City Plaza in Los Angeles, and the World Trade Center in Manhattan. Ieoh Ming Pei, better known as I.M. Pei, was born in Guangzhou, China, and came to the United States in 1935, studying at the University of Pennsylvania, Massachusetts Institute of Technology, and Harvard University. After teaching at Harvard 1945–48, he joined the firm of Webb and Knapp, where he designed the Mile High Center in Denver. He established his own firm in 1955 and gained prominence designing the Government Center and the John Hancock Tower in Boston, the Jacob Javits Exposition and Convention Center in New York City, the East Wing of the National Gallery of Art in Washington, D.C., the Rock-and-Roll Hall of Fame in Cleveland, and the expansion of the Louvre in Paris.

In the field of physics, Chien-shiung Wu, a native of Shanghai, gained a reputation as the First Lady of Physics for her work on the Manhattan Project to develop the atomic bomb; her groundbreaking experiments confirmed the theories of Richard Feynman and Murray Gell-Mann, and demonstrated the violation of the law of conservation of parity in particle physics. In 1958 she became the first female recipient of the Research Corporation Award, and the first female awarded an honorary doctorate in physics by Princeton Universi-

An Wang

Born in Shanghai on February 7, 1920, Wang came to the United States in 1945 to enroll in graduate studies at Harvard University. After earning a Ph.D. in applied physics in 1948, he continued to work at Harvard where, along with another Chinese immigrant, Way-dong Woo, he invented a device for controlling electronic pulse transfers that made magnetic core memory ion computers possible. Patented in 1955, this device was used for nearly all computer memory until the invention of the microchip. In 1951 Wang used $600 in savings to found Wang Laboratories in Tewksbury, Massachusetts, to manufacture and sell electronic calculators, word processors, office automation systems, and later, microcomputers. His company eventually grew to employ over 30,000 people, with sales in excess of $2.4 billion, making him one of the richest people in the United States. Wang held more than 40 patents, contributed generously to the restoration of Boston's Metropolitan Theatre, which was renamed the Wang Theatre in his honor, and the Wang Center for the Performing Arts. In 1986 he was honored with the Medal of Liberty in a presentation by President Ronald Reagan, and in 1988 he was inducted into the National Investors Hall of Fame.

ty. She also received the National Medal of Science, the nation's ultimate award for scientific achievement, and was the first female to be elected president of the American Physical Society and to receive the Cyrus B. Comstock Award of the National Academy of Sciences.

In 1957 two Chinese Americans, Tsung-dao Lee and Chen Ning Yang, shared the Nobel Prize in Physics for their work demonstrating that the theory of the conservation of parity was not always valid. Both graduates of the Southwest Associated University in Kunming, China, Lee joined the faculty of Columbia University in 1953, and Yang joined the Institute of Advanced Study at Princeton in 1948.

Nobel Prize–winning Chinese-American physicist Tsung-Dao Lee in 2003.

In engineering, the most significant contribution came from Shanghai native An Wang, who came to the United States in 1945 to further his education. After inventing a means of storing electronic memory, he opened Wang Laboratories with only $600, parlaying the sale of electronic calculators, office equipment, and desktop computers into a business that employed thousands of people worldwide. Annual revenue that grew to in excess of $2 billion a year made him one of the richest people in the United States.

SPORTS

Athletics was one field in which immigrant or poor children could aspire to success—in the 1920s and 1930s, sports had become increasingly professionalized, with average salaries high enough to support a family. Amateur athletics could lead to popularity that also brought subsequent job offers. By the 1950s, Asian Americans were moving into athletics and becoming increasingly successful. Tamio "Tommy" Kono, a Nisei, won a gold medal in weightlifting at both the 1952 Helsinki Olympics and the 1956 Melbourne Olympics. In 1960 he won silver in the Rome Olympics, but what made his performance especially noteworthy—in addition to three medals in three separate Olympics—was that he achieved the feat in three different weight classes, an accomplishment unmatched in Olympic history. After setting world records in four weight classes, he was inducted into the U.S. Olympic Hall of Fame.

The 1952 Olympics were particularly important for Asian-American athletes. In addition to Kono's performance, Japanese American Yoshinobu Oyakawa set an Olympic record to win a gold medal in the 100-meter backstroke swimming event, and Ford Konno set another record to win a gold medal in the 1,500-meter freestyle. Konno also won a gold medal in the 800-meter freestyle relay, and a silver in the 400-meter freestyle at the same Olympics. In the 1956 Olympics, he added a silver in the 4 x 200 freestyle relay. Evelyn Kawamoto, who later married Konno, won two bronze medals in swimming in 1952.

But the first Asian American to win a gold medal at the Olympics was Korean American Sammy Lee in platform diving in 1948. He repeated his achievement in 1952, adding a bronze in three-meter springboard diving. Named the outstanding American athlete by the Amateur Athletic Union in 1953, Lee was the first nonwhite to receive the James E. Sullivan Memorial Award for outstanding achievement in sports. He was later inducted into the International Swimming Hall of Fame, served on the President's Council on Physical Fitness and Sports, and opened a private practice as a physician.

MARTIAL ARTS

Aside from individual performances, Asian Americans also contributed their own sports to the growing popularity of athletics in the United States. Chief among them have been various forms of the martial arts. *Kendo*, or the Japanese Way of the Sword, became a popular form of swordsmanship, combining physical and mental tests of strength. Within the next four decades, it is estimated that more than one million people in the United States actively pursued the sport of kendo. Even more popular were the various forms of unarmed competition. Among the first to become popular in the United States was jujutsu, which also became a generic reference to the variety of individual martial arts. Based on techniques derived from the feudal Japanese *samurai, jujutsu* involves various techniques for using the opponent's energy against him through a variety of leverages and grappling techniques, including such things as throws, holds, joint locks, pins, striking, and kicking. In friendly contests, elements such as gouging and biting, found in samurai warfare techniques, are disallowed. The idea behind the martial art form can be clearly seen in its component words, *ju* meaning to "give way" or to "move from harm's way" and *jutsu* meaning "understanding how something works." A sport derived from jujutsu is *judo*, a competition found today, both in local gymnasiums and the Olympic games. In this version of jujutsu, the object is to throw the opponent to the ground, or otherwise subdue the opponent through various grappling techniques.

A particular form of martial art developed in Okinawa and the Ryukyu Islands by merging techniques from China is popularly known in the United States as *kung fu*, and in the Ryukyus as *karate*. This very popular martial arts form differs from judo in that it emphasizes striking the opponent, rather than grappling. Punching, kicking, throws, and striking with the open hand in the familiar karate chop are all key features of karate. This form became particularly popular among U.S. armed forces personnel stationed in Okinawa after World War II, who brought it home with them. Tsutomu Ohshima, captain of the karate club at Waseda University in Japan, moved to the United States in 1955, began offering lessons in 1956, and the next year established the first university karate program in the United States at the California Institute of Technology. Two years later, he founded the Southern California Karate Association.

The popularity of martial arts films, often featuring forms of karate, began in the 1950s and spread interest in the sport and in martial arts in general, with the result that karate is often used as a generic term to refer to all martial arts.

JAPANESE-AMERICAN LITERATURE

Journalism provides a community with information, but in the case of an ethnic community, it serves a dual function—keeping alive the ties with and the culture of the country of origin, and serving as a bridge providing information to immigrants that will help them to understand their new environment, the opportunity it provides, and the avenues to citizenship. Literature provides a means of preserving the ethnic culture of a people, as well as exploring their experiences in their new homeland. The contributions of Asian Americans to these two important creative arts during the 1950s can be explored by examining the two largest groups—Japanese and Chinese.

Some of the early literature authored by Japanese-American writers after World War II deals with their experience of the wartime internments. Monica Sone, a Nisei whose birth name was Kazuko Itoi, published an autobiographical memoir titled *Nisei Daughter* in 1953. In addition to describing her personal experiences growing up in Seattle, Washington, during the 1920s and 1930s, she dealt extensively with life in the internment camps. A recurring theme in the book is the conflict between her Japanese heritage and her U.S. citizenship, and Sone's efforts to understand who she is and where she belongs. Another such book that appeared during the decade was John Okada's *No No Boy* (1957). Also a native of Seattle, Okada was likewise interned during the war, but chose to enlist in the U.S. Army. He later earned two bachelor's degrees from the University of Washington, and a master's from Columbia University. The title of his novel derives from the two questions asked of Japanese in the internment camps: would they be willing to serve in the U.S. armed forces, and would they swear allegiance to the United States and faithfully defend it from all attack? The protagonist of the novel, Ichiro Yamada, answers "no" to each question, and is sent to a federal prison. The question is one that divided Japanese Americans both during and after the war, the consequences of which Okada explores through Yamada's struggle to understand both his own decision, and the resulting schisms in the ethnic community.

Another common theme among Japanese-American authors during the 1950s is the attempt to explore their ethnic heritage. The Nisei author Yoshiko Uchida, whose internment during the war encouraged her to explore her heritage, went to Japan to collect folk tales under the sponsorship of a Ford Foundation Fellowship in 1952. The result of her research was the publication of a series of books on Japanese folk tales and Japanese heritage designed especially for young people. The series begins with *The Magic Listening Cap—More Folk Tales from Japan* (1955), followed by *The Full Circle* (1957); *Takao and Grandfather's Sword* (1958); and the story of a young girl growing up, *The Promised Year* (1959). *The Magic Listening Cap* earned the Festival Honor Award from the *New York Herald-Tribune*. Atsushi Jun Iwamatsu was another prominent author and illustrator of children's books. Born in Kagoshima, Japan, he immigrated with his wife to New York in 1939 and worked for the U.S. Office of War Information and the Office of Strategic Services during the war, writing and illustrating pro-American publications. To protect his family in Japan from retaliation, he adopted the pen name Taro Yashima. After the war, when his young daughter began asking questions about Japan, he embarked on a career writing and illustrating children's books. His early efforts included the well-received stories *Village Tree* (1953), *Plenty to Watch* (1954), *Crow Boy* (1955), *Umbrella* (1958), and *Momo's Kitten* (1960). A runner-up for the prestigious Caldecott Medal for both *Crow Boy* and *Umbrella*, he was later recognized with best children's book awards by the *New Yorker* magazine and the *New York Times*. Shelley Ayame Nishimura Ota authored *Upon Their Shoulders* (1951), the first novel in English to depict the experiences of Issei and Nisei family life in Hawaii.

CHINESE-AMERICAN LITERATURE

Chinese Americans were also interested in preserving and presenting their culture to both the Chinese and Americans. One of the first novels to gain significant attention was Jade Snow Wong's autobiographical *Fifth Chinese Daughter* (1950). Born in San Francisco and raised in Chinese tradition, she became a successful ceramic artist and authored a memoir about her struggles to succeed while growing up in the city's Chinatown. A kind of Chinese Horatio Alger story, her depiction of gaining success as one of nine children in a Chinese immigrant family was translated into several languages, and led the U.S. State Department to send her on a goodwill tour of Asia in 1953. Better known is Chin Yang Lee's *Flower Drum Song: A Novel of San Francisco's Grant Avenue* (1957). Its portrayal of life in Chinatown, though sometimes criticized as unrealistic, was the basis for Richard Rodgers and Oscar Hammerstein's very popular musical and a film, both by the same name. *Flower Drum Song* sparked great interest among the general public in all things Chinese.

An academic look at Chinese Americans resulted from the research of Northwestern University anthropologist Frances Lang Kwang Hsu, who published *Americans and Chinese: Two Ways of Life* (1953), in which she contrasted the cultures of the two societies as a theory for understanding differing outlooks and values between Chinese and Americans. Her work contained references to many autobiographical incidents that were used to explain the differences produced by the two cultures.

FINE AND PERFORMING ARTS

The fine and performing arts have long been associated with Asian cultural traditions. During the 1950s, Asian performers began to break barriers in theater and film, while Asian topics also appeared that popularized Asian culture and led to increased interest in Asian themes and opportunity for Asian performers. Several community-based organizations, such as the Chung Lau Drama Club, founded in San Francisco in 1958, were established to present Chinese plays to American audiences. The largest boost to popularity came from the Broadway productions *Teahouse of the Autumn Moon* (1953), and *Flower Drum Song* (1958).

One of the first Asian actors to play a significant role on Broadway, Yuki Shimoda was a Nisei actor who had experienced the internment camps during World War II. From its opening in 1953 until 1956, Shimoda starred in *Teahouse of the Autumn Moon,* which uses comedy to explore the conversion of an American following government policy to Americanize the inhabitants of Okinawa, into someone who comes to appreciate the preservation of the native culture. In the process, the Okinawans use their foresight and ingenuity to foil government plans. The play presents Okinawan culture in a sympathetic light. Shimoda went on to roles in the Broadway production of *Auntie Mame,* and in films including: *The Horizontal Lieutenant* (1962), *Midway* (1976), *MacArthur* (1976), *The Last Flight of Noah's Ark* (1980), and *The Octagon* (1980).

The hit musical *Flower Drum Song* (1958) marked the first time that a largely Asian cast had appeared in a Broadway production and included, among others, many who would go on to establish successful careers—Miyoshi Umeki, Jack Soo, Reiko Sato, Keye Luke, and Pat (Chiyoko) Suzuki. The story of generational and cultural conflict based on San Francisco's Chinatown nightclub Forbidden City, the play was very popular among non-Asian audiences. Umeki and Suzuki were featured on the cover of *Time* magazine in December 1958, and Suzuki's rendition of *I Enjoy Being a Girl* is generally considered to be the best version of the song among

The Japanese-American actor Yuki Shimoda on set in the early 1960s.

the many actresses who later played the role of Linda Low. Umeki went on to reprise the role of Mei-Li in the 1961 film version of the story.

Best known as the creator of the monster Godzilla, Tomoyuki Tanaka produced over 200 films during his career, including the classic *Godzilla, King of the Monsters* (U.S. release 1956), the first of 21 films featuring the gigantic amphibian. In 1957 James Wong Howe, a Chinese American, received the Academy Award in cinematography for *The Rose Tattoo* (1955). Members of the International Cinematographers Guild voted him one of the 10 most influential cinematographers in history. Best known for his work in black and white films, he also received an Academy Award nomination for the color movie *The Old Man and the Sea* (1959).

The 1950s saw several Asian film and television stars win acclaim for their roles. Miyoshi Umeki played Katsumi in *Sayonara* (1957) opposite Marlon Brando, winning the Academy Award for Best Supporting Actress. Sessue Hayakawa starred in *Bridge on the River Kwai* (1957), gaining a nomination for an Academy Award for Best Supporting Actor in his role as Colonel Saito. James Shigeta starred as Detective Joe Kojaku in *The Crimson Kimono* (1959), and Anna May Wong became the first Asian American to play the featured role in a U.S. television series (*The Gallery of Madame Liu-Tsong*, 1951).

FESTIVALS AND CULTURAL EVENTS

With the growth of Asian-American communities in the 1950s, ethnic festivals and cultural traditions began to appear regularly in places like Hawaii, California, and New York. Various Asian religions such as Buddhism, Confucianism, Shintoism, and Taoism grew with the Asian populations. Temples and other religious facilities began to appear in the larger metropolitan areas, and many in the "beat generation" of the 1950s, attracted to Buddhism, spread its influence among non-Asian Americans.

Probably the most widespread Asian holiday is the celebration of Chinese New Year. Traditionally beginning on the first day of the first month of the Chinese lunar calendar, it lasts until the 15th of the month, and is a time for cleaning the house to sweep away bad luck, visiting relatives and friends, giving presents, decorating the home, and sitting down to a family meal on the eve of the New

The pioneering Chinese-American actress Anna May Wong around 1940.

Miyoshi Umeki

A native of Otaru, Japan, where she was born on May 8, 1929, Umeki began her professional career as a nightclub singer in Japan. She recorded several records in Japan and appeared in the film *Seishun Jazu Musume* before moving to the United States in 1955. There she appeared on *Arthur Godfrey and His Friends* and released several recordings on Mercury Records. In 1957 she played the role of Katsumi opposite Red Buttons in *Sayonara*, becoming the first Asian to win an Academy Award when she garnered the Oscar for Best Supporting Actress. She received a Tony nomination as Best Leading Actress in a Musical for her role as Mei-Li in the Broadway musical *Flower Drum Song*, a role she also played in the 1961 film by the same name for which she earned a Golden Globe Award nomination. She later had roles in the movies *Cry for Happy* (1961), *The Horizontal Lieutenant* (1962), and *A Girl Named Tamiko* (1963). In 1958 she appeared on the television variety show *The Gisele MacKenzie Show*, and she later played the housekeeper, Mrs. Livingston, in *The Courtship of Eddie's Father* (1969–72), for which she again received a Golden Globe Award. Her numerous other television appearances included guest appearances on a wide variety of shows over three decades.

Year. Firecrackers traditionally usher in the New Year, with abundant good wishes to family and friends.

Another celebration that spread outside the Asia community was the Cherry Blossom Festival, which in the United States began to take on the appearance of a cultural festival first for Japanese, and later for Asian cultures in general. These festivals generally include folk arts, cuisine, music, and other traditional ethnic customs. Educational programs later became frequent elements of these celebrations. Another celebration in Japanese culture is the Obon Festival, which originated in the Buddhist custom of honoring the spirits of one's ancestors. A three-day event taking place in the summer, it is celebrated primarily in Hawaii and California, where most of the Japanese-American population reside, and is often accompanied by cultural events.

Filipinos celebrate Rizal Day every December 30 in honor of José Protasio Rizal, a national hero and martyr killed by the Spanish in 1896 during their occupation of the Philippine Islands. A national holiday and time to celebrate ethnic identity, it is usually accompanied by fiestas, traditional cultural events, parades, dinners, and picnics.

During the 1950s, American taste for Asian cuisine became more sophisticated, with increased demand for previously exotic foods such as *sushi* (raw fish served over rice), *sashimi* (thinly sliced raw fish served with a horseradish mix called *wasabe*, or a ginger and soy sauce), *soba-ya* (buckwheat noodles), *sukiyaki* (grilled fish or meat), *yakitori* (skewered, grilled chicken), *tempura* (battered deep-fried seafood, vegetables, or meat), *ramen* (a noodle dish with meat or fish flavored with soy or *miso*), *dim sum* (hors d'oeuvres), Peking duck (roasted, crispy duck), *wonton* (stuffed dumplings), and the California roll (an American adaptation of sushi credited to Ichiro Manashita of the Tokyo Kaikan restaurant in Los Angeles). Along with the growing appetite for Asian food, Americans also adopted the *wok*, a traditional Chinese cooking vessel that channels the heat for fast cooking.

CONCLUSION

The decade of the 1950s brought exceptions and a general easing of immigration regulations that led to a rapid increase in the Asian-American population, especially with the admission of Alaska and Hawaii as states in 1959. Although some Asians Americans were the subject of the anticommunist "witch hunts" of the era of McCarthyism, others were successful in affirming their civil rights and, in doing so, reaffirmed these same rights for all Americans. The vast majority of Asian Americans settled into generally middle-class lives, mostly in the states bordering the Pacific Ocean, and in New York City and Chicago. As educational and professional levels rose, Asians broke important barriers in a wide range of professions, politics, and athletics. By the end of the decade, the group as a whole was well on the way toward earning the nickname The Model Minority.

JAMES S. PULA
PURDUE UNIVERSITY NORTH CENTRAL

Further Reading

Chin, Tung Pok, with Winifred C. Chin. *Paper Son: One Man's Story.* Philadelphia, PA: Temple University Press, 2000.

Hsu, Francis Lang Kwang. *Americans and Chinese: Two Ways of Life.* New York: H. Schuman, 1953.

Knoll, T. *Becoming Americans: Asian Sojourners, Immigrants, and Refugees in the Western United States.* Portland, OR: Coast to Coast Books, 1982.

Kwong, Peter, and Dusanka Miscevic, *Chinese Americans: The Untold Story of America's Oldest New Community.* New York: New Press, 2005.

Lee, Robert G. *Orientals: Asian Americans in Popular Culture.* Philadelphia, PA: Temple University Press, 1999.

Lee, Rose Hum. *The Chinese in the United States of America.* Hong Kong: Hong Kong University Press, 1960.

Melendy, H. Brett. *Asians in America: Filipinos, Koreans and East Indians.* Boston, MA: Twayne Publishers, 1977.

Okada, John. *No No Boy.* Rutland, VT: C.E. Tuttle, 1957.

Sone, Monica. *Nisei Daughter.* Boston, MA: Little, Brown, 1953.

Takaki, Ronald. *Strangers from a Different Shore: A History of Asian Americans.* Boston, MA: Little, Brown, 1989.

Uchida, Yoshiko. *The Magic Listening Cap—More Folk Tales from Japan.* New York: Harcourt, Brace, 1955.

Uchida, Yoshiko. *Takao and Grandfather's Sword.* New York: Harcourt, Brace, 1958.

Wilson, Robert A., and Bill Hosokawa. *East to America: A History of the Japanese in the United States.* New York: Morrow, 1980.

Wong, Bernard P. *Chinatown: Economic Adaptation and Ethnic Identity of the Chinese.* New York: Holt, Rinehart and Winston, 1982.

Wong, Jade Snow. *Fifth Chinese Daughter.* New York: Harper, 1950.

Zhao, Xiaojian. *Remaking Chinese America: Immigration, Family, and Community, 1940–1965.* New Brunswick, NJ: Rutgers University Press, 2002.

CHAPTER 7

A Decade of Expansion: 1960 to 1969

THE 1960s WERE characterized by the expansion of the Asian-American population, especially after the 1965 Immigration Act became law. The decade also witnessed two important trends that would continue for the rest of the 20th century. Native-born white Americans often did not recognize the diverse origins and histories of Asians, so they began to forge a new racial identity—Asian American—in the United States. Second, Asian Americans from some backgrounds were stereotyped in damaging ways. By the end of the decade, Asian Americans had become a presence in the U.S. Congress, in ethnic enclaves and even suburbs, and on college campuses throughout the United States. Asian Americans of many different backgrounds were active participants in the struggle for civil rights and ethnic identity that roiled U.S. society in the last years of the 1960s.

STATISTICAL OVERVIEW

Asian-American immigration in the 19th and early 20th centuries had many different sources, mainly: China, Japan, Korea, India, and the Philippines. Most of these sources of immigrants were closed by legislative measures or other means, such as the Chinese Exclusion Act, the Gentlemen's Agreement, and the Immigration Act of 1924. The Immigration Act was designed to lessen the influence of "less desirable" immigrants, and to encourage immigrants

Young Chinese-American women carrying ice skates on Mott Street in New York City's Chinatown in 1965. In the 1960s, Chinese Americans on the East Coast continued to cluster in large urban centers, with established Chinatowns like the one in New York.

from northern Europe in a blatant attempt to whiten the United States. The 1924 act was modified to allow immigration from China during World War II, when that nation joined the United States and the Allies in their fight against Japan. The Communist Revolution in China spurred a new wave of immigration to the United States. The result of this history of exclusion was a relatively small number of Asian Americans living in the United States at the beginning of the 1960s. The 1960 census listed just 980,337, representing only one-half of one percent of the total population of the United States. Of these nearly one million Asian Americans, about 700,000 were either Japanese or Chinese (473,170 and 236,084, respectively).

By 1970 the total number of Asian Americans had risen dramatically, to 1,538,721, representing 0.8 percent of the total population of the United States. In 1960 both Chinese and Japanese Americans were more likely than not to have been born in the United States. The sex ratio of the Japanese-American population was roughly equal between men and women, though women constituted a slight majority of the population. The population of Chinese Americans was skewed in favor of men, though this factor was mitigated by increased female immigration that began in the 1950s and continued into the 1960s.

Geographically, Asian Americans were spread throughout the United States in the 1960s, though some areas featured much higher concentrations of Asian Americans than others. Hawaii, a relatively new state in 1960, boasted 207,000 Japanese and 39,000 Chinese Americans. Although at least a handful of Asian Americans could be found in every state, over 80 percent of Japanese Americans lived in Hawaii, California, Washington, and Oregon. Similarly, just over 60 percent of Chinese Americans lived in the same geographic region. Significant clusters of Asian Americans also lived in Chicago, Boston, Washington, D.C., Philadelphia, and New York City.

As far as income and education are concerned, census data from 1960 indicates that Chinese Americans were slightly less educated than Japanese Americans (11.1 years of schooling as compared to 12.1 years). Asian-American income in 1960 was lower than might be expected, given the population's overall level of education. Japanese-American men had a median income of $4,304, and Japanese-American women had a median income of $1,967. Among Chinese Americans, men had a median income of $3,471, and women had a median income of $2,067. These depressed incomes can be traced to a variety of factors: discrimination, losses during World War II (in the case of Japanese Americans), and exclusion from certain sectors of the economy, such as the professions and unionized trades, that might have guaranteed higher incomes. Both Japanese and Chinese Americans were overrepresented in services, wholesale and retail, agriculture, forestry, and fishing.

HAWAII AND NATIONAL-LEVEL POLITICS

Hawaii became a state in 1959, and the island chain was a natural launching pad for Asian-American politicians onto the national level. According to the 1960 census, Japanese Americans slightly outnumbered whites on the island, 203,455 to 202,230. Sizable Filipino and Chinese minorities were present as well. These numbered 69,070 and 38,197, respectively. Native

Hawaiians were counted separately, and lumped into the "Other Races" category. Together, Chinese, Japanese, and Filipino citizens could form a powerful voting bloc to ensure that Asian-American voices were heard in the halls of power in Washington, D.C. Hawaii cannot claim the first national-level Asian-American politician, as that honor belongs to California, which sent the India-born Democrat Dalip Singh Saund to the House of Representatives in 1957.

As soon as Hawaii was a state, it began sending Asian Americans to represent it in Congress. The first U.S. representative from Hawaii was Daniel Inouye, who had begun his career in politics in the 1950s even before statehood. After serving as Hawaii's first congressman 1959–63, Inouye was elected to the U.S. Senate (he was still serving in that capacity in 2010). Hiram Fong, the first Asian American to serve in the U.S. Senate, was also from Hawaii. He had been elected as a Republican U.S. Senator from Hawaii in 1959, and then was reelected in 1964 and 1970. He retired from the Senate in 1977.

Another Hawaii Nisei, Masayuki "Spark" Matsunaga, had served in the 442nd Regimental Combat Team just like Inouye. Matsunaga was wounded and received the Bronze Star—and went on to a distinguished career in politics. He was first elected to the U.S. House of Representatives as a Democrat in 1962, and served there until his election to the U.S. Senate in 1976. He became a power broker in the Senate, where he served until his death in 1990.

In 1964 Patsy Takemoto Mink, a Sansei (or third-generation Japanese American), became the first woman of color elected to the U.S. House of Representatives. Prior to that accomplishment, Mink had served as a territorial representative and a state senator in Hawaii. She was a member of the Democratic Party. In Congress, Mink was a tireless advocate of the rights of women, children, minorities, and immigrants. As a legislator, Mink is perhaps best remembered for her support of Title IX, which ensured athletic equity at U.S. high schools, colleges, and universities.

Patsy Mink, shown here in 1972, was the first minority woman to serve in the U.S. House of Representatives.

Kimm v. Rosenberg

In the 1950s, American intelligence officials monitored the associations of Asian Americans who they suspected might harbor loyalties to foreign governments, especially if those governments were communist. Many Americans were the targets of these investigations. Ill treatment in this regard continued in the 1960s. In 1960 a Korean immigrant, known in court documents simply as Kimm, was ordered to be deported from the United States when he refused to answer a question about whether or not he had ever been a communist, seeking Fifth Amendment protection.

In this case, Kimm did not directly contest the order of deportation, but rather requested that it be suspended because of his good character (this was one of the exceptions granted in the Immigration Act of 1917). Kimm argued that his decades of work in the United States and high reputation ought to count for something. In the decision excerpted below, the Supreme Court ruled that Kimm's refusal to answer the question about Communist Party membership was an absolute disqualification for the kind of suspension Kimm was seeking. An excerpt of Justice William O. Douglas's dissent follows:

Petitioner applied for suspension of an order directing his deportation to Korea or permitting his voluntary departure. He does not question the validity of the deportation order, but contends that he is within the eligible statutory class whose deportation may be suspended. . . . Before the hearing officer, petitioner was asked if he was a member of the Communist Party. He refused to answer, claiming the Fifth Amendment privilege against self-incrimination. The officer refused the suspension on the grounds that petitioner had failed to prove that he was a person of good moral character and that he had not met the statutory requirement of showing that he was not a member of . . . the Communist Party. . . . He contends that the disqualifying factor of Communist Party membership is an exception . . . which the Government must prove. We think not.

Mr. Justice Douglas . . . dissenting.
It has become much the fashion to impute wrongdoing or to impose punishment on a person for invoking his constitutional rights. . . . Today we allow invocation of the Fifth Amendment to serve, in effect though not in terms, as proof that an alien lacks the "good moral character" which he must have . . . . there is not a single shred of evidence in the record of bad character against this alien. . . . He entered as a student in 1928 and pursued his studies until 1938. He planned to return to Korea but the outbreak of hostilities between China and Japan in 1937 changed his mind. Since 1938 he has been continuously employed in gainful occupations. That is the sole basis of his deportability. . . . No one came forward to testify that he was a Communist. There is not one word of evidence that he had been a member of the Communist Party at any time.

IMMIGRATION ACT OF 1965

After his electoral triumph in 1964, Lyndon B. Johnson set four major policy goals—the Big Four, as some policymakers referred to them. They included federal aid to education, a voting rights act to ensure the gains of the civil rights movement would not slip away, Medicare and Medicaid, and immigration reform. Of these, immigration reform often took a back seat, but it was crucially important to Asian Americans.

In 1965 the basis for U.S. immigration law remained the 1924 Immigration Act. This act set quotas for legal immigrants from many nations, with the quotas frozen at two percent of the number of people representing the nation at the time of the 1890 U.S. census. As 1890 was at the very beginning of the wave of new immigration from eastern and southern Europe, the racial intent of the act was clear in this regard. The act had been modified several times to make exceptions for various groups (restrictions on Chinese immigration were relaxed in the World War II era, for instance). Still the quota system remained more or less intact, and seemed outmoded in light of the civil rights revolution that was sweeping the United States in the 1960s.

The legislative fight for the 1965 Immigration Act, also known as the Hart-Celler Act, was led in the House of Representatives by Emanuel Celler, a congressman from Brooklyn, who had devoted decades of legislative energy—he gave an impassioned speech against the 1924 Immigration Act—to overturning what he perceived to be a grossly unjust law.

The 1965 Immigration Act allowed 20,000 immigrants from each country in the Eastern Hemisphere, and set a total limit of 170,000 immigrants per year. The quota system was weakened in favor of a list of seven preferences, which are described by Franklin Odo in *The Columbia Documentary History of the Asian American Experience* as follows:

First preference: adult, unmarried sons and daughters of citizens.

Second preference: spouses and unmarried sons and daughters of lawful permanent resident aliens. Green card holders (permanent residents) may send for relatives in this category only.

Third preference: members of the professions or those with exceptional ability in the sciences or the arts—who can benefit the economy, cultural interests or welfare of the United States.

Fourth preference: married sons or daughters of citizens.

Fifth preference: brothers or sisters of citizens.

Sixth preference: skilled or unskilled workers, not temporary, for which a shortage of employable persons exists.

Seventh preference: persons fleeing the Middle East, uprooted by natural calamity, and because of persecution due to race, religion, or political opinion from Communist or Communist-dominated countries.

The Hawaiian Schoolchildren's Petition to Congress

Hiram Fong from Hawaii, who was the first Asian American to serve in the U.S. Senate, was an early advocate of a federal civil rights act, a stance that put him at odds with some members of his party. He had this petition from children at Manoa Elementary School in Hawaii read into the *Congressional Record* in October 1963. The students, who ranged in age from 9 to 11, had some help from their teachers in preparing the petition, but that fact does not detract from the feelings the document represents, and it stands as an early example of a rising racial consciousness among young Asian Americans.

Honorable Sirs: May we have a moment of your precious time to discuss a matter of extreme consequence to us?

We are 64, 9- to 11-year-olds from Manoa Elementary School in Honolulu, Hawaii. In this nice school of ours we have all kinds of faces.

There are Filipino, Japanese, Chinese, Irish, Korean, Norwegian-German, Scottish-Irish, French-Japanese, and Hawaiian-Chinese faces. Religiously we represent Episcopalians, Buddhists, Friends, Baptists, Methodists, Protestants, and Catholics. We have fun learning and living together. (We have disagreements, too.) We would miss the different races and religions if they were gone.

. . . How grateful we are to our country, the United States of America, for such equal opportunities. We have always been proud of our country. Now that we are a State, our pride and love are overflowing.

The civil turmoil that is presently afflicting America deeply troubles us. When you love a thing very much and it is in trouble you feel a need to help.

We are aware that our brains cannot encompass the entire problem. We have tried to read as much available material as possible and have carried on numerous discussions in school, with friends, and at home. But of these reasons we are certain, and upon these principles we urge you, the lawmakers of our land, for the passage of the civil rights bill.

. . . In today's world too many people are oppressed and unhappy. Many are merely struggling to exist day by day. Let democracy radiate hope for all men.

Let us begin at home. Let us begin with something as fundamental as civil rights. Let us begin to lift all men upward. Let us make real democracy. . . .

Then truly can we sing; our hearts lifted in pride, our minds unconfused, our voices singing true:

"This is my country
Grandest on earth . . . !"

Family reunification became the overriding concern of U.S. immigration policy, followed closely by the preference for skilled workers. At a signing ceremony in the shadow of the Statue of Liberty, President Johnson reportedly remarked that the bill was not all that revolutionary, and simply a common-sense measure to make American immigration policy match American ideals. Earlier supporters had pointed out that, as the United States waged a cold war against communism around the world, and African Americans fought for equality at home, an immigration policy based on notions of racial purity and eugenics looked questionable at best.

The bill's advocates wrongly assumed that it would not alter American society dramatically, but within just a few years, and certainly by the 1970s, it had begun to change the face of the United States. Many of the bill's supporters greatly underestimated the pull of the U.S. economy and educational system for a new class of skilled immigrants from around the world, especially from Asia. Chinese immigration was slowed by Chinese policies in the 1960s and early 1970s, but warming relations between the countries would allow increasing numbers of Chinese to immigrate to the United States. In places with less repressive emigration policies, such as South Korea, India, and the Philippines, the response was enthusiastic. Within just a few years, Asian America, and America in general, was transformed.

CHINESE IMMIGRATION

The post-1965 immigrants were a diverse and large group. The population of Asian Americans doubled, from one to two million, in the two decades following the Hart-Celler Act. These new immigrants were predominantly urban in origin, as opposed to their mostly rural predecessors. Their ethnic makeup was also different. Prior to 1965, the Japanese and the Chinese were the largest groups of Asian Americans. From 1965 to 1984, Japanese people represented only 1.7 percent of all Asian immigrants to the United States. The reasons for this shift are complex, but one of the major factors was the miraculous Japanese economy of the postwar period, with its massive demand for skilled labor. During this same time

Many new Asian immigrants worked for low wages at sites like this Chinese laundry in San Rafael, California, shown here in 1964.

400,000 Chinese entered the United States. The 1965 Immigration Act would eventually result in a large number of Vietnamese immigrants to the United States, though the majority of this population arrived after 1975.

The Chinese and the Filipinos became the largest Asian-American immigrant groups. The change in Chinese America was particularly noticeable—within a few years, the community shifted from majority native-born to majority foreign-born. Commentators noted the change in Chinatowns throughout the United States, as women and children began to appear in larger numbers and, consequently, to play a more public role in Chinese-American society. In the late 1960s, many Chinese immigrants were refugees from the People's Republic of China, who stopped first in Taiwan or Hong Kong before crossing the Pacific to the United States. One of the major draws for the Chinese was the U.S. university system. Once Chinese Americans had secured jobs, they could send for siblings, spouses, children, and even parents under the family reunification preferences outlined in the 1965 Immigration Act. The Asian-American population doubled in the space of two decades. The leading scholar of this migration, the late Ronald Takaki, has argued that post-1965 immigration created a Chinese-American community divided along class lines, between a "colonized working class and an entrepreneurial-professional middle class." In the 1960s, Chinese immigrants who picked up a little English could quickly land jobs cleaning offices or similar work. Many more, especially women, ended up working in sweatshop conditions in garment factories for very low wages. On the same side of the class divide described by Takaki, many Chinese men went to work for low wages in restaurants. By the 1980s, about 25 percent of Chinese Americans lived below the poverty line in New York City (the overall poverty rate in New York at this time was about 17 percent).

FILIPINO AND KOREAN IMMIGRATION

Filipino immigration to the United States far outstripped Chinese immigration in the 1960s, 1970s, and early 1980s. Many of the new Filipino immigrants were professionals (65 percent professionals to 10 percent laborers, by one estimate), and they were more likely to be urban than rural before their move to the United States. The corrupt Marcos regime acted as a push factor, as did the souring Philippine economy. Skilled Filipino immigrants during this era included large numbers of doctors, nurses, and pharmacists. By the end of the 1960s and the beginning of the 1970s, Filipinos accounted for nearly a quarter of all foreign physicians entering the United States (Canada and India sent eight percent, South Korea seven percent). The transition to life in America was not easy. Many Filipino doctors found they had to accept temporary positions while they waited for tests to be administered and scored, and in some states, foreign-educated pharmacists were barred from practicing their trade altogether, since they had not attended one of

Ferdinand and Imelda Marcos at the White House with President Lyndon Johnson in September 1966. The Marcos regime was an important push factor in the Filipino immigration.

the state-accredited pharmacy schools. Many Filipino immigrants were underemployed in the 1960s. Because of their geographic distribution and lack of Manila Towns, or primarily Filipino suburbs, the Filipino presence in the United States seemed smaller than the Chinese presence in the years after the Hart-Celler Act.

Before 1965 there were very few Koreans in the United States, and they were spread thinly throughout the country. Between 1965 and the 1980s, however, the Korean population leaped from 10,000 to about 500,000. Some neighborhoods, notably Olympic Boulevard in Los Angeles's Koreatown, were packed with Korean-owned businesses and institutions, such as churches, barbershops, nightclubs, restaurants, and grocery stores. Like other groups of post-1965 immigrants, Koreans were mainly from professional or middle-class backgrounds, and less likely to be from laboring or agricultural backgrounds. Many were medical professionals, paralleling the experience of the post-1965 Filipino immigrants. However even among highly skilled professionals, a class system developed after 1965. Korean doctors were more likely than their white counterparts to work in hospitals in depressed urban settings, and were more disproportionately overrepresented in specialties like anesthesiology and radiology and under-represented as surgeons. The same licensing headaches that faced Filipino doctors, nurses, and pharmacists frustrated Korean immigrants as well.

The new wave of Korean immigrants were most visible as shopkeepers. As white ethnics retreated from central cities, and African Americans continued to lack the capital and access to credit necessary to start businesses in their neighborhoods, Korean immigrants, with moderate amounts of capital, stepped into the void. Racial tensions would develop in the 1980s and 1990s as Korean-American shopkeepers and their African-American customers misunderstood each other's experiences, and mistrusted each other. Korean-American entrepreneurs after 1965 generally worked extremely hard for little money, relying on family labor, sometimes without insurance, and occasionally sleeping in their shops at night.

As the result of restrictive immigration policies prior to 1965, Asian Indians formed a tiny minority of the Asian-American population. In 1946 the point at which some restrictions on immigration were eased, fewer than 2,000 Indians lived in the United States. The effect of the 1965 Immigration Act was immediate and dramatic. Between 1965 and 1970, for example, 20,000 Pakistanis entered the United States. The Indian population of the United States climbed from 10,000 to 525,000 in the two decades following the 1965 Immigration Act. Many Indian and Pakistani immigrants were skilled workers from south Asia's large cities. By the 1980s, there were 40,000 south Asian engineers, 25,000 doctors and dentists, and 20,000 scientists in the United States.

THE MODEL MINORITY

As early as the 1960s, a damaging stereotype had come to identify Asian Americans in the minds of their white neighbors. Because of their academic success and their visibility as professionals and entrepreneurs, white commentators and cultural critics began to refer to Asian Americans as a "model minority." Asian Americans were not the first immigrant group so designated. Prior to World War I, German Americans were perceived as the ideal immigrants. The implication behind such ranking of immigrants in terms of desirability is that while some ethnic groups in the United States achieve success, others—usually African Americans—are left behind. Some writers went beyond implying this, to posing the question more directly.

The model minority stereotype distorts reality. It downplays real incidents of racism targeting Asian Americans, and places an undue burden on Asian Americans to live up to an artificially high standard. Some scholars have also argued that it may reinforce white privilege by pitting different groups of people of color against one another (one famous 1960s article referred to Japanese immigrants "outwhiting the whites," for instance). It uses race to explain phenomena that are more properly explained by educational level and economic status. One enduring stereotype praises the educational achievement of Asian Americans as a whole, as if having Asian heritage is a predictor of stunning academic success. Besides denigrating the hard work of

The Model Minority

The model minority stereotype was first applied to Asian Americans in the 1960s. A series of articles in the *New York Times Magazine* and other publications searched for ways to explain the remarkable success of some Asian Americans and, sometimes, the frustrating failures of groups who had been in the United States much longer. African Americans were sometimes cast as the foil in these pieces: the one minority group that couldn't seem to "get its act together." The long-term implications of dividing the United States into successful and unsuccessful races are disheartening. The article excerpted below appeared in *U.S. News and World Report* in 1966.

At a time when Americans are awash in worry over the plight of racial minorities—

One such minority, the nation's 300,000 Chinese Americans, is winning wealth and respect by dint of its own hard work.

In any Chinatown from San Francisco to New York, you discover youngsters at grips with their studies. Crime and delinquency are found to be rather minor in scope.

Still being taught in Chinatown is the old idea that people should depend on their own efforts—not a welfare check—in order to reach America's "promised land."

Visit "Chinatown U.S.A." and you find an important racial minority pulling itself up from hardship and discrimination to become a model of self-respect and achievement in today's America.

At a time when it is being proposed that hundreds of billions be spent to uplift Negroes and other minorities, the nation's 300,000 Chinese-Americans are moving ahead on their own—with no help from anyone else.

. . . What you find, back of this remarkable group of Americans, is a story of adversity and prejudice that would shock those now complaining about the hardships endured by today's Negroes.

. . . Dr. Sollenberger [Richard Sollenberger, a Mount Holyoke psychology professor] said: "The Chinese people here will work at anything. I know of some who were scholars in China and are now working as waiters in restaurants. That's a stopgap for them, of course, but the point is that they're willing to do something—they don't sit around moaning."

. . . And Chinatown . . . remains a haven of law and order. Dr. Sollenberger said:

"If I had a daughter, I'd rather have her live in Chinatown than any place else in New York City."

. . . Overall, what observers are finding in America's Chinatowns are a thrifty, law-abiding, and industrious people—ambitious to make progress on their own.

The model minority stereotype began to be applied to Asian Americans in the 1960s. This Chinese-American man worked in a government library in Washington, D.C., in the 1960s.

Asian students, the stereotype also fails to recognize that a child's parents' educational status is a prime factor in determining whether or not that child will succeed in school. Asian-American children are more likely to have parents with college educations (and beyond) than some other groups of Americans. Children of all races whose parents went to college perform similarly in school.

RACE CONSCIOUSNESS IN THE LATE 1960s

Asian Americans both benefited from the gains made by people of color in general in the 1960s, and forged a racial consciousness at the same time. This racial consciousness was not nearly as developed as it would be during the 1980s, during a surge of anti–Asian and Asian-American sentiment. Chinese, Japanese, Filipinos, and Indians came to the United States from different nations, with different histories, speaking different languages. There was no unified Asian-American consciousness yet.

The movement toward race consciousness among Asian Americans can be traced to developments on college campuses in the 1960s. College campuses in the 1960s were the backdrop for many different dramatic confrontations. These concerned the war in Vietnam, human and civil rights at home and abroad, free speech, poverty, and the role of women in society. They

Ethnic Studies

Berkeley was not the only campus to erupt over the inclusion of Ethnic Studies. The following statement comes from the San Francisco State incarnation of the Third World Liberation Front. Strikes on that campus, which had established the nation's first Black Studies Department, also led to an Ethnic Studies program. The document demonstrates not just the intellectual bent of Ethnic Studies in the 1960s, but also the fact that the protesters viewed themselves as grounded in communities outside the campus, and that college campuses had become isolated from the communities that surrounded them.

Throughout the entire educational systems in California, a complete and accurate representation of minority peoples' role in the past and the present conditions of this state is nonexistent. In every aspect from lectures to literature the educational facilities do not contain the information necessary to relate any facet of minority peoples' history and/or culture. Such an institutionalized condition of negligence and ignorance by the state's educational systems is clearly a part of the racism and hatred this country has perpetuated upon nonwhite peoples. The consistent refusal of State Education to confront its inadequacies and attain an equitable resolution between our peoples, makes it mandatory for minority people to initiate and maintain educational programs specifically based upon their people's background and present situation at intra and international levels.

The Third World Liberation Front is demanding a school of Ethnic Area Studies specifically organized to establish area studies of nonwhite peoples within the United States. At the present there are being developed area studies of Mexican American, Latin American, Filipino America, Chinese American, and Japanese American peoples.

The school's function is as a resource and an educational program for those minority peoples actively concerned with the lack of their peoples' representation and participation in all levels of California's educational institutions.

The school clearly intends to be involved in confronting the racism, poverty and misrepresentation imposed on minority peoples by the formally recognized institutions and organizations operating in the State of California . . .

San Francisco State, a community college, exists in a moral vacuum, oblivious to the community it purports to serve. It does not reflect the pluralistic society that is San Francisco; it does not begin to serve the 300,000 people who live in this urban community in poverty, ignorance, and despair. The Chinese ghetto, Chinatown, is a case in point. WE, THEREFORE, SUPPORT THE ESTABLISHMENT OF A SCHOOL OF ETHNIC AREA STUDIES and further submit . . . our proposal for the establishment of a Chinese Ethnic Studies Department within that school that will begin to attack the problems that exist in the Chinese community at large . . . .

also included calls for Ethnic Studies programs. The most notable protests in this regard came from California. In the late 1960s, students at both San Francisco State and the University of California, Berkeley, launched major protests against the lack of ethnic diversity of faculty and course offerings. The protests were part of two larger critiques: one of the ongoing military misadventure in Vietnam and colonialism in general, and one against the specific grievances of people of color in the United States. The coalitions that protested in the late 1960s cut across the color line in dramatic fashion, including Asian Americans, Native Americans, Hispanic Americans, and African Americans.

The Third World Liberation Front at Berkeley was comprised of a number of different student organizations, including the Afro-American Studies Union, the Mexican-American Student Federation, and the Asian American Political Alliance. On January 22, 1969, the Third World Liberation Front established picket lines at the major entrances to the campus. The student strikers, who received support from some white students and faculty as well, demanded a Third World College, increased minority hiring, recruitment, and financial aid, and increasing minority control of minority programs on campus. For nearly two months, strikers faced off against national guardsmen and police, some of whom were not in uniform, and others of whom used mace against the strikers. The use of tear gas prompted violence between strikers and police. By the fall of 1969, however, Berkeley was offering more than 30 new courses in a new Ethnic Studies program.

CONCLUSION

For Asian Americans, the 1960s were truly a remarkable decade. A relatively small, native-born Asian-American population was revitalized by new arrivals. These new arrivals came from the traditional sources of China and Japan, but increasingly from the Philippines and south Asia as well. Renewed immigration from Asia was one of the major effects of the landmark Hart-Celler Immigration Act of 1965. Many of the post-1965 immigrants were professionals and city dwellers before they came to the United States, and many came to the United States for professional training and stayed for job opportunities. By the end of the decade, a nascent race-consciousness was developing among this extraordinarily diverse group of immigrants. Asian Americans continued to face discrimination in housing and employment, but the generation of the 1960s pointed the way toward future developments.

MATTHEW JENNINGS
MACON STATE COLLEGE

Further Reading

Alba, Richard, and Victor Nee. *Remaking the American Mainstream: Assimilation and Contemporary Immigration.* Cambridge, MA: Harvard University Press, 2003.

Chen, Jack. *The Chinese of America.* San Francisco, CA: Harper & Row, 1980.

Daley, William, and Sandra Stotsky, ed. *The Chinese Americans.* New York: Chelsea House, 1996.

Daniels, Roger. *Asian America: Chinese and Japanese in the United States since 1850.* Seattle: University of Washington Press, 1990.

Do, Hien Duc. *The Vietnamese Americans.* Westport, CT: Greenwood Press, 1999.

Fuchs, Lawrence H. *The American Kaleidoscope: Race, Ethnicity, and Civic Culture.* Hanover, NH: Wesleyan University Press, 1990.

Kitano, Harry H.L. *Japanese Americans: The Evolution of a Subculture.* Englewood Cliffs, NJ: Prentice-Hall, 1969.

Odo, Franklin, ed. *The Columbia Documentary History of the Asian American Experience.* New York: Columbia University Press, 2002.

Spickard, Paul R. *Japanese Americans: The Formation and Transformations of an Ethnic Group.* New York: Twayne Publishers, 1996.

"Success Story of One Minority Group in U.S.," *U.S. News and World Report*, December 26, 1966. Available online, URL: http://www.dartmouth.edu/~hist32/Hist33/US%20News%20&%20World%20Report.pdf. Accessed July 2009.

Takaki, Ronald. *A Different Mirror: A History of Multicultural America.* Boston, MA: Little, Brown, 1993.

———. *Strangers from a Different Shore: A History of Asian Americans.* New York: Penguin Books, 1989.

Tong, Benson. *The Chinese Americans.* The New Americans. Westport, CT: Greenwood Press, 2000.

White-Parks, Annette, et al., eds. *A Gathering of Voices on the Asian American Experience.* Fort Atkinson, WI: Highsmith Press, 1994.

Wu, Frank H. *Yellow: Race in America Beyond Black and White.* New York: Basic Books, 2002.

Zia, Helen. *Asian American Dreams: The Emergence of an American People.* New York: Farrar, Straus & Giroux, 2000.

CHAPTER 8

New Immigrants: 1970 to 1979

THE 1970s WAS a period of political upheaval followed by economic crisis. First, Vice President Spiro Agnew was forced to resign under a cloud of misdeeds. Then President Richard Nixon resigned under allegations of wrongdoing. Gerald Ford replaced Nixon, but lost a bid for his own election to Jimmy Carter, ushering in four years of international reversals and domestic economic disarray. The Vietnam War ended, but in a chaotic fashion, while at home crime rates increased steadily. Yet despite the political turmoil, science recorded major advancements with the introduction of such innovations as the microprocessor, the computer chip, the videocassette recorder, low-cost video games played through a television, e-mail, bar codes, laser printers, and MRI scanners.

For Asian Americans, changes in the immigration laws in 1965 began to be felt with increases in the number of Asians entering the country, but the end of the war in Southeast Asia led to the first really large-scale Asian emigration from places like Vietnam, Laos, and Cambodia. President Nixon's trip to China and the subsequent normalization of relations between the two countries led to an easing of scrutiny of Chinese immigrants in the United States, and eventually to the immigration of some mainland Chinese as either students or residents. During the 1970s the term Asian American came into general use. The older term, Orientals, began to be viewed by civil rights

President Jimmy Carter meeting with Chinese Vice Premier Deng Xiaoping on January 29, 1979, after the normalization of U.S. relations with the People's Republic of China. This development led to an increase in immigrants from mainland China.

activists during the 1960s as a pejorative term, conjuring up images of colonialism. Historian Yuji Ichioka is usually given credit for popularizing the use of Asian American.

According to the 1970 census, there were 1,439,562 people of Asian heritage in the country, comprising 0.7 percent of the total population. The largest groups of Asians were 591,290 people of Japanese ancestry, 436,062 Chinese, 336,731 Filipinos, and 69,150 Koreans, with smaller numbers of other groups. Of those born outside the United States, 122,500 were Japanese, and 204,232 were Chinese. Of the Japanese, 67.9 percent were females; the percentage of females in the Chinese population was only 48.1 percent. The disparity in the percentage of females among the Japanese population born outside the United States is explained by the large number of war brides who were married to non-Asians. Chinese immigrants during this period included a much higher percentage of families in which both spouses were of Asian descent. The overwhelming majority of the Asian population resided in urban areas, chiefly San Francisco, New York, Los Angeles, and Honolulu. Among Japanese and Chinese, urban dwellers accounted for more than 95 percent of the total. During the 1970s, the Asian groups with the largest number of new immigrants were from the Philippines (354,987), Korea (267,638), China (237,793), Vietnam (172,820), and Japan (49,775).

Ending Executive Order 9066

Although the internment of Japanese aliens and Japanese-American citizens had ended more than three decades previously, by the mid-1970s the issue was not only still hotly debated but remained a rallying point for Asian civil rights organizations. As the Bicentennial year began, President Gerald Ford moved to address the old wound by ending the official existence of Executive Order 9066 under which the internments occurred. The Proclamation read in part:

February 19th is the anniversary of a sad day in American history. It was on that date in 1942, in the midst of the response to the hostilities that began on December 7, 1941, that Executive Order 9066 was issued, subsequently enforced by the criminal penalties of a statute enacted March 21, 1942, resulting in the uprooting of loyal Americans. Over one hundred thousand persons of Japanese ancestry were removed from their homes, detained in special camps, and eventually relocated.

The tremendous effort by the War Relocation Authority and concerned Americans for the welfare of these Japanese-Americans may add perspective to that story, but it does not erase the setback to fundamental American principles. Fortunately, the Japanese-American community in Hawaii was spared the indignities suffered by those on our mainland.

We now know what we should have known then—not only was that evacuation wrong, but Japanese-Americans were and are loyal Americans. On the battlefield and at home, Japanese-Americans—names like Hamada, Mitsumori, Marimoto, Noguchi, Yamasaki, Kido, Munemori and Miyamura—have been and continue to be written in our history for the sacrifices and the contributions they have made to the well-being and security of this, our common Nation.

The Executive order that was issued on February 19, 1942, was for the sole purpose of prosecuting the war with the Axis Powers, and ceased to be effective with the end of those hostilities. Because there was no formal statement of its termination, however, there is concern among many Japanese-Americans that there may yet be some life in that obsolete document. I think it appropriate, in this our Bicentennial Year, to remove all doubts on that matter, and to make clear our commitment in the future.

Now, therefore, I, Gerald R. Ford, President of the United States of America, do hereby proclaim that all authority conferred by Executive Order 9066 terminated upon the issuance of Proclamation 2714, which formally proclaimed the cessation of hostilities of World War II on December 31, 1946.

I call upon the American people to affirm with me this American Promise —that we have learned from the tragedy of that long-ago experience forever to treasure liberty and justice for each individual American, and resolve that this kind of action shall never again be repeated."

IMMIGRATION

The 1970s brought legal and diplomatic changes that greatly affected Asian immigration. South Vietnam collapsed in April 1975; that same month President Gerald Ford authorized the entry of 130,000 refugees from Vietnam, Laos, and Cambodia into the United States. To meet the escalating refugee crisis, Congress passed the Indochina Migration and Refugee Assistance Act of 1975, which broadened the definition of "refugee" to include people from Asia. In 1977 the act was amended to permit refugees permanent residency status after two years in the United States, and to allow any time spent in the United States after April 1, 1975, to count toward the required five-year residence to qualify for citizenship. In addition to the 130,000 already approved for entry, this led to the admittance of another 11,000 Southeast Asians in 1976, 15,000 in 1977, and 34,500 in 1978. In total, some 750,000 refugees from Southeast Asia entered the United States during the decade following passage of the legislation in 1975.

Among the new arrivals, in addition to the Vietnamese, were sizable numbers of refugees from Cambodia and Laos, two nations with little previous presence in the United States. The predominant religion among the Cambodians and Laotians was Buddhism. Among the refugees from these areas were a number of small ethnic groups such as the Hmong, Montagnards, Muong, Nung, and Yao. About 4,600 Cambodians arrived in 1975, and about 8,000 had emigrated by the end of the 1970s. Because of their assistance to U.S. forces during the Vietnam War, Congress agreed in 1975 to admit 3,466 Hmong, most of whom were resettled in California, Minnesota, and Wisconsin. About 50,000 Laotians entered the United States by the end of the decade; this group included some Hmong and other ethnic minorities who were not recorded separately. Aside from the Hmong, they mostly settled in California, Texas, Minnesota, and Washington. Most of these early Laotian immigrants had been government officials, military personnel, or shopkeepers, but later arrivals among the "boat people" tended to be less-educated farmers and villagers.

The U.S. Immigration and Naturalization Service recorded only 650 Vietnamese arriving in the United States 1950–74, about 75 percent of them spouses and children of U.S. armed forces personnel. This changed dramatically in 1975, when some 126,000 Vietnamese fleeing the fall of South Vietnam entered the United States. Studies have shown that this group was mostly male (55 percent), heavily skewed to the young (82 percent under age 35, and 65 percent under age 25), and generally well educated (only two percent had less than an elementary school education). More than 30 percent had trained in medical, technical, or managerial occupations; 16.9 percent had been employed in transportation; 11.7 percent had held clerical or sales positions in their homeland; and only 4.9 percent had been farmers or fishermen, the two largest occupations in South Vietnam. Over 70 percent were from urban locales, whereas the overwhelming number of Vietnamese resided in rural districts. Although only 10 percent of South Vietnamese were Catholic, some 40 percent of the initial refugee group was Catholic, probably a reflection of the close tie between the Catholic community and South Vietnam's ruling political group.

Vietnamese immigration continued, with 21,000 arriving in 1977, but a new wave began with the arrival of 106,500 in 1978, and over 150,000 in 1979. They became known as "boat people" because so many had fled Vietnam in dangerous, dilapidated old boats. It has been estimated that some two million people fled Vietnam beginning in 1978, most of them hoping to reach refugee camps in Thailand, Malaysia, Singapore, Indonesia,

These refugees escaping Vietnam in a boat with a homemade sail were rescued by the U.S. Navy.

Hong Kong, and the Philippines. This second wave that began in 1978, and continued into the mid-1980s, contained a much higher percentage of rural farmers and fishermen with limited education. Most knew no English, and were not prepared for life in the United States. Though they were dispersed under the provisions of refugee resettlement, within a decade they began a secondary immigration to urban centers with Asian and Vietnamese communities, primarily in California and Texas.

Two other groups that began to immigrate to the United States in very modest numbers during the 1970s were Indonesians and Thais. During the decade, an average of about 500 Indonesians were admitted to the United States each year. Most immigrated as families; the majority were between 20 and 40 years of age, with the males holding mostly professional, technical, white-collar, or skilled worker positions. By 1980 some 5,000 Thais had entered the United States, most residing in Los Angeles and New York City. Unlike the Indonesians, about 75 percent of Thais were women, the majority of them wives of U.S. service personnel. The males tended to be physicians and entrepreneurs, and the women who were not spouses of Americans were mostly nurses.

The establishment of normal diplomatic relations between China and the United States in 1979 had dramatic ramifications for Chinese Americans because it led to easier reunification of families long separated by cold war politics. Between 1970 and 1979, 97,987 Chinese entered the country due largely to the elimination of the nationality quotas in 1965. The vast majority of the new immigration was from Hong Kong or Taiwan, with only a few from mainland China. After the normalization of relations in 1979, emigration from mainland China began to increase.

Although Japanese Americans constituted the largest Asian group in the United States according to the 1970 census, immigration from Japan during the 1970s was not as high as from other nations due to Japan's positive economy. But the increase in business ties brought Japanese business people, especially to New York and Los Angeles, as well as increased importation of Japanese products. The largest concentrations of Japanese Americans continued to be in Honolulu, Los Angeles, San Francisco, New York, and Chicago.

The largest Asian group to arrive during the 1970s came from the Philippine Islands. Referred to in the Philippines as the "brain drain" migration because it contained a very high percentage of physicians, attorneys, engineers, and nurses, it also included a large number who came to the United States via enlistment in the navy. By 1970 some 17,000 Filipinos were serving in the U.S. Navy; this offered them a path to citizenship, educational benefits, and other advantages. With a growing shortage of trained nurses in the United States, a large number of Filipinas took this route to America. During the 1970s, schools in the Philippines were graduating approximately 2,000 nurses per year. In response to some hospitals' aggressive recruitment in the Philippines, about 20 percent of these graduates immigrated to the United States. By 1973 there were more than 12,000 Filipina nurses in the United States, a movement that helped raise the percentage of females among the Filipino-American population from 37 percent in 1960, to 46 percent during the 1970s. A study the following year revealed that there were nearly 7,000 Filipino physicians in the United States—about 40 percent of all the Filipino physicians in the world.

RESETTLEMENT

With the rapid influx of refugees forced to flee their countries because of the war in Southeast Asia, Congress passed the Indochina Migration and Refugee Assistance Act of 1975 to provide funding for a resettlement program designed to assist the new arrivals in their transition to life in the United States. To facilitate processing of the immigrants, President Ford established a receiving center on the island of Guam. After processing, the refugees moved to reception centers at Camp Pendleton (California), Fort Chaffee (Arkansas), Eglin Air Force Base (Florida), and Fort Indiantown Gap (Pennsylvania). Although the reception centers tended to be crowded, new immigrants were given medical examinations, treatment for any ailments, clothing, and other supplies. After a security processing, they received Social Security and alien registration numbers. The centers provided classes in English, as well as instruction in American social customs and citizenship. Meals were taken communally, and recreational activities were available. However because a number of the lessons on American social customs

The Chinese YMCA building in Philadelphia's Chinatown stands beside a Filipino shop in this 1974 photo. In the 1970s, Filipinos were the largest group of Asian immigrants to come to the United States.

tended to clash with their traditional cultures, some parents were reluctant to allow their children to participate.

To facilitate assimilation, a primary goal of the government resettlement program, nine Voluntary Assistance Groups (VOLAGS) were approved to assist in placing the immigrant families into local communities. As official sponsors, the VOLAGS—which included the U.S. Catholic Conference, the International Rescue Committee, the Church World Service, the Lutheran Immigration and Refugee Service, the American Council for Nationalities Service, the United Hebrew Immigration Aid Society, the Tolstoy Foundation, the American Fund for Czechoslovak Refugees, and the Travelers Aid International Social Services of America—accepted responsibility for the immigrants once they left the reception centers. The federal government provided $500 per immigrant to assist with resettlement costs. The VOLAGS were responsible for providing housing, food, clothing, medical care, and financial assistance until the immigrants obtained employment and were able to support themselves. Sponsoring organizations also acted as intermediaries with state and federal agencies, provided translation services, and assisted in enrolling children and adults in school or educational classes. Most of the organizations published newsletters for informational purposes. Although the government resettlement officials promoted assimilation as quickly as possible, resettlement progressed slower than anticipated, because it proved difficult to place the larger Asian extended families with local sponsors.

SECONDARY MIGRATION

Federal policy was to spread out the refugees among as many communities as reasonably possible to lessen the impact on any one location. As a result, 27,199 were placed with sponsors in California, 9,130 in Texas, 7,159 in Pennsylvania, 5,322 in Florida, 4,182 in Washington, 3,696 in Illinois, 3,689 in New York, and 3,601 in Louisiana. Over 52,000 were settled through the United States Catholic Conference. Problems quickly arose because of the rush to move immigrants to local communities, whether or not they were ready to cope with their new environment. Most of the exiles were from urban areas in their native lands, and most had been at least middle class in income, many of them professionals or government workers. In the United States, they generally found employment in lower-paying positions than they previously had, and a large number were placed in smaller communities where they felt isolated from anything familiar. Because of their low wages, many families found themselves below the poverty level. Once it became apparent that long-term assistance would be needed, many local sponsors withdrew. Because of the increasing sense of isolation among those resettled in rural communities or small towns, within six months many had already begun a secondary migration to larger urban areas with existing Southeast Asian populations, chiefly Los Angeles, San Francisco, New Orleans, and Dallas.

CIVIL RIGHTS

By the 1970s, Asian Americans had become more assertive in defending their legal rights. Community organizations such as the Asian Law Caucus founded in Oakland, California, in 1972; Asian Americans for Equality established in New York in 1974 (originally named Asian Americans for Equal Employment); and the Asian Law Alliance organized in San Jose, California, in 1977, were designed to inform immigrants of their legal rights and to provide low-cost legal services to Asian Americans to ensure equal access. The Organization of Chinese Americans, established in Washington, D.C., in 1973 to promote Chinese history and culture, asserted Chinese-American civil rights and opposed negative stereotypes. Similar roles were played by the San Francisco–based Chinese for Affirmative Action, the Washington, D.C.-based Organization of Chinese Americans, the Korean American Political Association of San Francisco, and similar organizations. Asian-American women also took an active part in promoting civil rights. Asian Women United, formed in San Francisco in 1976, promoted equality for Asian women; as did the Organization of PanAsian American Women organized in Washington, D.C., in 1976, and the Organization of Chinese American Women founded in Washington, D.C., in 1977.

In 1978 a national convention of the Japanese American Citizens League adopted a resolution proposed by Edison Uno to pursue legal remedies to compensate victims of forced relocation during World War II. This led to the establishment of the National Council for Japanese American Redress in 1979. Although the process was lengthy, eventually these efforts succeeded in gaining a formal government apology, and $20,000 in reparations for each person who had been interned. In 2001 Congress also set aside funds for the preservation of the larger relocation camps as historical landmarks.

Asian Americans continued to seek legal remedies for other forms of discrimination. In *Hampton v. Mow Sun Wong* (1976), Chinese immigrants in San Francisco sued the U.S. Civil Service Commission over its regulation requiring U.S. citizenship as a prerequisite for employment. The Supreme Court held that the requirement violated the due process clause of the Fifth Amendment when applied to legal permanent residents. But the most significant case involving Asian Americans to be decided by the U.S. Supreme Court during the decade was *Lau v. Nichols* in 1974. At the time, there were approximately 2,800 Chinese students enrolled in the San Francisco Unified School District who were not fluent in English. These included about 1,000 who did not speak English; the remainder had limited English skills—insufficient for them to keep up in their classes. A group of families filed suit in federal court, arguing that the school district's failure to provide sufficient support for students with limited English ability violated Section 601 of the Civil Rights Act of 1964, which prohibited discrimination based on race, color, or national origin. The Court agreed, ordering the district to provide English-language support and special assistance to non-English speakers. The decision formed the legal basis for the Bilingual Education Act (1974) designed to promote equal educational opportunity.

ETHNIC COMMUNITIES

By the 1970s, the Asian-American population was largely concentrated in urban areas—about 40 percent of all Asian Americans lived in the Los Angeles, San Francisco, New York, and Chicago Metropolitan Statistical Areas. Almost 57 percent lived in communities whose populations were 2.5 million or more, and half of all Asian Americans lived in California, Hawaii, or the other Pacific Coast states. Within these urban communities, a majority of Asians lived in traditional ethnic communities known locally as Chinatown, Japantown, Koreatown, Little Tokyo, Little Manila, or Little Saigon. As with other ethnic groups, by the 1970s, the urban ethnic enclaves were populated largely by working-class people, small entrepreneurs, the lower and middle economic classes, and more recent arrivals. In San Francisco, it was estimated that 74 percent of its Chinatown residents were born abroad, while 80 percent of New York's Chinatown and 88 percent of Los Angeles's Chinatown were born outside the United States.

Most professionals and other well-educated people of the upper-middle- and upper-class income groups had begun to move to the more affluent suburbs, leading to socioeconomic divides and often generational gaps between Asian Americans living in the urban ethnic communities and those living in the surrounding suburbs. In New York, a similar dichotomy occurred between the Downtown Chinese, comprised mostly of waitstaff, seamstresses, and those with lower-paying unskilled jobs, and the Uptown Chinese that included the more affluent professionals and people with managerial, technical, and other white-collar jobs. The divisions between socioeconomic classes also fueled conflicts between the values immigrants brought with them from their Asian origins, and the new cultural landscape they found in America. One example of this was the issue of caring for the elderly residents of the community. In Asia, great responsibility was placed on the younger generations to care for the elderly in their extended families, yet in the United States an entire industry existed, devoted to maintaining retirement communities, assisted-living facilities, and other services designed to care for the elderly outside the traditional home. Whether or not to make use of these options often stirred controversy and feelings of guilt within Asian-American communities.

The urban ethnic enclaves served to keep the various Asian cultures alive in the United States. With Asian Americans concentrated in geographically small urban communities, sufficient population existed to support Buddhist temples, Shinto shrines, or other Asian religious places of worship, and particularly Asian houses of Christian worship spread rapidly. By the 1970s, the uniquely

Asian-American communities began to interest the greater U.S. society, becoming tourist attractions in many of the larger cities. Chinese restaurants, in particular, began to attract increasing numbers of non-Asian clientele and to spread beyond the confines of the ethnic enclaves, even appearing in cities and towns with only modest Asian populations. It has been estimated that by 1970, there were already some 9,400 Chinese restaurants in the United States. Not quite as ubiquitous, but growing in popularity were Japanese, Vietnamese, Thai, and other restaurants offering Asian cuisine, including those specializing in Cantonese, Szechuan, or other subdivisions of larger groups.

Yet despite the growing popularity of Asian cuisine and other aspects of Asian culture, these communities, like other urban ethnic communities during the 1970s, were subject to pressures from outside. Buildings in the older urban communities, often founded more than a century ago, had begun to decay by 1970. In San Francisco's Chinatown, for example, a study revealed that two-thirds of the people were living in substandard housing. This, coupled with the skyrocketing value of urban real estate, led to efforts at "revitalization" that often meant the displacement of residents, and the effective elimination of the traditional neighborhoods.

In 1973 the San Francisco Redevelopment Agency unveiled plans to renovate Japantown as a tourist area. In the process, buildings were identified for demolition, and traditional businesses and low-income residents were pushed out. Local activists comprised mostly of Sansei, business owners, and community residents formed the grassroots Committee Against Nihonmachi Evictions, but its success was limited because of a lack of funds and disagreements within the community. In Los Angeles, the Little Tokyo Redevelopment Project led to similar divisions. Aimed at developing the area into a tourist attraction, plans resulted in the eviction of businesses and elderly residents of a 67-acre area. Joined by young Japanese-American radicals, these groups fought the project, but often found themselves arrayed against Japanese-American investors bidding for building sites and businessmen from Japan looking for investment opportunities. As a result of these and similar conflicts, some of the older traditional urban ethnic areas were redeveloped into tourist areas at the expense of their original character, and residents.

POLITICAL INFLUENCE

The addition of a large Asian-American population that came with the admission of Hawaii as the 50th state in 1959, combined with increased immigration, a high rate of naturalization, and the voluntary settlement of Asian Americans in relatively small geographic areas, all led to an unprecedented increase in the election of Asian Americans to political office. In California, Norman Mineta was elected mayor of San Jose, the first Asian-American mayor of a major city. The popular Nisei was elected to the U.S. House of Representatives in 1974, where he served for some 20 years until appointed secretary of commerce by

President Bill Clinton and secretary of transportation by President George W. Bush. In 1974 March Kong Fong Eu was elected California's secretary of state, the first Asian-American woman elected to that office in the United States. She won reelection four times, then served as U.S. ambassador to Micronesia.

Hawaiian-born Herbert Young Cho Choy became the first Korean American admitted to the bar, and the first Asian American to hold a federal judgeship when President Richard Nixon appointed him to the U.S. Court of Appeals for the Ninth Circuit in 1971. That year, the Hawaii legislature included 13 Japanese Americans and four Chinese Americans in the state Senate, and 33 Japanese and five Chinese in the House, where the speaker was Taddu Beppu. In 1974 George Ryoichi Ariyoshi became the first Japanese American elected governor of Hawaii, and the first Asian American elected governor of any U.S. state. His lieutenant governor was another Japanese American, Nelson Doi. By the mid-1970s, approximately one-half of Hawaii's state representatives and senators were Japanese Americans.

In 1976 Samuel Ichiye Hayakawa of California became the second Japanese American to be elected to the U.S. Senate, joining Daniel Inouye and Spark Matsunaga of Hawaii, the first and third Japanese Americans elected to the U.S. Senate. An English professor who had served as president of San Francisco State College (later University), Hayakawa rose to national prominence by opposing student demonstrations on the San Francisco State campus, but lost significant support among Asian Americans for founding U.S. English, an organization that worked toward the establishment of English as the official language of the United States. Matsunaga remained in the Senate until his death in 1990. His portrait appears on the $10,000 denomination of U.S. Series I Savings Bonds.

The growing political influence of Asian Americans led to the recognition, for the first time, of Hawaiians as native peoples under the Native American Program Act of 1974. Included in the groups eligible to apply for funding were public and nonprofit private agencies, community colleges, and universities serving native Hawaiians, as well as native peoples in American Samoa, Guam, Palau, and the Commonwealth of the Northern Mariana Islands. Four years later, Representatives Frank Horton of New York and Norman Y. Mineta of California introduced in the House of Representatives a resolution calling on the president to designate the first 10 days in May as Asian/Pacific Heritage Week. The same resolution was introduced in the U.S. Senate by Daniel Inouye and Spark Matsunaga. With both houses of Congress concurring, President Jimmy Carter signed the joint resolution on October 5, 1978, designating the annual celebration of Asian/Pacific Heritage Week.

EDUCATIONAL AND ECONOMIC PROGRESS

Asian Americans have often been referred to as the model minority. With a strong family structure that has traditionally placed a high value on education,

U.S. Secretary of Commerce Norman Y. Mineta speaking in Santa Cruz, California, in 2000. Mineta was the first Asian American to hold a cabinet-level post in the U.S. government.

Norman Yoshio Mineta

Born November 12, 1931, in San Jose, California, Norman Mineta was interned with his family during World War II. In 1953 he earned a degree in business administration from the University of California, Berkeley, and joined the army, serving as an intelligence officer in Korea and Japan. Upon discharge, he joined his father's Mineta Insurance Agency. In 1967 the mayor of San Jose appointed him to a vacant seat on the city council, to which he was later elected. He was the first Asian-American mayor of a major U.S. city. Elected to the House of Representatives in 1974, he served 1975–95, cofounding the Congressional Asian Pacific American Caucus and chairing the House Public Works and Transportation Committee (1992–94). Highlights of his congressional career were authoring the Intermodal Surface Transportation Efficiency Act of 1991, and his vigorous support of the Civil Liberties Act of 1988, which finally offered an apology and redress for the internment of citizens of Japanese ancestry during World War II.

In 2000 President Bill Clinton appointed Mineta secretary of commerce, the first Asian American to hold a cabinet-level position. Although a Democrat, he was appointed in 2001 to Republican president George W. Bush's cabinet as secretary of transportation. When the attacks of September 11, 2001, commenced, Mineta issued the first order in U.S. history to immediately ground all civilian air traffic. For his many services, Mineta received the Presidential Medal of Freedom (2006), and his hometown airport was named in his honor—the Norman Y. Mineta San Jose International Airport.

virtually every Asian group has fared well in America. Like all immigrant groups, many members of the initial waves of immigration were not well educated, and took the only jobs that were available to them—low-paying manual labor or service positions. As late as 1970, a survey of Chinese Americans aged 25 and older revealed that fully a quarter had not advanced beyond a seventh-grade education, while another quarter had already earned college degrees. The difference lay in the age of the respondents. Among the older generation, few had the opportunity for secondary or advanced education. Yet such value was placed on education by this same older generation that they sacrificed to make sure that their children had the opportunity they had not enjoyed.

Disadvantages were overcome quickly. Among the two largest groups, in 1970, 68.8 percent of Japanese Americans aged 25 and older had achieved high school diplomas, as had 68.1 percent of Chinese Americans. By 1979 the median annual income for Japanese-American workers was $16,829, compared with $15,572 for Caucasians. In the same year, only 4.2 percent of Japanese-American families were at or below the poverty line, significantly less than the seven percent of Caucasian families. In 1970 the census disclosed that professional and technical employment among Chinese men had risen from only seven percent in 1950, to 26 percent 20 years later. In addition to those in professional and technical positions, another 8.3 percent held managerial jobs, 20.4 percent were service workers, 15.9 percent operatives, and 17.2 percent clerical. While 12.2 percent of all adult Americans were college graduates in 1970, the ratio for Chinese Americans was 27.6 percent. Further, with the high rate of professional and white-collar jobs, the median income for a Chinese-American family was approximately $1,000 higher than the national average.

FESTIVALS AND FOODS

With the growth in the number and variety of Asian immigrants during the 1970s, the prominence of Asian ethnic festivals grew to attract media coverage and attendance from outside the traditional ethnic communities. Chinatowns had long celebrated the Chinese New Year with colorful parades, fireworks, family dinners, and other festivities ending on the 15th day of the month with the Lantern Festival. The second most important festival in Chinese-American communities is the Mid-Autumn (or Moon) Festival. Celebrated on the 15th day of the eighth Chinese month, ordinarily in September, it marks the equinox, and is celebrated by eating traditional "mooncakes" of

Mooncakes like the one at left are made with many variations, but are often filled with lotus seed paste and whole salted egg yolk.

many varieties, and carrying lanterns. Another Chinese festival celebrated in larger communities is the Dragon Boat Festival on the fifth day of the fifth Chinese month. This celebration typically involves eating rice stuffed with different fillings and wrapped in bamboo or other leaves called *zongzi*, drinking realgar wine (said to ward off illnesses), and staging races of long, narrow, decorated boats known as dragon boats.

Japantowns had long celebrated the Cherry Blossom and Obon Festivals. Also called the Feast of Lanterns, the Obon Festival was traditionally a time for families to reunite in their ancestral village where they would remember the spirits of their ancestors. Since this was not practical for Issei in the United States, the festivals became occasions for family reunions and remembering departed or separated ancestors without the traditional trek to the family village. In the urban Little Manilas, Filipinos celebrated Flores de Mayo (a Roman Catholic harvest feast), Philippine Independence Day, and José Rizal Day in honor of a Filipino patriot killed by the Spanish in 1896. All of these are occasions for parades, feasts, and other public and private customs.

A decorative carving of a dragon's head from the bow of a dragon boat.

With the arrival of large numbers of Koreans and Southeast Asians, new celebrations also took root. In addition to celebrating the lunar New Year, some Korean communities celebrate *Chusok*, a traditional Korean holiday occurring on the 15th day of the eighth month of the lunar year. The name translates into English as "harvest moon." It is a time for family reunions, remembering ancestors, and giving thanks for a good harvest. Vietnamese, Cambodian, Laotian, Thai, and other immigrants from Southeast Asia also celebrate the Lunar New Year holiday, the Mid-Autumn Festival, and various other local holidays. And a new holiday was added—Ngay Quoc Han—commemorating the exodus of Vietnamese from their homeland following the fall of Saigon.

Prominent in all of these celebrations is food. Until the 1970s, Chinese cuisine, the most widely known Asian cuisine in the United States, consisted mostly of Americanized chop suey, egg foo yung, chow mein, and a few other dishes prepared to resemble only superficially their Chinese origins. With the renewed diplomatic emphasis on China in the 1970s, and with the appearance of some favorable images of Asian film and television productions, Americans became more discriminating in their enjoyment of Asian foods. Cantonese,

Growing numbers of immigrants from Korea in the 1970s increased the availability and popularity of dishes like bul-kogi and kimchi, which are both featured in the meal shown above.

Szechuan, and other regional Chinese cooking became popular outside the ethnic communities. Adventurous Americans began to move beyond the "Japanese steak house" to acquire a taste for *sushi*, *sashimi*, *tempura*, and other authentic Japanese cuisine. Dishes that accompanied the new waves of immigration from Korea and Southeast Asia also became popular.

Koreans brought with them *bul-kogi*, a thinly sliced and seasoned beef that is grilled over charcoal and served with rice, and *kimchi*, a very spicy dish made of fermented cabbage, shredded radish, red chili peppers, scallions, garlic, and ginger. Foods native to Southeast Asia reflect a wide variety of influences from China, Thailand, and other surrounding areas, as well as their own uniqueness. They tend to use fresh fruits and vegetables, pork, chicken, shrimp, and a variety of seafood. Dipping sauces based on soy, fish, or other oils are common, as is the use of fresh herbs such as basil, coriander, lemongrass, and mint. Various forms of spring rolls are also common in Asian foods.

SCIENCE AND ENGINEERING

Asian Americans have been among the foremost in discoveries and innovations in fields relating to science and engineering. George Nakashima, a native of Spokane, Washington, earned a graduate degree in architecture from the Massachusetts Institute of Technology in 1930. While interned during World War II, he studied carpentry, from which he developed a unique style that combined Shaker simplicity with more modern craft techniques. In 1973 he was hired to design some 200 pieces for Governor Nelson Rockefeller of New York. His famous *Altar of Peace* adorns the Cathedral of St. John the Divine in New York City, and his book *Soul of a Tree* (1981) is considered a classic on the art of woodworking.

Another architect, Minoru Yamasaki, was also born in Seattle, Washington. After studying architecture at the University of Washington and New York

University, he worked for firms in New York and Detroit until 1951, when he opened his own firm. He gained special notice with his design for the U.S. consulate in Kobe, Japan (1954), followed later by the Science Pavilion in Seattle (now the Pacific Science Center), Century City Plaza in Los Angeles, and the Lambert air terminal in St. Louis, Missouri. His two most famous designs were both completed in the 1970s—World Trade Center One in 1972, and Chicago's Sears Tower (now the Willis Tower) in 1974. At the time of their construction, each was the tallest building in the world.

In the field of medicine, Choh Hao Li, a native of Guangzhou, China, gained an international reputation for synthesizing the pituitary growth hormone in 1970, and for his discovery in 1978 of the beta-endorphin, a robust pain-killing drug produced in the brain. He was also the first researcher to isolate a means of stimulating the growth of bones and cartilage in humans.

In 1972 Makio Murayama, a native of San Francisco, received the Martin Luther King Jr. Medical Achievement Award for his research on sickle cell anemia. Asian-American immigrants also brought with them traditional medical practices that gained acceptance within non-Asian U.S. society. During the late 1970s, traditional Chinese acupuncture began to be studied seriously as a treatment for chronic pain and other ailments. Eventually it was included in many health insurance programs. Meditation techniques first became popular first among counterculture groups, and by the end of the 1970s, they were accepted by medical practitioners as well. Herbalism, massage therapy, and yoga were also widely adopted for their health benefits.

In the field of physics, Leo Esaki, a native of Osaka, Japan, shared the 1973 Nobel Prize

Japanese-American architect Minoru Yamasaki's Willis Tower (formerly the Sears Tower) was finished in 1974.

Mission Specialist Ellison Shoji Onizuka appears at far left in this November 15, 1985, group photograph of the crew of the ill-fated Challenger space shuttle mission.

Ellison Shoji Onizuka

Born in Kealakekua, Hawaii, on June 24, 1946, Onizuka earned his undergraduate and graduate degrees in engineering at the University of Colorado before joining the U.S. Air Force, where he served as a test pilot and flight test engineer. He joined the astronaut program in 1978, completing his training in August 1979, and was assigned to the Orbiter test team at the Kennedy Space Center in Florida. Onizuka became the first Asian American in space on January 24, 1985, when he served as part of the crew of the space shuttle *Discovery,* and was responsible for its primary payload activities.

Assigned to a follow-up operation as a mission specialist aboard the *Challenger,* Onizuka perished with the other crew members in the disaster that occurred shortly after launch on January 28, 1986. Among his many honors were the Air Force Commendation Medal, the Air Force Meritorious Service Medal, Air Force Organizational Excellence Award, National Defense Service Medal, and the Congressional Space Medal of Honor.

for his discovery of the tunneling effect in semiconductors, a breakthrough that was essential for the invention of the Esaki diode used in computers. Samuel Chao Chung Ting,was a graduate of the University of Michigan, where he earned a doctorate in physics in 1963. He went on to work at the Brookhaven National Laboratory, where he led a team that discovered a new heavy subatomic particle, J/ψ. His work earned him the Ernest Orlando Lawrence Award in 1976, and in the same year, the Nobel Prize in Physics. He was the first Nobel recipient to give his acceptance speech in Mandarin Chinese.

Among those who gained recognition for their application of science and technology to successful businesses was Chinese-born David Lee, who cofounded the Qume Corporation in 1973 to manufacture daisy-wheel printers. The company was purchased by the ITT Corporation in 1978, and Lee became president of the subsidiary ITT Qume. Thomas C.K. Yuen, along with college roommates Albert C. Wong and Safi U. Qureshey, all three immigrants, pooled their meager resources of $2,000 to found AST Research Incorporated in 1979. Using new technical innovations, they built the company into the third-largest manufacturer of personal computers using microprocessing chip technology, with sales in excess of $13 million per annum within five years. Yuen went on to become CEO and board chair of SRS Labs, an innovator in audio, voice, and semiconductor technology. Shanghai-born Charles B. Wang founded Computer Associates in 1976, using money borrowed on credit cards. Building it into a multimillion-dollar business, he later became owner of the New York Islanders professional hockey team, and donated some $50 million to the State University of New York at Stony Brook to fund the Charles B. Wang Center.

JOURNALISM AND PUBLISHING

During the 1970s, Asian Americans made great strides in journalism and literature. Within the mainstream media, Connie Chung became one of the first nationally televised Asian-American news correspondents when she began reporting on CBS in 1971, and later coanchored the *CBS Evening News*. Meanwhile at ABC, Ken Kashiwahara began reporting nationally in 1974. Within ethnic communities, journalism also proliferated. This was especially true of activists who sought to unify the Asian-American communities with bilingual and English-language publications designed for political impact.

In 1970 the I Wor Kuen, a Maoist-oriented group, began publishing the bilingual newspaper *Getting Together* in New York's Chinatown. A year later, it moved to San Francisco, where it provided radicals with an alternative to the *San Francisco Journal*, a bilingual Chinese-American newspaper founded in 1972, or the English-language *Asian Week*, founded by John Fang in 1979. Among the other influential publications originating during these years were *Bridge* (New York, 1971), the *Asian American Review* (University of California, Berkeley, 1972), *Jade* (Los Angeles, 1974), and the intellectual *Hsintu* (New Soil, 1978).

One of the most important periodicals was the *Amerasia Journal* founded at Yale University in 1971 with Lowell Chun-Hoon as editor. Described as a "national interdisciplinary journal of scholarship, criticism, and literature on Asian and Pacific Americans," it moved to the Asian American Studies Center at the University of California at Los Angeles after its first issue. As the first refereed, interdisciplinary publication on Asian-American studies, it wielded significant influence on the development of this emerging field of study. *Amerasia Journal* was soon joined by other academic publications investigating Asian-American history and culture.

In 1972 Korean Americans inaugurated the journal *Insight, Korean American Bimonthly,* edited by Brenda Paik Sunoo, with a focus on identity issues, poetry, and literature. In 1974 the Asian American Arts Center began publication of its annual *Artspiral* as a forum for the arts. *Bamboo Bridge: The Hawaii Writers' Quarterly* was established in 1978 by Eric Chock and Darrel H.Y. Lum to promote writing by and about the people of Hawaii. In the same year, Janice Mirikitani, an influential literary voice of the Asian-American ethnic pride movement in the 1970s, published *Awake in the River* to focus on socially conscious poetry and identity issues.

The collection and preservation of Asian-American writing was important to a growing number of individuals and organizations. The Demonstration Project for Asian Americans, established by Dorothy Laigo Cordova in Seattle, Washington, in 1971, collected stories, photographs, oral histories, and other documentation of the Asian experience in the Pacific Northwest. Her research eventually formed the basis for the book *Filipinos: Forgotten Asian Americans, A Pictorial Essay, 1763–Circa 1963.* Other documentary studies resulted in the publication of Victor and Brett Nee's *Longtime Californ': A Documentary Study of an American Chinatown* (1973), Alexander Saxton's *The Indispensable Enemy: Labor and the Anti-Chinese Movement in California* (1971), and *Roots: An Asian American Reader* (1971). Pioneering anthologies of Asian literature included *Asian-American Authors* (1972), edited by Kai-yu Hsu and Helen Palubinskas, and the acclaimed *Aiiieeeee! An Anthology of Asian-American Writers* (1974), edited by Frank Chin. Equally important was the outcome of the 1978 "Talk Story, Our Voices in Literature and Song: Hawaii's Ethnic American Writers' Conference," organized in Honolulu by Marie M. Hara, Arnold T. Hiura, and Stephen H. Sumida, which led to publication of *Asian American Literature in Hawaii: An Annotated Bibliography* (1979).

LITERATURE

In literature, one of the most celebrated Asian-American authors of the decade was Maxine Hong Kingston, born in Stockton, California, the daughter of Chinese immigrants. Skillfully blending fiction and non-fiction into novels reflecting her cultural heritage, her writing found receptive audiences in both the Asian and non-Asian communities. Her memoir *The Woman Warrior: Memoirs of a Girlhood Among Ghosts* (1976) was recognized with the National Book Critics Circle Award for nonfiction, while the later *China Men* on the nature of Chinese life in America received a National Book Award in 1981. Laurence Yep's *Dragonwings* (1975), a story of the power of imagination and freedom set in early-20th-century San Francisco, won the Newbery Award, while his *Child of the Owl* (1977), focusing on issues of Chinese identity, was honored with the Boston Globe/Horn Book Award. Shawn Hsu Wong's first novel, *Homebase* (1979), received the Pacific Northwest Booksellers Award and the Governor's Writers Day Award in Washington. In nonfiction, one of the more interesting contributions was by Jim Yoshida, who related in *The Two Worlds of Jim Yoshida* (1972) his story about being stranded in Japan, conscripted into the Japanese army, and fighting to regain his U.S. citizenship after the war.

ARTS ORGANIZATIONS

Within the Asian ethnic communities, efforts to collect, preserve, and disseminate Asian arts crystallized around new organizational support. One of the first efforts of the decade was formation of the Kearny Street Workshop, an artists' collective for Asian-American writers, filmmakers, and photographers in San Francisco in 1972. Four years later, the Association of Asian/Pacific American Artists was founded as an educational and cultural organization. Its mission was to monitor media productions for their portrayal

Josie Natori

A native of the Philippines, where she was born Josefina Almeda Cruz in Manila in 1947, designer Josie Natori immigrated to the United States, where she graduated from Manhattanville College in 1968. Launching a career in investment banking, she took a position with Bache Securities, and within six months had been charged with opening a new branch office in Manila. She soon left Bache for a position at Merrill Lynch, where she became vice president of investment banking by the exceptionally young age of 27. By 1977 the initial excitement of high finance had vanished, leaving her feeling unfulfilled. At the pinnacle of her career, she resigned to turn her talents to fashion design. Her lingerie and daywear creations won her a contract with Bloomingdale's. The founder and CEO of the Natori Company, her professional and community achievements have been recognized with the Peopling of America Award from the Statue of Liberty–Ellis Island Foundation, and an appointment to the White House Conference on Small Business.

of Asians, and to advocate for realistic, balanced representations. In 1977 San Francisco became home to the Japantown Art and Media Workshop, a grassroots community organization dedicated to preserving and publicizing Asian culture and materials relating to the Asian-American experience. On the East Coast, the Asian American Resource Workshop, founded in Boston in 1979, similarly sought to document the Asian-American experience through the collection of documents, library resources, and visual media. These and similar efforts to preserve and promote both Asian and Asian-American culture were evident in virtually every Asian-American community by the end of the decade.

PERFORMING ARTS

With the growth in the number and diversity of the Asian-American population during the 1970s, interest in Asian fine and performing arts and mainstream opportunities for Asians expanded. Spurring much of the development were local theater groups such as the Asian American Theatre Company established in San Francisco by Frank Chin. Founded as a playwrights' workshop, it became a professional theater company in 1975, and changed its name to the Asian American Theatre Workshop two years later. Chin won praise for his production and direction of *The Chickencoop Chinaman* and *The Year of the Dragon*, both of which dramatized Chinatown culture. The former became the first play written by an Asian American to be staged in mainstream New York City venues when it opened at the American Palace Theater. *The Year of the Dragon* became the first Asian-American play to be broadcast on national television.

Lisa Ting, director of the hit *Return of the Phoenix* (1973), was determined to provide Asian actors with an opportunity to play parts beyond mainstream stereotypes by forming the Chinese Theatre Group in New York City. In 1977 it became the Pan Asian Repertory Theatre (still later it was renamed the Asian Exclusion Act). Similar groups included the Northwest Asian American Theatre Company in Seattle, Washington, and the Los Angeles–based East West Players. One of the most successful plays staged by the Los Angeles group was Wakako Yamauchi's short story *And the Soul Shall Dance*, which explored the struggles faced by Issei farmers in California.

FILM AND TELEVISION

The 1970s witnessed an explosion of Asian Americans in the film industry. One of the catalysts was Visual Communications, a community-based media resources and production facility founded in Los Angeles in 1970 to portray in more realistic fashion the history and culture of Asian and Pacific Island Americans. Originally conceived as a photographic exhibit on Japanese Americans during World War II by Robert Nakamura, Eddie Wong, Alan Ohashi, and Duane Kubo, in 1971 it became a nonprofit corporation to promote and produce work on Asian themes. By the end of the decade it had produced 10 films on the Asian-American experience, and a book of photographs titled *In Movement* (1974). A similar success was Asian Cine Vision, a nonprofit national media arts center founded by Peter Chow, Christine Choy, and Tsui Hark in New York City in 1976 to promote the development of Asian-American film and video arts. In 1978 they organized the first Asian American International Film Festival, a three-day exhibit of some 50 films. In its first 15 years, the festival exhibited more than 500 Asian films.

Among the growing number of films produced by Asian Americans about their own experience was producer Robert A. Nakamura's *Manzanar* (1972), a powerful personal documentary about the Japanese-American internment. Christine Choy's documentary *From Spikes Spindles* (1976) focused on New York's Chinatown. Asian Americans with roles in mainstream films included James Shigeta, who played in *Lost Horizon* (1973) and *The Yakuza* (1975), and portrayed Vice Admiral Chuichi Nagumo in *Midway* (1976). Yuki Shimoda played Ambassador Hahn in *Girls Are For Loving* (1973), a Japanese naval officer in *Midway* (1976), and Prime Minister Shidahara in *MacArthur* (1976), later going on to roles in television series such as *Ironsides, Hawaii Five-O,* and *Kung Fu*.

Asian Americans were responsible for a new movie genre that began sweeping the country in the 1970s. Due largely to the popularity of Jun Fan Lee, better known to American audiences as Bruce Lee, martial arts films gained widespread popularity, and Lee became an iconic figure for his starring roles in *The Big Boss, Fist of Fury, Way of the Dragon, Enter the Dragon,* and *The Game of Death*. The popularity of the new martial arts genre propelled it to the television screen when Caucasian actor David Carradine starred in *Kung Fu* (1972–75). Set in the United States in the late 19th century, the show featured a Chinese martial arts monk in the Old West. Keye Luke, best known for his earlier role as "Number One Son" in the Charlie Chan movies, played the role of Po, the master-teacher.

Among the most popular television programs of the 1970s was the futuristic *Star Trek* that gained cult status as one of the most enduring television series of all time. George Takei portrayed Hikaru Sulu, the helmsman in the series, and he later reprised the role in several *Star Trek* movies. Another exceptionally popular series was *Happy Days*, with Noriyuki "Pat" Morita playing the role of Matsuo "Arnold" Takahashi, owner of Arnold's Diner. Morita went on to star as the philosophical karate master Keisuke Miyagi in the series of *Karate Kid* films. Jack Soo, who was born Goro Suzuki, landed a role on the sitcom *Barney Miller* that premiered in 1975, playing Sergeant Nick Yemana. Another popular entertainer was Hawaiian Donald Tai Loy Ho, who hosted *The Don Ho Show* (1976–77), and became a successful featured nightclub performer.

VIDEO ARTS

Nam June Paik was largely responsible for the development of another genre in video arts. Born in Seoul, Korea, he studied art, history, and music at the

University of Tokyo before moving to New York City. Recognized for innovations such as the video synthesizer, Paik gained a reputation as the Father of Video Art for his extensive use of television monitors to present his comic experimental works. Often employing up to 300 screens at a time, he gained widespread praise for *Global Groove* (1973) and *Guadalcanal Requiem* (1977). His credits also include composition of the electronic music in *TV Buddha* (1974) and *Video Fish* (1975). He was later named one of the 25 most influential artists of the 20th century by *ARTnews*.

MUSIC

In the field of music, local ethnic groups preserved Asian music, gained interest from the non-Asian community, and adapted Asian musical traditions to emerging American musical forms. Established in 1972, the Flowing Stream Ensemble of San Francisco used Chinese and Western instruments to play classical, folk, and contemporary Chinese music. The following year, Don Kin formed the Korean Classical Music and Dance Company in Los Angeles. In 1974 Asian American Dance Performances opened in San Francisco to support Asian-American performing artists, while the Asian American Dance Theatre, founded in the same year, offered two repertoires, one traditional, and one modern. Later expanded to include visual arts, it became the Asian Arts Institute in 1980.

Among the groups formed to preserve Asian musical art forms was San Jose Taiko, formed in 1973 by Sansei to preserve the art of Japanese *taiko* drumming. Long associated with Shinto and martial arts traditions, in the United States it was mostly linked to Buddhist temples and Obon celebrations. Unlike in Japan, where taiko drumming was strictly a male preserve, in the United States most of the drummers were female, and they were often accompanied with flutes, shell horns, and bells. Experimentation with Latin, African, and other rhythms extended taiko drumming far beyond Japanese tradition. *Karaoke*, derived from the Japanese slang for "empty orchestra" or "orchestra empty of vocals," is another imported Japanese musical form in which amateur singers perform to recorded music. Very popular in Japanese bars, restaurants, and nightclubs, it began to appear in Hawaiian and Pacific Coast ethnic communities in the 1970s, later erupting into a non-Asian fad.

With the Vietnam War raging at the beginning of the decade, singers Chris Iijima, Joanne Miyamoto, and Charlie Chin were leaders in the protest movement, with Iijima and Miyamoto writing *Yellow Pearl*, the signature song of the Asian American Music Movement (1972). After the war, their focus changed to promoting solidarity among Asian-American communities to resist discrimination. Iijima and Miyamoto again collaborated to write *We Are the Children* (1975), which employed historical stereotypes in an attempt to cement a pan-Asian political movement allied with Native Americans, Hispanics, and other minority Americans.

The early 1970s also witnessed the formation of Hiroshima, a pop group blending traditional Japanese music with jazz and other Western musical forms. Founded by June Okida Kuramoto and Danny Kuramoto, their first album—*Hiroshima* (1979)—earned them a Grammy nomination and recognition as the Best Live Jazz Group by *Cashbox* magazine.

Among the most prominent Asian-American musicians of the era were Seiji Ozawa and Yo-Yo Ma. Born in Manchuria, Ozawa had already gained an international reputation when he was hired as assistant conductor by the New York Philharmonic. After a stint as director of the Toronto Symphony Orchestra, he led the San Francisco Symphony Orchestra (1970–73), before moving on to be music director of the Boston Symphony Orchestra in 1973. He remained in Boston for nearly 30 years. Ozawa was the first person of Japanese ancestry to lead a major American orchestra. Yo-Yo Ma was born in Paris, the son of a Chinese musicologist. In 1963 his family moved to New York, where he began attending the Juilliard School of Music at age nine. The prodigy won the prestigious Avery Fisher Prize in 1978, launching a career as one of the era's premier cellists.

CONCLUSION

During the 1970s, Asian immigration to America increased over previous decades and became more diversified, including groups such as the Vietnamese, Cambodians, Laotians, Thais, and Hmong, whose previous numbers in the United States were negligible. With the new arrivals, urban ethnic communities were revitalized, bringing new cultural elements to non-Asians in the form of cuisine, music, festivals, and the arts. At the same time, Asian Americans made notable contributions to science, engineering, the fine and performing arts, music, film, television, and a wide variety of other professions in mainstream America. Asian Americans continued the fight for civil rights, attained influential elected offices, and were widely recognized for their educational and economic achievements.

JAMES S. PULA
PURDUE UNIVERSITY NORTH CENTRAL

Further Reading

Caplan, Nathan. *The Boat People and Achievement in America: A Study of Family Life, Hard Work, and Cultural Values.* Ann Arbor: University of Michigan Press, 1989.

Chin, Frank. *Aiiieeeee! An Anthology of Asian-American Writers.* Washington, DC: Howard University Press, 1974.

Cordova, Fred, Dorothy Laigo Cordova, and Albert A. Acena. *Filipinos: For-gotten Asian Americans, A Pictorial Essay, 1763–Circa 1963*. Dubuque, IA: Kendall/Hunt Publishing, 1983.

Fawcett, James T., and Benjamin V. Cariño. *Pacific Bridges: The New Immi-gration from Asia and the Pacific Islands*. Staten Island, NY: Center for Migration Studies, 1987.

Gardner, Robert W., Bryant Robey, and Peter C. Smith. *Asian Americans: Growth, Change, and Diversity*. Washington, DC: Population Reference Bureau, Inc., 1985.

Kingston, Maxine Hong. *The Woman Warrior: Memoirs of a Girlhood among Ghosts*. New York: Knopf, distributed by Random House, 1976.

Kwong, Peter, and Dusanka Miscevic. *Chinese America: The Untold Story of America's Oldest New Community*. New York: New Press, 2005.

Liu, William T., Mary Ann Lamanna, and Alice Murata. *Transition to Nowhere: Vietnamese Refugees in America*. Nashville, TN: Charter House, 1979.

Nee, Victor, and Brett de Bary Nee. *Longtime Californ': A Documentary Study of an American Chinatown*. Boston, MA: Houghton Mifflin, 1973.

Strand, Paul J., and Woodrow Jones, Jr. *Indochinese Refugees in America: Problems of Adaptation and Assimilation*. Durham, NC: Duke University Press, 1985.

Tachiki, Amy. *Roots: An Asian American Reader*. Los Angeles, CA: UCLA Asian American Studies Center/Continental Graphics, 1971.

Takaki, Ronald T. *Strangers from a Different Shore: A History of Asian Ameri-cans*. Boston, MA: Little, Brown, 1989.

Tsai, Shih-Shan Henry. *The Chinese Experience in America*. Bloomington: Indiana University Press, 1986.

Wilson, Robert A., and Bill Hosokawa. *East to America: A History of the Japanese in the United States*. New York: Morrow, 1980.

Yoshida, Jim. *The Two Worlds of Jim Yoshida*. New York: Morrow, 1972.

CHAPTER 9

Pursuing the American Dream: 1980 to 1989

THE 1980s WAS a profoundly important decade for Asian Americans. The changes in immigration law of previous decades had brought about a dynamic, diverse mix of Asian Americans, tracing their roots to many more countries than just Japan and China. In addition the racial consciousness of Asian Americans, that is to say, the willingness of Chinese, Vietnamese, or Filipino Americans to identify as Asian Americans was heightened. The 1980s saw the continuance of several stereotypes about Asian Americans—that they were perpetual foreigners, or that they were a gifted race when it came to academic success in the United States. This sort of soft racism combined with more obvious forms of prejudice in the 1980s. As Asian economies, particularly Japan's, rose to dizzying heights in the 1980s; the U.S. economy continued the painful process of deindustrialization, and the 1980s were a grim financial decade for many Americans. Some non-Asian Americans vented their frustration on Asian Americans in horrifying episodes. However Asian Americans ended the decade hopefully. They had gained access to crucial American institutions, and many had reshaped American entrepreneurship and culture, but damaging stereotypes continued to haunt them on the eve of the 1990s.

The 1980 census counted 3,500,439 Asian Americans and Pacific Islanders in the United States. By 1990 this number had increased to 7,273,662. The Asian-American percentage of the population nearly doubled during the same period, jumping from 1.5 to 2.9 percent of the total U.S. population. Immigration scholars believe that approximately three-fourths of this growth was caused by immigration (2.9 million new Asian immigrants came to the United States in the 1980s), and the largest groups of immigrants came from China, the Philippines, Japan, India, Korea, and Vietnam. Immigration from India, Korea, and Vietnam doubled during this decade, while the Japanese rate of immigration rose by 20 percent. Broken down along regional lines, the west's population was about five percent Asian American, and the northeast's population was about one percent. Other regions were less than one percent Asian American. California ranked first in total number of Asian Americans, with 1.3 million, followed by Hawaii with almost 600,000, and New York approximately 330,000. Other states with high numbers of Asian and Pacific Islander Americans included Illinois, Texas, Washington, and New Jersey. Hawaii was 61 percent Asian and Pacific Islander American—the only state with a majority Asian-American

A row of shops and restaurants along H Street in Washington, D.C.'s Chinatown in August 1980. Asian Americans worked in service jobs in large numbers in the 1980s, in part because of discrimination.

population. After California, which was about six percent Asian American in 1980, no other state was more than three percent Asian American in 1980. This small population endured the vicious anti-Asian rhetoric and violence that characterized the 1980s.

EMPLOYMENT AND INCOME

Asian Americans were employed in a wide, and widening, variety of fields in the 1980s, but they were disproportionately working in low-paying jobs, as cooks, waiters, gardeners, shopkeepers, and technicians. In the 1980s, Asian Americans had a difficult time breaking into management positions, in part because they were stereotyped as too passive to lead and make decisions. Asian-American labor activism and entrepreneurial activity showed that Asian Americans would fight for their rights in the 1980s. Shopkeepers, many of whom were first-generation Korean Americans in the 1980s, founded an organization to protect their interests, for example. KAGRO, or the Korean American Grocers Organization, was founded in 1989, and flexed its muscles in the early 1990s by spearheading a successful boycott of St. Ides malt liquor when one of its spokespeople, rapper Ice Cube, recorded the viciously anti-Korean *Black Korea* on his *Death Certificate* album.

Income statistics from California in 1980 indicate that achieving economic parity with whites was an ongoing struggle. Only Japanese-American men earned the same median income as white men, though they had to stay in school longer and work longer hours to do so. White men in California had a mean income of $23,400. In the same study, other Asian-American men fared worse than Japanese Americans. Korean-American men earned $19,000 (82 percent of white income), Chinese men earned $15,900 (68 percent of white income), and Filipino men earned $14,500 (62 percent of white income). Filipino men in New York State earned just over half of what white men earned. Taken as a whole, Asian-American men could expect to earn roughly what African-American men and Mexican-American men earned.

ANTI–ASIAN AMERICAN SENTIMENT: VINCENT CHIN

Vincent Chin was a promising young man of just 27 years old when he was beaten to death by racist white men in Detroit. The early 1980s, a time of economic pain in the United States and boom times in Asia, saw a jump in the number of hate crimes against Asian Americans. Chin's murder was just the most galling of a number of crimes, and spurred a protest movement that cut across lines of ethnicity to help forge a racial consciousness among Asian Americans.

Vincent came to the United States as a child; his parents were from Guangdong Province in China. He originally intended to study architecture, but had a change of heart when he thought he might not be able to get a steady job in the field. Instead he studied computer operations at a technical school, and found work as an engineer. On the weekends, he worked as a waiter to earn extra money. He and his fiancée, Vikki Wong, planned to marry in June 1982, which is what brought Vincent and two friends to a strip club in June 1982.

Two white patrons in the bar were upset at the attention that Vincent was receiving from one of the dancers, and they taunted Chin, calling him "Chink" and "Nip," and informing him that "it's because of [expletive] like you that we're out of work." Chin confronted the men, and a scuffle ensued. Chin and his friends left the bar and were pursued by Ronald Ebens and Michael Nitz. Ebens was superintendant at a Chrysler plant, and Nitz was unemployed. After retrieving a Louisville Slugger baseball bat from the trunk of their car, Nitz pinned Chin to the ground and Ebens struck him repeatedly with the bat. Chin died four days later as the result of his injuries. As horrifying as the event was, the trial was worse. Ebens and Nitz each received probation, and were ordered to pay a $3,000 fine and court costs. At the sentencing, Judge Charles Kaufman proclaimed, "these aren't the kind of men you send to jail . . . We're talking here about a man who's held down a responsible job for 17 or 18 years, and his son is employed and is a part-time student. You don't make the punishment fit the crime, you make the punishment fit the criminal."

COMMUNITY RESPONSE

The response by Detroit's Asian-American community to this gross miscarriage of justice was immediate. In March 1983, just after Ebens and Nitz received their sentences, a group of Asian Americans representing a wide spectrum of that community began to meet to address the rising tide of anti-Asian-American sentiment and to fight for Asian civil rights. The organization took the name American Citizens for Justice (ACJ). One of its founders, the Chinese-American labor activist and journalist Helen Zia, remembered the diverse crowd at the meeting: there were "liberals and conservatives, youths and seniors, scientists, businessmen, Chinese, Japanese, Filipinos and Koreans, Christians and Buddhists, Cantonese- and Mandarin-speakers, American-born and immigrants—all of us put aside the differences that kept us apart and agreed that night to form a new organization to protect our rights."

ACJ began to press immediately for another trial based on violations of Vincent Chin's civil rights. Many outside the Asian-American community were skeptical that civil rights laws could even be applied to Asian Americans. Combining noisy pickets with calls to launch a federal investigation, the ACJ and allied groups pressured the federal government to indict Ebens and Nitz on civil rights charges. Though this effort failed, a civil suit against the men resulted in Ebens being held liable for Chin's death, and he was ordered to pay $1.5 million. He never paid the money, and disappeared.

Documenting the Aftermath of Vincent Chin's Murder

King Fong Yu, also known as Lily Chin, penned this letter to the Chinese Welfare Council of Detroit to get support for continuing prosecution of her son's killers.

I, King Fong Yu (the wife of Bing Heng Chin), grieve for my son, Vincent Chin, who was brutally beaten to death by two assailants with a baseball bat. The two killers were apprehended by police and prosecuted in court. During the court proceedings, I, because I am widowed and poor, with no money in my bed, could not retain legal counsel to press the case for my deceased son. As a result, the murderers' attorneys had the say. Yesterday, I read in the newspaper, the sentence was only a fine and probation; and the killers were set free. There was also no compensation for the victim's family. This is injustice to a terrible extreme. My son's blood had been shed; how unjust could this be? I grieve in my heart and shed tears of blood. Yes, my son cannot be brought back—and I can only wait for death. It is just that my deceased son, Vincent Chin, was a member of your council. I therefore plead to you to please help me. Please let the Chinese American community know about this case so they can help me raise funds to hire legal counsel for an appeal. You must help put the killers in prison so my son's soul may rest and my grief be vindicated. This old woman will be forever grateful.

In addition to the activism that crossed lines in the Asian-American community after Chin's death, some tentative steps toward interracial alliance building were taken as well. The following is excerpted from the National Association for the Advancement of Colored People (NAACP) Detroit chapter's statement on the Chin case.

WHEREAS the Detroit Branch of the NAACP has fought for civil rights and justice for all minorities; and

WHEREAS the Detroit Branch of the NAACP is aware of the brutal and senseless death of Chinese-American Vincent Chin; and

WHEREAS Judge Charles Kaufman has sentenced those responsible for Vincent Chin's death to probation; and

WHEREAS a probationary sentence for the brutal killing of any human being is reprehensible; NOW, THEREFORE, BE IT RESOLVED that the Detroit Branch of the NAACP deplores the probationary sentence pronounced by Judge Charles Kaufman for the killers of Vincent Chin and supports all efforts to have said sentence rescinded and a new sentence rendered mandating appropriate incarceration. . ..

One of the long-term effects of the Vincent Chin murder was the unity it brought about among disparate communities of Asian Americans. To anti-Asian American mobs or individuals, it did not matter so much whether one was Vietnamese, Chinese, or Japanese. Though some whites had conflated all Americans of Asian descent into one category, and ascribed extremely negative characteristics to them, Asian Americans themselves could find strength in numbers, and use the lessons learned in the protests over Chin's killing to forge a positive, Asian-American racial identity.

Anti-Asian and anti-Asian-American sentiment ran rampant in the 1980s, and was not limited to the kind of violent bigotry exhibited in Detroit. Throughout the United States, a wave of hate crimes was unleashed against Asian Americans. In a reprise of the "yellow peril" hysteria of the late-19th and early-20th century, non-Asian Americans began to fear a takeover of American industry and real estate by faceless Asian hordes. When the Japanese corporation Mitsubishi bought a stake in Rockefeller Center in New York City in 1989, protests poured in, comparing the purchase to the attack on Pearl Harbor. While commentators fumed, British investment in the United States was more than double that of Japan, and no public outcry arose over that fact, or the fact that Germany and Italy also had substantial investments in the United States. Other troubling incidents of the 1980s included the violent assaults of a group calling itself the Dotbusters, after the *bindi* worn by some Indian women. In 1987 in Hoboken, New Jersey, a mob beat Navroz Mody to death outside a restaurant, shouting "Hindu, Hindu" at him. American popular culture in the 1970s and 1980s seemed to reinforce these kinds of actions in films like *The Deer Hunter* and *Rambo*, which relied on the basest of Asian stereotypes when it came to Asians.

NEW IMMIGRANTS FROM SOUTHEAST ASIA

During the 1980s, significant changes in the makeup of the Asian-American population that began in the 1960s and 1970s continued to pick up steam. One of the most noticeable changes was the increasing numbers of Laotians, Cambodians, Hmong, Mien, and Vietnamese refugees. Many of these immigrants had sided with the United States during the cold war and the Vietnam War, and had paid a high price in their countries of origin. Many of these immigrants had no choice in the matter; they were forced out by political events. Their migrations were not at all smooth; some of the thousands of boat people were attacked by pirates as they fled political turmoil. By 1985 643,200 Vietnamese were living in the United States. They faced the same kind of hostile response that some native-born white Americans had given to previous generations of immigrants from Asia. Recent immigrants who spoke little or no English entered the job market at the very bottom, if they were fortunate enough to find employment. In 1983 a study of Vietnamese employment patterns found that 19 percent of Vietnamese immigrants had been professional or technical workers before their immigration, but that fewer than 10 percent of them had been able to find similarly well-paying employment in the United States. Hmong and Mien immigrants from Laos left their homeland for similar reasons, and faced similar situations in the United States. Minnesota and California became centers of Hmong settlement in the 1980s. Cambodian immigrants came from an especially traumatized land, and many suffered from post-traumatic stress disorder as a result of their interactions with the murderous regime of Pol Pot.

CONTINUING STEREOTYPES: WHIZ KIDS AND PERPETUAL FOREIGNERS

The 1980s saw another installment of the model minority stereotype, and this latest one focused on the educational achievements of Asian-American children. News magazines lauded the Asian-American Whiz Kids, whose hard-driving parents imbued them with superhuman study skills. According to the myth, their proficiency was especially noticeable in math and science, and less in the humanities.

Asian Americans continued to be perceived as perpetual foreigners in the United States, as a group that was too different to be able to fit in. Native-born Asian Americans were sometimes complimented on their skills in English (the Japanese-American historian Ronald Takaki began his seminal *A Different Mirror* with one such anecdote). Governmental officials were not immune from such blunders. In one story that Senator Spark Matsunaga particularly enjoyed telling, Secretary of State Alexander Haig mistakenly assumed that Matsunaga was part of a visiting Japanese delegation in 1981. Haig asked Matsunaga if he spoke any English, and Matsunaga replied by saying "Yes, Mr. Secretary, I do—and I had the honor of voting for your confirmation the other day."

REPARATIONS FOR WORLD WAR II INTERNMENT

In the Senate, Spark Matsunaga was one of a number of lawmakers who led the fight for reparations for the unconscionable internment of Japanese Americans during World War II. Soon after the Japanese attack on Pearl Harbor, U.S. policymakers, citing national security, placed 110,000 or so Japanese Americans, two-thirds of whom were U.S. citizens, in detention camps away from the Pacific Coast. In 1988 Congress passed and President Ronald Reagan signed the Civil Liberties Act of 1988. In the congressional hearings that led up to the bill's passage, the wounds of internment were reopened in a profound way. Hundreds of internees came forward with their stories, and these stories, sometimes little known even in Asian-American communities, entered the public consciousness. The Civil Liberties Act, sometimes known as the Japanese American Redress Bill, provided $20,000 to each survivor of the camps. In addition the survivors received signed letters of apology from the president. As Ronald Takaki relates, at the signing ceremony,

Korematsu v. United States, Round Two

In 1984 Fred Korematsu again fought his conviction for disobeying exclusion orders, which were announced through posters like these seen in San Francisco in April 1942.

Fred Korematsu was at the center of one of the worst Supreme Court decisions of all time in the 1940s. As a young man, he had resisted Japanese-American internment, and in the 1944 case *Korematsu v. United States,* the Supreme Court determined that the internment of Japanese Americans (or any people suspected of disloyalty) was constitutional. In 1984, though the statute of limitations had passed, Fred Korematsu sued the United States, hoping to vacate his conviction and win a confession of error (referred to here as a writ of *coram nobis*) on the part of the Court. The Court did this, but also left the door open for future detentions.

. . . Fred Korematsu is a native born citizen of the United States. He is of Japanese ancestry. On September 8, 1942 he was convicted in this court of being in a place from which all persons of Japanese ancestry were excluded pursuant to Civilian Exclusion Order No. 34 . . . His conviction was affirmed. Mr. Korematsu now brings this petition for a writ of coram nobis to vacate his conviction on the grounds of governmental misconduct. . . .

It was uncontroverted at the time of conviction that petitioner was loyal to the United States and had no dual allegiance to Japan. He had never left the United States. He was registered for the draft and willing to bear arms for the United States. . . . Korematsu remains on the pages of our legal and political history. As a legal precedent it is now recognized to have very limited application. As historical precedent it stands as a constant caution that in times of war or declared military necessity our institutions must be vigilant in protecting constitutional guarantees. It stands as a caution that in times of distress the shield of military necessity and national security must not be used to protect governmental actions from close scrutiny and accountability . . . In accordance with the foregoing, the petition for a writ of coram nobis is granted.

Reagan remarked that Japanese Americans had remained "utterly loyal" to the United States. He continued: "Indeed, scores of Japanese Americans volunteered for our Armed Forces—many stepping forward in the internment camps themselves. The 442nd Regimental Combat Team, made up entirely of

Japanese Americans, served with immense distinction to defend this nation, their nation. Yet, back at home, the soldiers' families were being denied the very freedom for which so many of the soldiers themselves were laying down their lives."

ACROSS RACIAL LINES AND INTO NATIONAL POLITICS

One of the most striking Supreme Court decisions of the 1980s was the ruling in the *Wards Cove* case. The case arose from the antidiscrimination efforts of Silme and Nemesio Domingo and Gene Viernes. The Domingo brothers and Viernes organized their own union to protest the disgusting, dangerous, and segregated working conditions at Alaska salmon canneries. Though there was a union in place, it appeared to be both corrupt and colluding with management to keep better-paying jobs white, and enforced a labor system reminiscent of an antebellum plantation. The Alaska Cannery Workers Association (ACWA) had been organized in the 1970s. The ACWA immediately began to rile cannery management, but also ran afoul of Filipino gangsters who ran gambling rings in Alaska towns, and depended on their cut of the proceeds. In June 1981 Silme Domingo and Gene Viernes were murdered by shadowy figures with connections to the military regime of Ferdinand Marcos. A civil suit brought damage awards, but Domingo and Viernes's families received very little compensation.

In the late 1970s and early 1980s, two of the first three major antidiscrimination cases were decided in favor of the workers. The *Wards Cove* suit continued to wind its way through courts in the 1980s. The *Wards Cove* plaintiffs were a diverse group of Asian Americans, including Samoan Americans, Japanese Americans, Chinese Americans, and Filipino Americans. The white family that owned the cannery engaged in all sorts of delaying tactics, one of which was to argue that the case should not be heard because one of the plaintiffs (Gene Viernes) was dead. The plaintiffs alleged systemic discrimination. The suit was originally filed in 1973, and was finally decided in favor of the cannery, and against the workers. The defeat led directly to a push for a new civil rights bill that would restore some of the balance destroyed by the Supreme Court in *Wards Cove*. The Civil Rights Act of 1991 did just that, but political maneuvering added an amendment that exempted any suit filed before 1975, and initially ruled upon after 1983. *Wards Cove* was the only case that fit this description. In the words of Helen Zia, "the only case in the nation that would not be covered by the new law was the very case that inspired it." Oddly when the bill went up for a final vote, a drafting error omitted the offensive amendment, so senators had to vote again. The delay allowed activists to mass support to end the exemption. The National Asian Pacific American Bar Association, the Organization of Chinese Americans, and the Japanese American Citizens League lobbied key senators and representatives, but failed to end the exemption. Subsequent efforts stalled

Wards Cove

The 1980s saw the U.S. Supreme Court shift decidedly to the right. In 1989 the Court ruled on *Wards Cove Packing Company, Inc.*, et al. *v. Atonio et al.* The case arose from a labor dispute at an Alaska cannery. At Wards Cove, the dirtiest and lowest paying jobs were performed almost exclusively by Native Alaskans and Filipino Americans, while the cleaner white-collar jobs appeared to be reserved for whites only. The split Supreme Court decision, and the dissent, are excerpted below. *Wards Cove* made it extremely difficult to prove discrimination, and placed the burden of proof on the workers.

Jobs at the canneries are of two general types: "cannery jobs" on the cannery line, which are unskilled positions; and "noncannery jobs," which fall into a variety of classifications. Most noncannery jobs are classified as skilled positions. Cannery jobs are filled predominantly by nonwhites: Filipinos and Alaska Natives.

. . . In 1974, respondents . . . alleged that a variety of petitioners hiring/ promotion practices—e.g. nepotism, a rehire preference, a lack of objective hiring criteria, separate hiring channels, a practice of not promoting from within—were responsible for the racial stratification of the work force. . . .

. . . As a general matter, a plaintiff must demonstrate that it is the application of a specific or particular employment practice that has created the disparate impact under attack.

. . . The persuasion burden here must remain with the plaintiff, for it is he who must prove that it was "because of such individual's race, color," etc., that he was denied a desired employment opportunity. . . .

Excerpts from the dissent:

. . . The harshness of these results is well demonstrated by the facts of this case. The salmon industry as described by this record takes us back to a kind of overt and institutionalized discrimination we have not dealt with in years: a total residential and work environment organized on principles of racial stratification and segregation, which, as Justice Stevens points out, resembles a plantation economy. This industry long has been characterized by a taste for discrimination of the old-fashioned sort: a preference for hiring nonwhites to fill its lowest level positions, on the condition that they stay there. The majority's legal rulings essentially immunize these practices from attack under a Title VII disparate-impact analysis.

Sadly, this comes as no surprise. One wonders whether the majority still believes that race discrimination—or, more accurately, race discrimination against nonwhites—is a problem in our society, or even remembers that it ever was . . .

(Note: Title VII refers to a section of the Civil Rights Act of 1964).

throughout the 1990s, but in 2009, the Justice for Wards Cove Workers Act was again in committee, and a Democratic president and Congress were more likely to look favorably on such a measure. Though the last-minute lobbying did not succeed, it led to a renaissance of Asian-American politics at the national level, and turned Asian Americans into a force to be reckoned with in Washington, D.C.

SPORTS FIGURES, ARTISTS, AND WRITERS

Asian Americans were more visible in U.S. culture in the 1980s than they had been in prior decades. On television and at the movies, Asian Americans continued to be stereotyped in damaging, negative ways. The increasing political clout of Asian Americans and the rising race consciousness described in this chapter combined to force more complicated, authentic Asian voices into the cultural mainstream of the United States. The achievements of individual Asian Americans such as Maya Lin, Yo-Yo Ma, and Amy Tan demonstrate the arrival of Asian Americans on the American cultural scene in the 1980s. In 1989 young tennis phenomenon Michael Chang, a Chinese American, won the French Open, defeating Ivan Lendl. Chang dedicated his victory to the students protesting China's repressive regime in Tiananmen Square. Some sports journalists chalked Chang's victory up to his "vicious Oriental mind," and referred jokingly to Chang's Asian features.

Maya Lin was born in Ohio in 1959, the daughter of a poet and literature professor at Ohio University, and a ceramicist. Lin garnered national attention when her design was selected from nearly 4,300 submissions for the Vietnam War Memorial on the National Mall in Washington, D.C., in 1981. The design, and Lin's heritage, sparked protests. Some critics thought the design veered too sharply from the monumental style of the other memorials on the mall. Arguments about the memorial's design sometimes seemed to parallel arguments about the morality of the war, or its legacy. Lin was also criticized for being an Asian American. Business leader Ross Perot, one of the sponsors of the project and spokes-

Chinese-American tennis champion Michael Chang at a match in August 1994.

Maya Lin Interview

Maya Lin, a Chinese American from Ohio, first came to national attention as an undergraduate at Yale when she won the international competition to design the Vietnam War Memorial in Washington, D.C. Her victory was not without controversy, largely because of her Asian heritage. She gave the interview excerpted below in Scottsdale, Arizona, in 2000.

What was your childhood like, growing up in a small town in Ohio as the daughter of Chinese immigrants?
It's funny, as you live through something you're not aware of it. It's only in hindsight that you realize what indeed your childhood was really like. Growing up, I thought I was white. It didn't occur to me that I wasn't white. It probably didn't occur to me I was Asian-American until I was studying abroad in Denmark actually and there was a little bit of prejudice—racial discrimination—because as I get a suntan I look like a Greenlander. And as the U.S. had a certain prejudice against Native Americans, the Danes had a similar read towards the Greenlanders, and all of a sudden they would be moving away from me on the bus. They wouldn't sit next to me. There would be these weird comments.

How much of your family's history were you aware of?
Not much. I think it happened with the first generation of a certain era. If you talk to Asian Americans now, they're probably brought up bilingual. Back then, our parents decided not to teach us Chinese. Now they'll say that we weren't interested, but I think part of it was they wanted us to fit in. It was an era when they felt we would be better off if we didn't have that complication. Ten years later, it had already switched. Now you want both cultures when you're very young. I think 30 years ago, it was more like, "Oh, let's make you comfortable in your new climate."

Were you more preoccupied with trying to be American?
I think I wanted to fit in. I didn't want to be different. I probably spent the first 20 years of my life wanting to be as American as possible. Through my 20s, and into my 30s, I began to become aware of how so much of my art, and architecture, has a decidedly Eastern character. I think it's only in the last decade that I've really understood how much I am a balance and a mix. There's a struggle at times. I left science, then I went into art, but I approach things very analytically. There's the fact that I choose to pursue both art and architecture as completely separate fields rather than merging them. I sometimes think the making of architecture is antithetical to the making of art. Then there's the East/West split. I think a lot of it is a struggle because I come from two heritages.

The dedication of the Vietnam Veterans Memorial, which was designed by Maya Lin, took place on November 13, 1982, and included this assembly of color guards from different branches of service.

person for a veterans' group, referred to Lin as an "eggroll," an anti-Asian epithet. Some non-Asian Americans were upset that an Asian-American woman had been chosen to memorialize one of the United States's Asian wars. Even after weathering the controversy and building the monument, the dedication ceremony made no mention of the artist whose work was on display. However the success of her work speaks for itself. To visit Washington, D.C., today and not pause to reflect at the stark granite wall that slices into the ground is to miss one of the most moving experiences in the national capital. The wall has promoted debate, discussion, and remembrance of one of America's most controversial wars. Following her triumph in Washington, D.C., Lin went on to a distinguished career as a sculptor and designer of memorials. Another particularly well-received Lin work graces the Civil Rights Memorial in Alabama.

Yo-Yo Ma, who had matured into one of most highly regarded classical musicians in the world, earned a series of awards beginning in the 1980s, including a string of 15 Grammys. He won in 1985 for *Bach: Unaccompanied Cello Suites,* and in 1986 and 1987 for ensemble performance, of Bach and Beethoven. Yo-Yo Ma's tastes and skills range beyond classical music, and he has recorded and performed with pop and bluegrass stars as well. His cosmopolitan outlook has brought him into contact with music and musicians

Yo-Yo Ma, who won a string of 15 Grammy Awards beginning in the 1980s, is shown here performing at the World Economic Forum in Davos, Switzerland, on January 25, 2008.

from around the world, and the United Nations named him a Messenger of Peace in 2002.

Chinese-American author Amy Tan also continued to achieve career milestones in the 1980s. Tan's life changed forever when her mother fell ill. After her mother's recovery, Tan traveled with her to China in 1987 to visit one of her siblings who had been left behind when the family fled. The trip proved revelatory, and inspired Tan to write *The Joy Luck Club* in 1987. The book follows the stories of four Chinese families in the United States, and revolves around mother/daughter relationships and the relationship between East and West, or China and America. The book is fictionalized, but it does contain deep insights into the relationship between Tan and her mother. *The Joy Luck Club* resonated deeply in the United States, as a story of immigrant experiences, a tale of moving between two worlds, and a powerful evocation of the relationship between all mothers and daughters. First published in 1989, the book was a major achievement. For eight months, it appeared on the *New York Times* best seller list, and it eventually spawned a film (for which Tan wrote the screenplay). Tan's fiction in the 1990s and 2000s continued to mine many of these same themes.

CONCLUSION

Asian Americans faced continuing struggles and discrimination throughout the 1980s. Asian Americans also continued to define themselves as a race within the United States, despite their diverse origins and histories. Doing so provided one means of strength during hard times. It did not preclude forging alliances with other people of color and immigrants in the United States, though such developments were limited in scope in the 1980s.

MATTHEW JENNINGS
MACON STATE COLLEGE

Further Reading

Alba, Richard, and Victor Nee. *Remaking the American Mainstream: Assimilation and Contemporary Immigration.* Cambridge, MA: Harvard University Press, 2003.

"Amy Tan Biography," *Women of Achievement.* Available online, URL: http://www.achievement.org/autodoc/page/tan0bio-1. Accessed July 2009.

Chen, Jack. *The Chinese of America.* San Francisco, CA: Harper & Row, 1980.

Daley, William, and Sandra Stotsky, ed. *The Chinese Americans.* New York: Chelsea House, 1996.

Daniels, Roger. *Asian America: Chinese and Japanese in the United States since 1850.* Seattle, WA: University of Washington Press, 1990.

Do, Hien Duc. *The Vietnamese Americans.* Westport, CT: Greenwood Press, 1999.

Fuchs, Lawrence H. *The American Kaleidoscope: Race, Ethnicity, and Civic Culture.* Hanover, NH: Wesleyan University Press, 1990.

Kitano, Harry H.L. *Japanese Americans: The Evolution of a Subculture.* Ethnic Groups in American Life Series. Englewood Cliffs, NJ: Prentice-Hall, 1969.

"Maya Lin Interview," *Women of Achievement.* Available online, URL: http://www.achievement.org/autodoc/page/lin0int-1. Accessed July 2009.

Odo, Franklin, ed. *The Columbia Documentary History of the Asian American Experience.* New York: Columbia University Press, 2002.

Spickard, Paul R. *Japanese Americans: The Formation and Transformations of an Ethnic Group.* New York: Twayne Publishers, 1996.

Takaki, Ronald. *A Different Mirror: A History of Multicultural America.* Boston, MA: Little, Brown, 1993.

———. *Strangers from a Different Shore: A History of Asian Americans.* New York: Penguin Books, 1989.

Tong, Benson. *The Chinese Americans.* The New Americans Series. Westport, CT: Greenwood Press, 2000.

White-Parks, Annette, et al., eds. *A Gathering of Voices on the Asian American Experience.* Fort Atkinson, WI: Highsmith Press, 1994.

Wu, Frank H. *Yellow: Race in America Beyond Black and White*. New York: Basic Books, 2002.

Yung, Judy, et al., eds. *Chinese American Voices: From the Gold Rush to the Present*. Berkeley, CA: University of California Press, 2006.

Zia, Helen. *Asian American Dreams: The Emergence of an American People*. New York: Farrar, Straus & Giroux, 2000.

CHAPTER 10

Asian Americans Today: 1990 to the Present

THE 1980S BROUGHT a boom in the Asian-American population, and a greater acceptance of Asians developed in the American cultural landscape into the 1990s. This included increased participation of Asian Americans in vital areas of American industry and business, such as in science and technology, finance, and government. More Asian names appeared not just in news journals and periodicals particular to Asians, but also in technical journals, academic studies, books, and web sites. Asian Americans were fast becoming a common sight in U.S. neighborhoods. At 7.3 million in the early part of the 1990s, Asian Americans constituted over three percent of the total U.S. population. This was the result of a doubling of their number in the 1980s, attributed to the influx of refugees and immigrants in that decade. According to the U.S. Census Bureau's findings in 1991, the largest subgroup was Chinese, which equaled 22.6 percent of the total Asian-American population. The next largest was Filipino, at 19 percent. Japanese, Indians, and Koreans followed with around 11 percent each. Vietnamese came next with 8.6 percent, followed by very small numbers of Laotians, Thai, and Hmong. Foreign-born Asian Americans numbered 4.5 million, compared to 2.3 million born in the country, showing that immigration was the biggest source of Asian-American citizens.

Since the 1990s, even more Asians have moved to the United States. The early years of the 21st century were a time of renewed immigration in the

Newer groups of Asian immigrants include Laotians, Thai, and Hmong peoples. This Thai-American man, who was born in the United States to immigrant parents, is a member of the U.S. Air Force, and is pictured working at Ramstein Air Base, Germany, in April 2006.

United States, with most subgroups significantly increasing in number. Between 1990 and 2000, the Asian-American population increased by five million. According to the U.S. Bureau of the Census, in 2000, Asian Americans comprised 3.6 percent of the population, a total of 11.9 million people. Another 1.7 million individuals identified themselves as part Asian American. By the beginning of the 21st century, two-thirds of all Asian Americans had been born in foreign countries. The historical pattern of clustering in Western states continued, but new Asian immigrants also settled in other parts of the country. In 2009 Asian Americans made up 9.3 percent of the population in the west, 4.4 percent in the northeast, 2.3 percent in the south, and 2.2 percent in the Midwest. In spite of their relatively small numbers, the Asian-American impact on U.S. society is strong, especially with media visibility and their increasing participation in politics.

The Asian-American community is composed of more than 23 racial and ethnic groups, each with its own distinct culture. Newer immigrant groups come from Bangladesh, Vietnam, Cambodia, Laos, Taiwan, Hong Kong, Pakistan, and Indonesia. By 2000 the Chinese-American population had grown to 2,314,537. The Chinese, at 22.6 percent of the total Asian-American population, remained the largest subgroup of Asian Americans. Of the 25,859 Japanese immigrants who arrived 2000–02, more than half came as spous-

The Case of Wen Ho Lee

In 1998 Wen Ho Lee was a Taiwan-born American employed at the Los Alamos National Laboratory, known as the place where the atomic bomb was developed. The laboratory at the time was operated under U.S. government oversight. In December 1998 Lee was suddenly arrested and indicted a year later for being a spy of the Chinese government. This event raised a rash of protests in the Asian-American community, which was shocked that one of their own serving the country had been singled out as a traitor. A story had appeared in the *New York Times* in March 1998—an article about Asian spies lurking in the country for secrets to atomic weapons. The *Times* article was inaccurate, but it was sensational and alarming enough to cause the government to embark on a hunt that led to Lee.

Among the things that the investigation uncovered was that during a meeting in the 1980s, Lee was asked by some scientists in China to help develop nuclear missiles. He refused, but he admitted to failing to report the incident immediately. The only other suspicious findings in the investigation were his unauthorized transfer of some classified information to other computers in the office. The files were then accessed by a student from the University of California at Los Angeles (UCLA), but the student could not be identified.

The prize at stake was the design secrets of the W-88 nuclear warhead, which was developed at Los Alamos. The government prosecutors alleged that Lee gave plans of the W-88 nuclear warhead to China. However no proof of this was presented. It was also argued that most of the information on the W-88 warhead was actually classified as restricted, rather than top secret, and some was already available to the public. When the information reached then Secretary of Energy Bill Richardson, he fired Lee from his post at Los Alamos. Upon arrest, Lee was held in solitary confinement for nine months, and his every move was monitored. He was made to undergo polygraph tests. The first one he passed, but the succeeding three tests were failures.

The media also joined in castigating Lee. His name was leaked to the public, and several major newspapers, including the *New York Times*, released articles decrying Lee as a traitor to the country. Richardson reported the investigation of Lee to Congress, although he was criticized for not having done so earlier.

Of the 59 counts against Lee, 58 were dropped, and the one regarding mishandling of information was settled with a plea bargain. He was released in September 2000, and Judge James A. Parker apologized to him for the government, calling the government's handling of him shameful. In June 2006 Lee won $1.6 million in damages and reparations from the U.S. government and media companies involved. In 2009 he had retired, and was living in Albuquerque, New Mexico.

es of American citizens. In 2000 there were more than 1,850,314 Filipino Americans living in the United States, and an estimated 2,385,120 Americans with some Filipino ancestry, making Filipino Americans the second-largest group of Asian Americans. In the 1990s, Korean immigration rose significantly with 311,733 Korean immigrants entering the United States 1990–2000. Most were middle class, settling in California, New York, and New Jersey.

IMMIGRATION LAW
There was a new upheaval of immigration law in 1990 in response to increased levels of immigration, resulting in strict control of admission into and removal from the United States. The chief criterion of the new law was to determine which immigrants could contribute to the United States, both economically and socially. The law also provided for the admission of 195,000 foreign temporary workers into the United States each year. Between 1990 and 1994, Asian immigration, except for South Korean immigration, reached its peak. Many Asian engineering and science students chose to establish permanent residency. In all, around 8.3 million Asians became permanent U.S. residents 1965–2002.

By 1996 the government had established strict guidelines concerning the eligibility of immigrants for social services. Over the next four years, the government further restricted immigration by placing even greater emphasis on allowing into the country only those immigrants who could demonstrate possession of skills already in demand in the United States. After the terrorist attacks of September 11, 2001, the U.S. government forcibly removed over 3,000 Asian immigrants, including 492 from China, 457 from the Philippines, 375 from India, 375 from Pakistan, 263 from Korea, and 222 from Indonesia who had been in the United States illegally.

SETTLEMENT PATTERNS
When the Immigration Act of 1965 created new immigration opportunities, people of all nationalities flocked to the United States. Some 220,000 Asian Americans came to the United States 1965–2000. Large numbers came to New York, where the Asian-American community included immigrants from China, Japan, the Philippines, Korea, India, Vietnam, Pakistan, Bangladesh, Cambodia, and Laos. Asian Americans of all nationalities began moving into old Chinatowns. Japanese Americans were less likely than other Asian Americans to live in ethnic enclaves. Only three such enclaves remained by the 21st century, and those were found in California and Hawaii. There are major Filipino settlement centers in Southern California, northern California, New York City, Chicago, Seattle, and Honolulu. In Long Beach, California, Santa Fe Avenue between 20th and Spring Streets has been officially recognized as a Filipino enclave. Despite these concentrations, Filipino

Americans are sometimes called the "invisible ethnic community" because they tend to assimilate into American life. Many Filipino Americans live in small towns. This population has been on the rise, however, in Chicago and New York City. Like the Japanese, Filipino Americans have a history of marrying outside their own community.

Recent immigrants to the United States from the Caribbean, Latin America, and Asia are much more likely than earlier immigrants to live in multiracial and multiethnic neighborhoods. In part because of comparatively high economic and educational levels, Asian Americans are more likely than other minorities to live in middle-class suburbia. Some 54.6 percent of Asian Americans live in the suburbs, compared to 32 percent of whites, 49.6 percent of Hispanics, and 38.8 percent of blacks. Historically Asian immigrants have settled in California, New York, and Texas; but in recent years, large numbers of Asian Americans have moved into the Sun Belt. According to the 2000 census, 71.2 percent of Asian Americans live in eight states: California, 36.1 percent; New York, 11 percent; Texas, 5.5 percent; Hawaii, 4.9 percent; New Jersey, 4.7 percent; Illinois, 4.1 percent; Washington, 3.1 percent; and Virginia, 2.6 percent.

ETHNIC ENCLAVES

The Los Angeles/Riverside/Orange County area of California, which is the largest Asian-American center in the United States, is home to 1.7 million Asian Americans. The area is dotted with Buddhist and Hindu temples. Koreatown in Los Angeles has become so well established that it is marked on highway exits. In Orange County, Indochinese refugees have established enclaves in Santa Ana, Garden Grove, and Westminster.

The second-largest Asian-American center is found in the New York/New Jersey/Long Island area. Within New York City, large Asian-American populations live in Woodside, Elmhurst, Jackson Heights, and Flushing. Significant Asian-American populations are also found in Nassau, Suffolk, Westchester, and Bergen counties in New York State. The city of Flushing in the Queens borough of New York is an excellent example of how the growth of Asian-American communities has changed U.S. demographics. In 1965 Flushing was a middle-class neighborhood, and 95 percent of its residents were white. By the late-20th century, Flushing had become a magnet for immigrants of all nationalities, and Asian Americans made up the majority of the population. By 2000 many signs on Flushing's Main Street were written in Chinese. Hundreds of stores on Union Street were owned by immigrant proprietors, many of them Korean Americans who established a Korean enclave in the area. The presence of the Asian-American community has had a strong influence on the culture of the entire area. At Lincoln Center, Asian dance, music, and cultural performances are regularly performed. Roughly half of the student body at Stuyvesant and Bronx Science High School in New York City is Asian American.

Chinese businesses in Sunset Park, Brooklyn, in 2007. Many of the neighborhood's recent immigrants work in retail.

Traditionally the Chinese have been more likely than any other group to live in ethnic enclaves. Sunset Park in Brooklyn, New York, has the third-largest concentration of Chinese Americans in New York State, outranked only by Manhattan and Flushing. In 1980 there were 5,211 Asian Americans living in Sunset Park. Over the next two decades, that number rose to 35,628. The average age of these immigrants is 34. Most adults are married, and they were employed before they immigrated to the United States. Most Sunset Park immigrants cluster in retail (28 percent), manufacturing (25 percent), and services (20 percent). The poverty rate among these immigrants is 19 percent, compared to 32 percent for Hispanic Americans and 18 percent for whites. For foreign-born Asian Americans, however, the poverty rate is 85 percent. Of the Chinese who live in Sunset Park, 91 percent are from China, eight percent are from Hong Kong, and one percent are from Taiwan.

The San Francisco/Oakland/San Jose area of California makes up the third-largest Asian-American center in the United States. This center is home to 1.3 million Asian Americans. In San Francisco, Asian Americans comprise almost a third of the total population. The fourth-largest number of Asian Americans in a single area is concentrated in Honolulu. With a population of 400,000, Asian Americans make up 57 percent of Honolulu's population. Despite the heavy concentrations in certain areas, Asian Americans have also made their homes in many other large cities. More than 40,000 Asian Americans reside in each of the following cities: Atlanta, Georgia; Tampa, Florida; Raleigh/Durham, North Carolina; Portland, Oregon; and Denver, Colorado. Austin, Texas; and Phoenix, Arizona, have also been identified as magnets for Asian Americans, boasting populations of 43,000 and 60,000, respectively. The Washington, D.C., area has also seen significant growth. Between 1990 and 2000, the Asian-American community grew from 202,000 to 400,000.

The growth of the Asian-American community in Las Vegas, Nevada, in recent years has been phenomenal. In 1990 the city's Chinatown covered three city blocks. By 2008 the area had grown to four miles, and was still expanding. Signs in both Chinese and Korean were prominently displayed. Newspapers were available in several Asian languages, and Asian Americans owned banks and real estate companies, in addition to stores and restaurants. The Asia Town Center, located in Las Vegas, covered 15 acres and encompassed 180,000 square feet of retail shopping. The center was touted as the largest Asian shopping center in the American southwest.

DEMOGRAPHICS

The makeup of the Asian-American community has been steadily changing since 1965. In 1990 34 percent of Asian Americans were born in the United States. Within a decade, that number had fallen to 31 percent. In 2000 Japanese Americans (60.5 percent) were more likely than Filipino (32.3), Chinese (29.1), Korean (22.3), or Indian (24.6) Americans to have been born in the United States. Outside of the Japanese-American community, the majority of native-born Asian Americans are second-generation children. There are significant differences in the accomplishments of native and foreign-born Asian Americans. The high school completion rate for native-borns is 93 percent, compared to 82 percent for foreign-borns. However the college completion rate for foreign-borns (46 percent) is slightly higher than that of native-borns (45 percent).

While Asian Americans generally have higher median household incomes than the general population, they also have a higher poverty rate. In 2000 the median wage for Asian Americans employed full-time was $72,000 for native-borns and $57,000 for foreign-borns. For whites, the median income was $48,500; for Hispanics, $36,000; and for blacks, $33,300. The poverty rate for individual Asian Americans was 10 percent, compared to six percent for whites.

For families, it was nine percent, compared to 5.2 percent for whites. Asian-American families (73 percent) are more likely to include two parents than either white families (67 percent) or black families (40 percent). The mean family size of Asian-American families is 4.2, compared to 3.5 for whites, and 3.9 for blacks. Fifteen percent of Asian-American families live in multigenerational households, but only 14 percent of black families and 3.5 percent of white families do so.

Asian-American women participate in U.S. society to a great degree, and approximately 70 percent of Asian women are in the labor force, compared to 73.2 percent of white American women. Asian-American men tend to marry Asian women. Among Chinese Americans, 89 percent of males marry Chinese women, and 83 percent of women marry Chinese men. Whenever there is a shortage of brides, Asian-American men look outside the United States for mates. In the 1940s, the Chinese solved the problem with picture brides. The technology of the 21st century has led some Asian Americans to search out internet brides. Unlike earlier Asian-American brides who came to the United States with limited resources, internet brides often have comfortable incomes. Consequently they have the ability to leave if a relationship does not work. Since there are no studies on this phenomenon, evidence for the growing practice of internet matches among Asian Americans is anecdotal.

Japanese Americans are more likely than any other Asian-American group to marry outside the Asian community. In some cases, a female may initiate a search for a groom with particular characteristics. For example one Japanese woman named Mami conducted an internet search for African-American males because she liked hip-hop music; Mami became engaged within two weeks of her arrival in New York.

According to the 2000 census, Asian Americans are likely to be employed in certain fields, including physical science (15.3 percent), life science (14.7 percent), medicine and dentistry (13.6 percent), computer science (13.2 percent), mathematics (11.1 percent), textile machine operation (10.1 percent), engineering (9.9 percent), and architecture (6.9 percent). Asian Americans (34 percent) are also more likely than whites (22 percent) to be employed in white-collar jobs. This is particularly true among native-born Asian Americans—nearly 40 percent identified their jobs as "professional" in the 2000 census. Even though Asian Americans are generally perceived as being engaged in high-status occupations, this is not always true, particularly for recent immigrants who have not entirely mastered the English language. Many of them find jobs waiting tables and washing dishes.

Mee Moua is the first Hmong immigrant to be elected as a state senator. She won a place in the Minnesota state legislature in 2002.

Taiwanese and Indians have exceptionally high levels of education. Japanese, Filipino, and Koreans also generally achieve higher levels of education than the white population. However Vietnamese, Cambodians, Bangladeshi, and Laotians all tend to have lower levels of education than the white population. The high school completion rate for Chinese Americans is only 79 percent, compared to 90 percent

There is wide variety in occupations among Asian Americans. This Vietnamese fisherman is discussing hurricane relief programs with a Federal Emergency Management Agency representative on his 85-foot shrimp boat in Biloxi, Mississippi, on February 6, 2006.

for white Americans. However for those who attend college, the completion rate is considerably higher: 49 percent, compared to 30 percent. These large differences within the Asian-American community create significant class divisions. One of the major reasons that Asian Americans are generally associated with high achievements in both education and employment is that high numbers of Asian Americans are recruited by the U.S. government and by multinational corporations to work in the United States in science and technology-oriented occupations. Asian Americans also receive advanced degrees in certain fields in greater percentages than might be expected from their presence in the total population. In 1995 4.2 percent of all master's degrees were awarded to Asian-American students. Within 10 years, that number had increased to 56 percent. Most of those degrees were in the fields of science, technology, engineering, mathematics, and the health professions.

Among prominent Asian Americans in business and industry are some of the many successful Indians and South Asians in the information technology (IT) industry, such as Anand Lal Shimpi. Shimpi became known as one of the foremost computer hardware reviewers, with his now well-known site Anandtech.com. Shimpi continues to be one of the American IT world's foremost personalities, appearing at conventions, and writing for IT publications.

Kristi Yamaguchi

After Japanese Americans were released from internment camps (1944–46), many continued to feel close bonds with others who had been interned. Carole Doi and Jim Yamaguchi, both of whom had been born in internment camps, married, and had a daughter, Kristi, in 1971. At the age of 21, Kristi Yamaguchi won a gold medal in Ladies Figure Skating in the 1992 Winter Olympics in Albertville, France. She also won two world championships, and a U.S. National Championship. After giving up her amateur status, Yamaguchi won the World Professional Championships four times. She began her skating career by competing in both pairs skating and singles. Her decision to devote her time to singles proved a wise move when she began garnering international attention for both artistry and technical skills.

Usually, winning Olympic gold brings in enormous sums in endorsements and television contracts. However, some advertisers and network executives were reluctant to select Kristi Yamaguchi for such activities because of her Asian name and appearance. She did sign deals with Kellogg's, Ray-Ban, Evian, Campbell's, and Kraft Products. Despite the lack of initial support, Yamaguchi was subsequently featured in the "got milk?" campaign, and won additional endorsements for Hallmark, General Motors, Heinz, and Smart Ones Food. She also continued to win accolades for her skating skills, and her down-to-earth personality. Yamaguchi has an extremely high "Q" rating with the public, proving that the initial reaction to her being an Asian American was unfounded. She has continued to draw large crowds, while appearing with the Stars on Ice tour and in television specials.

In 1996 Yamaguchi was named Skater of the Year by the U.S. Figure Skating Association. Three years later, she was inducted into the World Skating Hall of Fame. In December 2005 she was inducted into the U.S. Olympic Committee's Hall of Fame. During the 2002 Salt Lake City Winter Olympics, she served as the official Goodwill Ambassador and has said that "winning the Olympic title is one of the proudest moments of my life." In 2008 she proved that her talents went beyond figure skating, winning the competition on *Dancing with the Stars*. She was only the second female in the show's history to do so. Now a wife and the mother of two daughters, Yamaguchi continues to work with the children's charity, Always Dream Foundation.

Olympic skater Kristi Yamaguchi in February 2009.

Other Asian-American corporate successes include Andrea Jung of Avon. Jung broke ground in two ways; first, as a member of an ethnic minority, and second, as a woman. Starting out in department stores after her education at Princeton, she worked first for high-end stores like Neiman-Marcus and I. Magnin. Her move to Avon came in 1993 as a consultant, and she became a regular employee some months later. In 1999 she was named Avon's chief executive officer, and she remained in this position in 2009. She is one of the few female CEOs in the U.S. business world.

Jerry Yang, a founder of the search engine Yahoo!, is perhaps the most well-known Asian Americans in business. He was born in Taiwan, and moved with his family to San Francisco at age eight. He claimed to have known only one word, "shoe," when he moved to the United States, but once he learned the language, he was put into an advanced program.

Yang cofounded Yahoo! in April 1994 under its original name, Jerry's Guide to the World Wide Web with colleague David Filo at Stanford University. The success of the search engine they created convinced them of its tremendous business potential, and they postponed their doctoral plans. Yahoo!'s model was based on its collection of information in a web directory, rather than having full-text copies of the web pages with the key words.

GENERATIONAL DIVIDES

Even though there are many similarities in Asian-American groups, there are also great differences. Many of these differences relate to time spent in the United States, English-language proficiency, and country of origin. Such factors influence the socioeconomic status of Asian Americans, as well as cultural orientation. Asian Americans also exhibit a great diversity of religion. Immigrants from Pakistan, Bangladesh, and India are likely to be Hindu, Sikh, or Muslim, while those from China, Korea, and Japan tend to be Buddhist. Each group practices religion in a distinct way, often building churches, temples, and mosques that reflect their particular faiths. Korean Protestants, for instance, have established more than 4,000 churches in the United States.

For decades, widening divides between native-born children and immigrant parents have created major problems in Asian-American families. This is due in great part to the fact that Asian-American parents have trouble understanding what they view as a lack of respect from American children. In 1978 poet Janice Mirikitani wrote in *Breaking Waves* of the chasm that had opened between her and her native-born daughter:

My daughter denies she is like me
her secretive eyes are walls of smoke
and music and telephones,
her pouting ruby lips, her skirts

swaying to salsa, teena marie, the stones,
 her thighs displayed in carnivals of color.
I do not know the contents of her room.
She mirrors my aging.
She is breaking tradition.

Some Asian Americans feel deeply alienated from the Asian-American community, and from the subgroups within it. For instance Asian war brides from Japan, Korea, the Philippines, and Vietnam who have been in the United States for decades often find little in common with recent immigrants from their own countries. Mixed-race Asian Americans may not feel entirely comfortable in any Asian-American community. Another group that may be isolated from the Asian-American community are Asian children who have been adopted by white families. Between 1948 and 2000, approximately 266,000 foreign children were adopted by U.S. citizens. Over 100,000 of those children came from Korea, and 24,005 from China. Others came from Japan, India, and the Philippines.

CULTURAL DIVIDES

There is also a good deal of variation in educational achievement of Asian Americans. Many Asian-American communities place great emphasis on educational and economic achievement. For this reason, large numbers of Asian-American students attend prestigious colleges and universities in the United States. Although Asian Americans make up only 3.6 percent of the total population, Asian-American students comprise more than 35 percent of student populations at the University of California's campuses at Los Angeles, Berkeley, and Irvine. Since the late 1960s, when Asian-American students at San Francisco State College and the University of California, Berkeley became active in winning student rights and making college curricula more inclusive, Asian-American student populations have tended to be politically active whenever they are present in significant numbers. The efforts of politically active Asian-American students have been partially responsible for the rise in multiculturalism. Most institutions of higher learning now offer classes in Asian-American studies, which provide an overview of Asian literature, history, culture, and the social sciences.

Ever since Asian Americans were allowed to become naturalized citizens in the 1940s, many have developed strong loyalties to the United States. Many also maintain close ties to their homelands. The strength of these ties often depends on how long immigrants have been in the United States, whether or not they have close family members still living in the homeland, particular countries of origin, and the country in which Asian Americans became socialized into adulthood. Although most Asian Americans also maintain close ties with members of their own nationality who live in the

United States, they also tend to interact with society as a whole on a more regular basis than do most other minorities.

The label Asian Americans is actually a relatively new concept in the United States—it was a result of changes that took place, along with a new recognition, of the civil rights of various subgroups of U.S. society. Since the 1970s, Asian Americans have pressured the federal government to compile more comprehensive statistics on Asian Americans so as to provide a clearer understanding of the issues that need to be addressed. Before 1990 when compiling census records, the federal government did not allow Asian Americans to indicate the race with which they identified. Since then, Asian Americans who identify themselves as Asian or Pacific Islander may also describe themselves as Chinese, Filipino, Hawaiian, Korean, Vietnamese, Japanese, Asian Indian, Samoan, Guamanian, or "other."

Asian Americans have often been referred to as "strangers in a foreign land." This is partly because of the large numbers of Asian immigrants who have come to the United States to work or to be educated before returning to their homelands. It is also due to distinct physical characteristics shared by many Asian Americans, which make them easy to identify.

Much of the hostility directed toward Asian Americans has come from other minority groups. A 2001 study of attitudes toward Chinese Americans conducted by K.C. Kang revealed that 43 percent of respondents had somewhat negative attitudes, and another 23 percent had very negative attitudes toward Asian Americans. Nearly a third of respondents felt that Asian Americans had too much influence in the fields of science and technology, and almost a fourth resented the fact that Asian Americans were taking jobs away from other Americans. Surprisingly, 28 percent responded that they felt Chinese Americans were more loyal to China than to the United States. A 2007 poll conducted by New America Media found that 46 percent of African American and Hispanic respondents felt that Asian business owners failed to treat them with respect. Asian Americans also held negative views of other minorities, associating African Americans with high crime rates, and relating Hispanic Americans to limited employment opportunities for other Americans. Respondents from all three groups expressed more trust for white Americans than for other minority groups.

HATE CRIMES

Since the 1990s, there has been a resurgence of hate crimes against Asian Americans, without consideration of birth or citizenship status. During the Los Angeles riots of 1992, which broke out after a jury exonerated police officers who had beaten African American Rodney King mercilessly, more than 3,000 Asian-owned stores were intentionally damaged by rioters. In New Jersey, organized hate groups such as Dotbusters and Edison Boys have targeted Southeast Asian Americans. In Massachusetts and Illinois, the targets have been Vietnamese and Cambodian refugees. In New York City and Los Angeles, violence has been committed against Korean-American store owners. Outrage against Japanese Americans as a result of the United States' trade war with Japan has resulted in increased incidences of "Japan bashing."

The Hate Crimes Statistics Act (28 USC 534) was passed in 1990. It mandated that statistics on crimes include the race, gender, religion, and other such background information on both the victim and the offender. Signed into law by President George H.W. Bush, it is also considered the first law to recognize gays and lesbians and identify them as victims of crimes. The Federal Bureau of Investigation provides the statistics to the Department of Justice.

The Hate Crimes Act had as one of its first major statistics a violent crime against a Laotian-American restaurant employee in Yuba City, California. As he was about to take two of his white female coworkers home, he was attacked by two white suspects using a hammer as a weapon. Although the employee survived, the suspects were never identified.

One of the more sensational crimes was the gang-related killing of five men in Boston's Chinatown in January 1991. Three men—identified as Siny Van Tran, Nam The Tham, and Hung Tien Pham—entered a gambling establishment, specifically rounded up six Vietnamese men, and summarily shot them in the head. Only one survived.

Aside from Asian Americans sometimes targeted in crimes, other acts of hate have been committed without taking lives, but are equally threatening. In 1992 the Japanese American Citizens League received 15 hate letters denouncing Japanese Americans in the United States, purportedly in connection with redress payments being made because of the 1988 act. The reparations were instituted to pay for the mistreatment of interned Japanese Americans during World War II. In 1993 the League's office in Sacramento, California, was firebombed. No one was injured or killed, but the cost of damage was $20,000.

The National Asian Pacific American Legal Consortium (NAPALC) in 1994 reported 63 incidents of Asian American–directed violent crimes; these rose to 113 incidents in 1995, and then to 188 incidents in 1996. The total number of confirmed and suspected anti-Asian hate crimes was 458 in 1995, and 534 in 1996.

SOCIAL AND POLITICAL MILESTONES

Probably one of the first major milestones for Asian-American culture in the 1990s was the proclamation of May as Asian Pacific American Heritage Month, creating an awareness and acknowledgment of Asian Americans and Pacific Islanders in the country. This initiative for this celebration started in June 1977, when Representatives Frank Horton of New York and Norman Y. Mineta of California filed a House resolution asking for the first 10 days of May to be devoted to celebrating Asian and Pacific culture.

A month later, Senators Daniel Inouye and Spark Matsunaga filed a bill with a similar thrust. Both bills were passed, and President Jimmy Carter in 1978 signed a Joint Resolution that officially established the celebration. President George H.W. Bush expanded this concept, and made it a month-long commemoration.

The celebration month is marked by community festivals, government-sponsored activities, and educational activities. In 1991 Bush signed the proclamation into law.

Another milestone in recognition of Asian Americans is the incorporation of NAPALC in 1991. It is an organization for the advancement of Asian Americans in legal matters; activities include promoting laws that support Asian Americans, and providing legal assistance and information. NAPALC is known today as the Asian American Justice Center (AAJA).

Senator Daniel Akaka of Hawaii, who is of both native Hawaiian and Chinese descent, won Spark Matsunaga's seat in the Senate after his death.

In 1993 a historical issue involving the state of Hawaii was resolved in the state's favor. It has long been recognized that the U.S. government overthrew the Hawaiian monarchy in the 1890s, paving the way for Hawaii's later inclusion in the United States. Some American businessman during the time of Hawaii's monarchy made up the story that the Hawaiians were about to become violent toward U.S. nationals. It prompted the annexation of the islands after the overthrow of Queen Liliuokalani. In 1993 the U.S. government apologized for the overthrow—the first apology the country made for taking over another country.

In 1996 Gary Locke of Washington was elected the first Asian-American governor of a U.S. state. He is a third-generation Chinese American. He served as governor until 2005. In 2009 Locke joined the Obama administration as secretary of commerce. Another Asian American in a significant government position was Bill Hann Lee, a second-generation Chinese American from New York. After a long career as a civil rights attorney, he was appointed assistant attorney general for civil rights in 1997.

In the military, the first Asian American to serve as a high-ranking staff official was Eric Shinseki, a Japanese American hailing from Kauai, Hawaii. He was a Vietnam War veteran, specializing in artillery and tanks, and he had been wounded to the point of near-death. He became the 34th Chief of Staff of the U.S. Army in 1999 and retired in 2003 and later served as President Barack Obama's Secretary of Veterans Affairs.

ENTERTAINMENT AND THE ARTS

Perhaps in no other field was the increasing Asian presence felt more in the United States than in the entertainment industry. Asians had been featured prominently in popular representations in the stereotypes of the evil oriental (in the guise of Fu Manchu) and the kung fu martial artist. Breaking these race stereotypes was one of the challenges Asian Americans faced in the entertainment world, which depended on such stereotypes to produce marketable material.

In 1991 a Broadway presentation with an Asian-centered theme opened to a wave of accolades—and protest. *Miss Saigon*, which featured Filipina singer Lea Salonga, drew protests outside the theater because a local Asian American had not been chosen for the role. However the show received rave reviews and was an instant hit, with Salonga receiving praise for her performance.

One of the groundbreaking Asian Americans in entertainment was Margaret Cho, a professional stand-up comedian and actress who starred in the first-ever TV series focused on Asian-American issues, the ironically named *All American Girl*, in 1994. A Korean American born and raised in San Francisco, she had been searching for a serious acting career, but found her place in comedy. *All American Girl* ran for one year, but was cancelled due to low ratings. Cho won the American Comedy Award for Best Female Comedian in 1994.

The movie industry also saw various Asian-American actors and actresses perform, such as Lucy Liu. She began in 1998 as Ling Woo in the TV series *Ally McBeal*, and later gained fame in *Shanghai Noon, Charlie's Angels,* and *Kill Bill*. In 1997 *The Hulk*, directed by Ang Lee, was released. Lee, a Taiwanese American, would prove to be one of the most versatile directors in the industry, filming everything from action movies to gay romance (*Brokeback Mountain*).

Another Asian director to make his mark in America was John Woo, known for making trademark action films. He started as an employee at Cathay Studios in Hong Kong, and gained more support upon his move to Taiwan in the 1980s. His first American movie was *Hard Target*, starring Jean-Claude Van Damme, in 1993. His most famous movies were *Broken Arrow, Face/Off,* and *Mission Impossible 2*. The 1980s had seen the proliferation of the now-famous GI Joe: A Real American Hero toy franchise by Hasbro. This GI Joe line was mostly written and conceptualized by Larry Hama, a third-generation Japanese American in the comic book business. By the 1990s, GI Joe was an established brand, and Hama had continually written for the series. With the revival of the franchise, he continues to do so in the 21st century.

Television Presence

Before the civil rights movement, Asian Americans were presented only as stereotypes in the American media. Women were seen as geisha types or domestic servants, and men were portrayed in the context of martial arts or the criminal world. In the early years of the 21st century, Asian Americans became a visible presence in a number of popular television shows. There are three Asian Americans in the regular cast of *Lost*, which premiered on ABC in the fall of 2004. Naveen Andrews, who appears as Sayid Jarrah, a former member of the Iraqi Republican Guard trained in interrogation and torture techniques, was actually born in London in 1969, and is of Indian descent. Yunjin Kim, who plays Korean Sun Kwon, was born in South Korea in 1973. Her husband, Jin, is played by South Korean actor Daniel Dae Kim (1968). Sandra Oh, who plays Dr. Cristina Yang on *Gray's Anatomy* (2005), is also of Korean descent. She was born in Ontario, Canada, in 1971.

In 2006 *Heroes* debuted on NBC with a multiethnic cast. Indian American actor Sendhil Ramamurthy, who appears as Dr. Mohinder Suresh and serves as the show's narrator, was born in Chicago in 1974. Japanese-American actor Masi Oka, who plays Hiro Nakamura, has achieved enormous success with both critics and the public. With an IQ of over 180, Oka is a true phenomenon in the entertainment industry. Although he was born in Tokyo in 1974, Oka moved to California at the age of six. In 1987 *Time* magazine identified him as an "Asian American whiz kid." Oka believes his success has produced a more positive image of Asian Americans, noting that people "treat me nicer. They don't say 'Yo, Asian dude.' They say, 'Hi, Masi. We love your show.'"

Another popular Asian-American actor began his career in the 1960s, but continued to be a presence on television in reruns and movies even after his death in 2005. When Pat Morita, who was born in 1932 in California, started as a stand-up comedian, he found that "The idea of a Japanese comedian was not only a rarity, it was non-existent." Morita spent part of his childhood in a World War II internment camp in Arizona. He established a career in film and television, playing Matsuo "Arnold" Takahashi on *Happy Days* (1974–84). However the four *Karate Kid* movies (1984, 1986, 1989, and 1994) made Morita a household name. In 1985 he was nominated for an Academy Award as Best Supporting Actor for his role as Kesuke Miyagi in the first *Karate Kid* film.

In music, perhaps the most iconic Asian-American artist of the decade was Coco Lee. Born in Hong Kong in 1974, she moved to California, where she graduated from the University of California at Irvine. She won the Chinese-America pageant in 1991, and returned to Hong Kong afterward, releasing several albums in her native Mandarin language. Her first English-language album was released in 2000. She was compared to Britney Spears and Christina Aguilera as a frontline diva representing Asia. In the comic book industry, the 1990s saw the founding of Image Comics—and one of its premier artists is Jim Lee. A Korean American, Lee was a staff artist for *Uncanny X-Men*, until his artwork received rave reviews, and he became one of the company's most celebrated artists. While at Image Comics, he founded Wildstorm as an imprint of Image, but later sold it to DC Comics. Another X-Men artist was Filipino American Whilce Portacio, who also joined Image at its founding, but he was mostly associated with Lee's Wildstorm imprint. Adrian Tomine is a fourth-generation Japanese American who draws editorial cartoons for *The New Yorker*; his Optic Nerve series was first released in 1995.

In literature, Amy Tan, who wrote *The Joy Luck Club* in 1989, saw her work made into a 1993 movie. Other notable Asian-American writers were Ha Jin, Jhumpa Lahiri, and Anita Desai. In sports, Kristi Yamaguchi in 1992 became the first Asian American to win an Olympic gold medal in figure skating. In 1998 Michelle Kwan took the limelight in figure skating, gaining the silver in the Nagoya Olympics. Famed golfer Tiger Woods is part-Thai and part-African American. His big break into the sport was in the 1997 Master's Open, which put him onto the world golfers' map.

In areas of entertainment, popular culture, and sports, Asian Americans attempted to break the stereotypes like Fu Manchu and Charlie Chan set in the previous decades, and found some success. However martial arts remain a fixture that is uniquely Asian, and it has influenced American movies like *The Matrix* and *Kill Bill*. These are aspects attached to Asian-American culture because of their unique nature, but in other respects, Asian Americans have come into their own in American culture.

CONCLUSION

Ever since the first immigrants arrived in white-dominated America, they were faced with the choice to assimilate, or not. Asian Americans continued to face this issue in the 1990s and into the 2000s. The issue deals with what one means by assimilation: either blend into America and lose one's ethnic identity, or stubbornly let one's ethnic identity oppose the face of another, more dominant culture. Many Asian Americans have mastered mixing the two. They have blended into the American landscape, and have become part of the country's industry, entertainment, and even government. But they have also retained their ethnic identities, using them to gain support and power. They are notable among the more successful subgroups of Americans, and yet they continue to face challenges related to their race and other issues that come with living in the United States.

CHINO FERNANDEZ
ELIZABETH R. PURDY
INDEPENDENT SCHOLARS

Further Reading

Ameredia. "Asian American Statistics." Available online, URL: http://www.ameredia.com/resources/demographics/asian_american.html. Accessed June 2009.

Fugita, Stephen S., and Marilyn Fernandez. *Altered Lives: Enduring Community: Japanese Americans Remember Their World War II Incarceration.* Seattle: University of Washington Press, 2004.

Jhou, Tom. "Scapegoat of the Century?" Johns Hopkins University. Available online, URL: https://jshare.johnshopkins.edu/tchou7/Wen_Ho_Lee.htm. Accessed June 2009.

Kang, K.C. "Study Finds Persistent Negative Perceptions of Chinese Americans." *Los Angeles Times* (April 25, 2001).

Lott, Juanita Tamayo. *Asian Americans: From Racial Category to Multiple Identities.* Walnut Creek, CA: AltaMira, 1998.

Ma, Sheng-Mei. *The Deathly Embrace.* Minneapolis: University of Minnesota Press, 2000.

Marquez, L. "Asian Americans Called the New 'Sleeping Giant' in California Politics." Asian American Studies Center. Available online, URL: www.aasc.ucla.edu/archives/sleepgiantspr.htm. Accessed May 2009.

Min, Pyong Gap. *Asian Americans: Contemporary Trends and Issues.* Thousand Oaks, CA: Pine Forge Press, 2007.

Mirikitani, Janice. "Breaking Tradition." *Ikon 9, Without Ceremony: A Special Issue by Asian Women United,* v.9 (1988).

Miyars, Ines M., and Christopher A. Airriess, eds. *Contemporary Ethnic Geographies in America.* Lanham, MD: Rowman and Littlefield, 2007.

New American Media. "Deep Divisions: Shared Destiny—A Poll of Black, Hispanic, and Asian Americans on Race Relations." Available online, URL: http://news.newamericamedia.org/news/view_article.html?article_id=28501933d0e5c5344b21f9640dc13754. Accessed June 2009.

Nguyen, Mimi Thi, and Thuy Linh Tu, eds. *Alien Encounters: Popular Culture in Asian America.* Durham, NC: Duke University Press, 2007.

Okihiro, Gary Y. *Margins and Mainstreams: Asians in American History and Culture.* Seattle: University of Washington Press, 1994.

Park, Edward J.W., and John S.W. Park. *Probationary Americans: Contemporary Immigration Policies and the Shaping of Asian American Communities.* New York: Routledge, 2005.

Scheer, Robert. "No Defense." *The Nation,* October 5, 2000. Available online, URL: http://www.thenation.com/doc/20001023/scheer. Accessed June 2009.

Siasoco, Ricco Villanueva. "Origins of APA Heritage Month: A National Celebration Established in 1977." Infoplease. Available online, URL: http://www.infoplease.com/spot/asianintro1.html. Accessed May 2009.

U.S. Census Bureau. 1990 and 2000 Decennial Census. "Asian Americans." History World.org. Available online, URL: http://history-world.org/asian_americans.htm. Accessed May 2009.

Wong, Frieda, and Richard Halgin. "The 'Model Minority': Bane or Blessing?" *Asian American Journal of Multicultural Counseling and Development,* v.34 (January 2006).

Zhou, Min, and James V. Gatewood, eds. *Contemporary Asian Americans: A Multidisciplinary Reader.* New York: New York University Press, 2000.

Zinn, Laura. "To Marketers: Kristi Yamaguchi Isn't as Good as Gold." *Business Week* (March 9, 1992).

ABCs: Abbreviation popular among members of the Chinese-American community that means "American-born Chinese."

accupuncture: Medical procedure originating in China that involves inserting needles into a person's body in order to relieve pain.

Apology Resolution: A joint resolution passed by Congress in 1993 that officially recognized that the overthrow of the Kingdom of Hawaii occurred with the active participation of agents and citizens of the United States.

boat people: Asian and other emigrants who travel in dangerously overcrowded and dilapidated vessels.

Boston Tea Party: Political protest where disgruntled colonists dumped Chinese-made tea into Boston Harbor in a revolt against British rule.

Chinatown: Area in New York City that is dominated by Chinese culture and evolved out of the first permanent Chinese settlement that was established in the early 19th century.

Chinese Exclusion Act of 1882: U.S. legislation that suspended Chinese immigration into the United States for what was originally intended to be 10 years. The act was not repealed until the United States needed military manpower in 1943.

chop suey: Chinese dish that was popular among non-Asians in 19th century California.

Chusok: Korean holiday that occurs on the 15th day of the eighth month of the lunar year.

coolie: Term for an unskilled manual laborer. The term later devolved into slang to mean any Asian American.

Dia Fou: Chinese phrase meaning "the big city" that was used to describe San Francisco.

Downtown Chinese: Chinese-American lower-class residents of New York City during the late 20th century.

dragon boat: A long, narrow canoe-style boat that is human-powered and originated in China.

Fan-tan: A popular Chinese board game.

fong: A group of people sharing a common origin, either through family or close proximity to one another.

Gam Saan: Chinese phrase meaning "gold mountain" that was used to describe California.

Ghadar: A weekly Indian-American newspaper published in the United States that advocated greater rights for Indian immigrants.

Haiku: A three-line type of Japanese poetry that uses syllable groupings of five, seven, and five to form a complete poem.

Hampton v. Mow Sun Wong: Court case in 1976 that resulted in the overturning of a law that required U.S. citizenship as a prerequisite for employment in the U.S. Civil Service Commission.

herbalism: Folk medicine practice popular in Eastern medicine that is based on the use of plants.

hindoo: Colloquial term for an Indian immigrant living in the United States.

hmong: Vietnamese word meaning "free."

huiguan: An association of Chinese Americans who usually share the same dialect and provide services to newcomers from China.

hui: An informal pool of capital that new Chinese immigrants could tap into to provide basic services and needs for themselves and their families.

ichi: Japanese word for "one."

Immigration Act of 1924: Legislation more commonly known as the Asian Exclusion Act that limited the number of immigrants allowed to enter the U.S. to two percent of the number of their countrymen already living in the United States.

Immigrant Act of 1965: Legislation that loosened immigration restrictions that were put in place after the passage of the Immigrant Act of 1924.

Indochina Migration and Refugee Assistance Act of 1975: Legislation that provided funding for a resettlement program for newly arrived immigrants from the area of Indochina.

issei: Japanese term for immigrant parents of natural-born citizens.

Japanese American Redress Bill of 1988: Legislation that provided $20,000 to each survivor of the World War II-era Japanese internment camps.

Jujitsu: A defensive form of Japanese martial arts that was later used to mean individual Japanese individual martial arts as a whole.

Jungle of Death: Phrase used to describe the Chinatown area of New York City as crime increased during the 1920s.

karaoke: A musical form, derived from Japan, where amateur vocalists sing over pre-recorded music.

karate: Martial arts form that originated in the Ryukyu Islands in Japan.

kendo: A popular Japanese form of swordsmanship. Translates literally into "the way of the sword."

keno: A Chinese game of chance that originated around 200 B.C.E.

kimchi: Spicy Korean dish featuring fermented cabbage, chili peppers, and ginger.

kris: A knife with a wavy blade that was popular among Chinese-Americans in the 19th century.

land bridge: A patch of land separating two bodies of water. DNA research conducted in 2006 concluded that there was an undisputable link between Native Americans and people living in East Asia, meaning that, theoretically, thousands of years ago a group of Asians crossed a land bridge on the Bering Strait and began to inhabit North America.

Lau v. Nichols: Supreme Court case in 1974 wherein the Court ruled in favor of a group of Chinese students who had sued, claiming they were not given special educational assistance in learning the English language.

li: A Chinese unit of measurement. Approximately 20,000 *li* equals 5,406 miles.

Manila Towns: Suburbs with a large amount of Filipino residents.

Mei Kuo: Chinese phrase meaning "flowery flag" that was used to describe the United States in the 19th century.

model minority: A class of immigrants who achieve greater success than the general population.

Muh Hey: A weekly newspaper published in the New York City area of Chinatown.

nisei: Japanese word for a native-born American.

Orientals: Word used to describe all Asians. The term was replaced with the preferred term "Asian Americans" during the Civil Rights era.

paper son: A Chinese immigrant claiming that he has familial ties to Chinese Americans already residing in the United States.

picture bride: The concept of a Chinese immigrant living in the United States employing a matchmaker to select a bride from his native country and bring her to the United States.

ramen: Japanese noodle dish.

samurai: Japanese term for the military nobility in Japan that existed before the onset of industrialization.

sashimi: Japanese dish featuring thinly sliced raw fish with horseradish sauce.

Sikhism: A popular religion that was founded near the border of India and Pakistan.

Six Companies: Chinese benevolent associations that provided services to newly arrived Chinese immigrants.

snakehead: Someone whose job it is to smuggle Asian immigrants into the United States.

soft racism: A perception of a group of people that is racist in nature but may seem benign, for example, the perception of the overwhelming success of Asian American in academia.

sushi: Japanese dish featuring raw fish and rice.

taehan toknip manse: Korean phrase meaning "long live Korean independence."

tae kwon do: The most popular martial arts form in the world, with over 70 million people participating in some form or another.

tempura: Japanese dish consisting of deep fried seafood or vegetables.

tong: A type of Chinese organization that had noble origins but was often involved in criminal activities, such as gambling and prostitution.

Uptown Chinese: Chinese-American upper class in New York City during the late 20th century.

VOLAGS: A group of voluntary organizations established in the 1970s that provided housing, food clothing, medical care and financial assistance to newly arrived immigrants.

wah gung: Chinese phrase meaning a Chinese immigrant who settles in the United States.

War Brides Act of 1945: Legislation allowing the spouses of U.S. military personnel to enter the United States after World War II.

wasabe: Japanese sauce consisting of ginger and soy sauce.

Webb Act of 1913: Prohibited any person who was "ineligible to naturalization" to purchase land.

wo: The ancient Chinese word for Japan.

wok: Japanese cooking device.

wonton: Chinese word for stuffed dumplings.

yakitori: Japanese word for grilled chicken.

Yellow Peril: Racist term popularized by Kaiser Wilhelm II that was used in the United States to describe the growing tide of Asian immigration.

Yoga: An Indian philosophy combining a physical and moral discipline to achieve spiritual enlightenment.

zongzi: A Chinese rice dish that is popular during Chinese American festivals.

INDEX

Index note: page references in *italics* indicate illustrations or pictures/captions; page references in **bold** indicate main discussion.

Produced by Golson Media
President and Editor   J. Geoffrey Golson
Layout Editor   Oona Patrick
Author Manager   Susan Moskowitz
Copyeditor   Barbara Paris
Proofreader   Mary Le Rouge
Indexer   J S Editorial